Everyday Surveillance

Everyday Surveillance

Vigilance and Visibility in Postmodern Life

William G. Staples

ROWMAN & LITTLEFIELD PUBLISHERS, INC.
Lanham • Boulder • New York • Oxford

ROWMAN & LITTLEFIELD PUBLISHERS, INC.

Published in the United States of America
by Rowman & Littlefield Publishers, Inc.
4720 Boston Way, Lanham, Maryland 20706

12 Hid's Copse Road, Cumnor Hill, Oxford OX2 9JJ, England

A previous version of this book was published in 1997 by St. Martin's Press as *The Culture of Surveillance*. *Everyday Surveillance* contains new chapters and updating throughout the text not included in the previous version.

British Cataloguing in Publication Information Available

Library of Congress Cataloging-in-Publication Data
Staples, William G.
    Everyday surveillance : vigilance and visibility in postmodern life / William G. Staples.
        p. cm.
    Includes bibliographical references and index.
    ISBN 0-7425-0077-2 (alk. paper)—ISBN 0-7425-0078-0 (pbk. : alk. paper)
    1. Social control—United States. 2. Electronic surveillance—Social aspects—United States. 3. United States—Social conditions—1980–. 4. Privacy—United States. I. Title.

HN59.2 .S698 2000
303.3'3'0973—dc21   00-040299

Printed in the United States of America

∞™ The paper used in this publication meets the minimum requirements of American National Standard for Information Sciences—Permanence of Paper for Printed Library Materials, ANSI/NISO Z39.48-1992.

For Lizette, my brave companion of the road

Contents

Preface

Entering a large discount store recently, I was struck at the contrast between the warm, welcoming, human smile of the "greeter" positioned in the lobby and, right behind her, the unblinking, mechanical stare of the videocam that was projecting my image on a nearby screen. As I stood taking in the scene, some little kids joined in, jumping up and down, watching themselves on the monitor. Mom spoiled the fun, however, protectively hustling them out of the range of the camera. Yet even she could not resist glancing back over her shoulder as her own image flashed across the screen.

As sociologist Wendy Griswold points out, we study culture when we observe a community's pattern of meanings; its enduring expressive aspects; its symbols that represent and guide the thinking, feelings, and behavior of its members as they go about their daily lives. The word *surveillance*, in the most general sense, refers to the act of keeping a close watch on people. The purpose of this book is to examine the meanings, attitudes, and behaviors surrounding the ways in which people in the United States are increasingly being watched, monitored, and controlled in their everyday lives.

Rejecting the idea of a highly coordinated, state-driven, Big Brother monopoly over the practice of watching people, I focus on the microtechniques of surveillance and social control that target and treat the body as an object to be watched, assessed, and manipulated. These are local knowledge-gathering activities often enhanced by the use of new information, visual, communication, and medical technologies that are increasingly present in the workplace, the school, the home, and the community. In this book I argue that, while our inherited, modern ideas about the nature of human beings, deviance, and social control continue to shape the ways in which we keep a close watch on people, a new set of meanings, attitudes, and practices is taking hold that is constituted by and indicative of conditions of postmodernity.

This book was written to be accessible to a wide audience. While deeply informed by the work of social theorists and historians, my approach is relatively free of academic jargon. It is particularly suited as a supplemental text for students taking classes such as Introduction to Sociology, Social Problems, Deviance and Social Control, Crime and Society, and American Society. Many of the positions I take will be considered provocative at the very least. My intent is to challenge the reader to come face-to-face with what I believe to be one of the most significant issues of our day and to consider it from what is likely to be an alternative vantage point. My hope is that you will find the book enjoyable, informative, and worthy of considerable discussion and debate.

This project was supported, in part, by the sabbatical leave program and a grant from the General Research Fund of the University of Kansas. I appreciate very much the work of my undergraduate research assistants Sarah Flood, Sharareh Hersemy, and Angela Marks. Thanks go to the students from my seminar in the History of Social Control, especially David Barney, Ben Coates, Kevin Gotham, Jennifer Hackney, Dan Krier, Frank Kunkle, Christine Robinson, and Ann Woodward. I would also like to recognize the people who were willing to share with me their work, lives, and experiences that have become part of this book. While many of their identities remain hidden, their impact has been profound.

Many friends and colleagues have offered valuable comments and suggestions on this and earlier versions of my work. They include David Altheide, Bob Antonio, Patricia Clough, Norman Denzin, Ted Frederickson, Mark Gottdiener, Travis Hirschi, John Kramer, Sue Lorenz, Roger Martin, Gary Marx, Joane Nagel, Lizette Peter, George Ritzer, Mike Schwalbe, David Smith, Cliff Staples, Ian Staples, and Carol Warren. I am grateful to all and absolve them of any responsibility for what I have written. And thanks to my editor, Dean Birkenkamp, and the staff at Rowman & Littlefield.

Everyday Surveillance

1

⤴

Everyday Surveillance

Throughout the U.S., thousands of criminals are placed under "house arrest," their movements monitored electronically by a transmitter attached to their ankle. In many states, criminal defendants and judges carry out proceedings on video monitors. In Arizona, a "welfare" mother has a court-ordered contraceptive device surgically implanted in her arm. In New York, a high-tech courtroom collects a myriad of information about a single defendant that is kept in an electronic file folder. Most "clients" in community corrections programs are subjected to random drug and alcohol testing.

At the same time:

Sixty-seven percent of major U.S. employers engage in some form of electronic monitoring of workers. In New York City, more than two thousand private surveillance cameras are taping citizens on public streets. In California, every citizen wishing to be issued a driver's license must have their thumbprint computer scanned. In Massachusetts, a company tracks the Web surfing habits of more than thirty million Internet users. Nearly 90 percent of U.S. manufacturers are testing workers for drugs.

The preceding examples illustrate a blurring distinction between the practices of the official justice system and the everyday lives of ordinary people. How are we to understand these developments? Are they simply "advances" in our struggle against illegal, deviant, or "troublesome" behavior, or do they signal the rise of what might be called a "culture of surveillance"? What kind of society has produced these practices, and why do we appear so willing to adopt them? The purpose of this book is to explore these and other questions about the emergence of new forms of social control in contemporary society.

Recently, I sat in the "café" section of a large, suburban bookstore talking with a friend. She asked me what I was working on these days, and I told her that I was writing a book about social control in contemporary life. At this she said, "You mean about crime and prisons?" "No," I said, "not really. More like the issue of surveillance." "Oh," she replied, "so you are looking into how the FBI spies on people?" To many of us, including my friend, issues of discipline, social control, and surveillance tend either to revolve around the criminal justice system or to invite the image of George Orwell's notorious Big Brother. Yet as important as the prison system and the activities of domestic "spying" organizations are, I am more interested here in the relatively small, often mundane procedures and practices—the Tiny Brothers if you will—that are increasingly present in our daily lives. These techniques exist in the shadow of large institutions such as prisons; they are not ushered in with dramatic displays of state power such as the Branch Davidian standoff in Waco, Texas, nor do they appear as significant challenges to constitutional democracy such as the FBI's COunterINTELligence programs of the 1960s and 1970s. The techniques I mean are the more commonplace strategies used by governmental and, increasingly, private organizations to "keep us in line," monitor our performance, gather knowledge or evidence about us, assess deviations, and, if necessary, exact penalties. For it is these daily activities that involve many more, if not all, of us than does life in a state prison or the latest FBI "sting" operation.

The techniques I have in mind range along a continuum. They begin with the "soft," seemingly benign and relatively inconspicuous forms of monitoring such as those used in the very bookstore where I sat with my friend. In that business, as in thousands across the United States, a security system monitored our interaction with video cameras, while the store's spatial arrangement was designed for optimal surveillance of customers and employees alike. Computerized checkout stations kept track of inventory, calculated store performance figures, assessed the credit worthiness of patrons through remote data banks, collected personal information about customers so they could be targeted for marketing campaigns, monitored the log-on and log-off times of employees, and calculated the average number of customers those employees processed per hour. All this was accomplished "behind the scenes" as it were, without disruption to the manufactured ambiance of soft leather chairs, melodic Muzak, and the sound and smell of cappuccino making.

At the "hard" end of the spectrum are the more obtrusive and confrontational practices that often begin with the assumption of guilt and are designed to uncover the "truth," to test an individual's character, and, more generally, to make people consciously aware that they are indeed being watched and monitored. Of course, this element was also evident at the corporate bookstore I visited with my friend, as they had "tagged" all the merchandise so that both of us could be electronically "frisked" as we walked through the sensor gates at the exit. These are what I call "surveillance ceremonies." They include random drug and alcohol testing, the use of lie detectors, pre-employment integrity tests, and "sobriety checkpoints" in the streets. They also include the practices of electronically monitored "house arrest," adolescent curfews, and the use of metal detectors.

Between these soft and hard types of social control lies a vast array of techniques and technologies—exercised on and by people both inside and outside the justice system—that are designed to watch our bodies, to regulate and monitor our activities, habits, and movements, and, ultimately, to shape or change our behavior. These procedures are often undertaken in the name of law and order, public safety, the protection of private property, or simply "sound business practice"; other procedures are initiated for an individual's "own good" or benefit. But no matter what the stated motivation, the intent of social control is to mold, shape, and modify actions and behaviors.[1]

The subject of this book, then, is the cultural practices that I will call "meticulous rituals of power." Most generally, I include those microtechniques of social monitoring and control that are enhanced by the use of new information, communications, and medical technologies. These are knowledge-gathering activities that involve surveillance, information and evidence collection, and analysis. I call them meticulous because they are "small" procedures and techniques that are precisely and thoroughly exercised. I see them as ritualistic because they are faithfully repeated and are often quickly accepted and routinely practiced with little question. And they are about power because they are intended to discipline people into acting in ways that others have deemed to be lawful or have defined as appropriate or simply "normal." In this way, meticulous rituals are the specific, concrete mechanisms that operate to maintain unbalanced and unequal authority relationships. These relationships exist between specific clusters of individuals (e.g., between managers and workers, police officers and suspects, probation officials and offenders, teachers and students, parents and children, and the like) and, in a larger sense, between individuals and the public and private organizations where these rituals take place.[2] Surveillance and social control of this type are not orchestrated by a few individuals; they are not part of a master plan that is simply imposed on us. Rather, in my view, *we are all involved and enmeshed within a matrix of power relations that are highly intentional and purposeful; arrangements that can be more or less unequal but are never simply one-directional.*

"OK," you may say, "so what is really new here? Hasn't society always had ways of keeping people in line? Aren't these meticulous rituals just newer, perhaps more effective ways of doing what we have always done to ensure social order?" In some ways, yes, they are logical extensions of "modern" solutions to the problems of crime, deviance, and social control, and they may indeed be more efficient. Yet, at the same time, they have qualities that make them fundamentally new, and, I want to argue, *post*modern in design and implementation, and I think it's important that we come to understand the implications of their use. I see at least four defining characteristics that set these practices apart from more traditional methods. In the first place, consider the following. In the past, the watchful eyes of a small shopkeeper may have deterred a would-be shoplifter; her surveillance was personal, not terribly systematic, and her memory, of course, was fallible. She was more likely to know her customers (and they her), to keep a "closer eye" on strangers, and to "look the other way" when she saw fit (and to make a call to the offending juvenile's parents later). This kind of "personal" social control was once typical of small communities or close-knit societies where people certainly watched one another very closely and where fear of ridicule or exclusion was a powerful inducement to conformity.

By contrast, the part-time, non-owning employees of the large corporate bookstore where I sat with my friend have less interest in watching for thieves; their huge number of customers is an anonymous crowd. So here, the store management relies on the hidden, faceless, and ever-ready video security camera. The videocam—one of the defining features of postmodern society—projects a hyper-vigilant "gaze," randomly scanning the entire store day or night, recording every event, and watching *all* the customers, not just the "suspicious ones." The cameras are also positioned to watch the vast number of employees, who must now be monitored both as "productive" workers and as potential thieves. In this way, surveillance and discipline have become oddly democratic; everyone is watched, and no one is trusted.

So the first characteristic of postmodern social control is that it tends to be systematic, methodical, and automatic in operation. It is likely to be impersonal in that the observer is rarely seen and is anonymous; further, the "observer" is likely to be a computer system, a videocam, a drug-testing kit, or an electronic scanner of some kind. Once more, the data that these devices collect may become part of a permanent record in the form of a videotape, a computer file, or some other digital format. In fact, the role played by efficient and inexpensive digital databases is crucial. Corporate personnel files, hospital, mental health, and substance abuse agency records, as well as insurance company data banks, join all those demographic, financial, credit, and consumer habits data to create "virtual" database identities of all of us.[3] Once created, these representations are, as Mark Poster suggests, "capable of being acted upon by computers at many social locations without the least awareness by the individual concerned yet just as surely as if the individual were present somehow inside the computer."[4] For example, credit ratings can be destroyed, loan applications rejected, or medical benefits denied, without personal notice, input, or influence.

Second, these new meticulous rituals of power often involve our bodies in new and important ways, and I want to distinguish two primary tactics of bodily social control. I agree with Donald Lowe when he states: "As living beings, we are more than body and mind, more than the representations and images of our body. We lead a bodily life in the world."[5] These bodily lives are shaped, manipulated, and controlled by a set of ongoing practices that compose our daily lives as workers, consumers, and community members.

The first tactic I want to distinguish has to do with types of monitoring and surveillance that enhance our visibility to others. We seem to be entering a state of permanent visibility where attempts to control and shape our behavior, in essence our bodies, are accomplished not so much by the threat of punishment and physical force but by the act of being watched—continuously, anonymously, and automatically. This kind of watching happens when people engage in such diverse activities as clipping on a company beeper, using a credit card to purchase something at a store, or parking their car in a garage with a security camera. These instances signify different forms of "visibility": the beeper enables an employer to remotely "check up" on and monitor an employee; the credit card purchase leaves an electronic paper trail of a person's activities and whereabouts; and the security camera identifies to the police, or anyone else who gains access to the tape, that a particular individual was indeed parked in that garage on a particular day at a certain time. The methodical, technology-driven, impersonal gaze, I argue, is quickly becoming a primary mechanism of surveillance and, by extension, social control in our society, and it is fixed on our bodies and their movements.

A second tactic of bodily surveillance and social control relates to new developments in science, technology, and medicine. These intersecting fields are making the human body infinitely more accessible to official scrutiny and assessment. This means that the ability of organizations to monitor, judge, or even regulate our actions and behaviors through our bodies is significantly enhanced. It also means that it becomes less important to trust suspects to "speak the truth" or convicted offenders to "mend their ways." Rather, it is the individual's body that will "tell us what we need to know," as in indicating that someone is using drugs or was at the scene of a crime or even has "deviant desires." In this way, the body is treated as an "object" that contains the evidence of any possible deviance. For example, on the soft side of our spectrum of social control, we see that corporations are using medical data collected on employees in their "wellness" and exercise clinics to confront the "unhealthy lifestyles" of those not conforming to prevailing standards (about, for example, tobacco use or obesity). Meanwhile, on the hard side, DNA samples are being systematically collected and stored and are increasingly presented as evidence in courtroom proceedings. The body, I contend, is a central target of many postmodern surveillance techniques and rituals.

The third defining characteristic of postmodern social control relates to a shift in the location of social control and surveillance and which behaviors are the subject of it. Since the early nineteenth century, our primary method of dealing with lawbreakers, those thought to be insane, other deviants, and even the poor has been to isolate them from everyday life—as in the case of the modern prison, mental asylum, poorhouse, and reformatory. Yet the kinds of practices I am most concerned with here attempt to impose a framework of accountability on an individual in everyday life. While, obviously, removing "troublesome" people from society is still a significant means of formal social control (after all, in the United States, we institutionalize more people than any other Western country does), this approach is increasingly considered, by various experts, to be an inefficient, ineffective, and undesirable practice. This is particularly true if we consider the idea that as a society we seem to be engaged in a far-reaching attempt to regulate not only the traditional crimes of person and property but also the behaviors, conditions, and "lifestyles" of substance (ab)use, alcohol and tobacco consumption, "eating disorders," forms of sexual expression and sexual "promiscuity" and "deviance," teenage pregnancy, out-of-marriage births, domestic violence, child abuse, "dysfunctional" families, various psychological or psychiatric disorders and other "medical" conditions such as "attention deficit disorder," and such diseases as AIDS. How can we possibly institutionalize and control everyone that falls into these rapidly expanding categories of "troublesome" individuals?

Given these conditions, it would appear that the segregative or quarantine models of social control of the nineteenth century are an invention whose time has simply passed. The incentive now is to develop new ways to control and "keep an eye on" what appears to be an increasing number of "deviants" through an expanding network of formal "community corrections" programs; regulatory welfare, health, and social service agencies; and even schools, workplaces, and other community institutions. New developments in the forensic, medical, and computer and information sciences—generated by corporate research and development departments and the post-Cold War military-industrial complex (which I believe is being converted rapidly into a "security-industrial complex")—are creating more remote, more flexible, and more efficient ways of making this happen.

Finally, as new forms of social control are localized in everyday life, they are capable of bringing wide-ranging populations, not just the official "deviant," under their watchful gaze. As I indicated earlier, trust is becoming a rare commodity in our culture. The notion of "innocent until proven guilty" seems like a cliché these days, when people are apt to be subjected to disciplinary rituals and surveillance ceremonies simply because statistics indicate that they have the potential for being offenders (for example the police tactic known as "racial profiling" as a justification for stopping motorists). Data generated through surveillance techniques produce "types" or whole classes of individuals who are deemed "at risk" for behavior, whether any one particular individual has engaged in such behavior or not. These data, of course, are then used to justify even closer surveillance and scrutiny of this group, thereby increasing the likelihood of uncovering more offenses; and so it goes. In the context of these changes, social control becomes more about predicting and preventing deviance—always assuming that it will, indeed, happen—rather than responding to a violation after it has occurred.[6] Therefore, when put in place, ritualistic monitoring and surveillance ceremonies often blur the distinction between the official "deviant" and the "likely" or even "possible" offender. Indeed, what separates the convicted felon, the college athlete, or the discount store cashier if each is subjected to random drug screening? One consequence of this blurring is that we may be witnessing a historical shift from the specific punishment of the individual deviant to the generalized surveillance of us all.

But by implying that social control is becoming more universal and thus oddly more democratic, I am not suggesting that we are all necessarily subject to the same quantity or quality of social control. Historically and cross-culturally, the amount and character of monitoring, discipline, and punishment that individuals are afforded have varied considerably by such defining characteristics as race, ethnicity, class, and gender. Without question, this continues today. My point is that there are more impersonal, more methodical, and more technology-driven forms of surveillance and social control in our society than ever before, and today's forms—and their sheer volume—are enveloping even those who might have been previously exempt. For those who have traditionally been the target of monitoring and control, these developments serve only to intensify and increase the amount of formal regulation already in their daily lives.

So, it would seem that while these meticulous rituals are "more of the same," they are, in other respects, strikingly new; and this, I propose, is how we should come to understand them. In other words, we need to see how the world we are creating today is a product of both our modern historical past and our postmodern cultural present. This historically grounded perspective has two advantages. First, if we connect these "new" disciplinary techniques to significant long-term processes and trends, we can see the continuity of social life and can understand that contemporary developments reflect an ongoing struggle to deal with problems and issues set in motion by the birth of the modern age. Second, by looking at how differently we have responded to the problems of social order in the past, we can also see that matters of deviance and social control are not fixed categories but are changing, socially constructed ideas. Therefore we begin to realize that what is defined as "deviant" or as "social problems" today—as well as what seem like appropriate responses to them—may not have been considered worthy of attention one hundred or even ten years ago.

These long-term changes I refer to are some of the major themes that have come to characterize the period of modernity (from around 1790 until the 1950s) and have had considerable influence on our strategies of social control. These themes include the increasing rationalization of social life; the rise of large centralized states and private organizations; and strongly held beliefs in reason, rationality, and the certainty of "progress." This modern faith in our power to shape the world was grounded in our apparent ability to control and to "know" nature through the physical sciences. This model of science was increasingly

applied to the manipulation of "man" through the knowledge of the "human sciences" such as medicine, criminology, psychology, sociology, and demography. In
other words, with the birth of the modern era, human beings—our bodies,
minds, and behaviors—became the subject or topic of scientific inquiry as well
as the object or target of its knowledge. Thus, we see in the modern era the gradual disappearance of public torture and stigmatization as the primary means of
punishment and social control, and their replacement by rationally organized reformatory institutions such as the prison, the poorhouse, and the asylum. Rather
than seek retribution and public punishment, these institutions would isolate
the offending individual and introduce behavioral modification—the transformation of the criminal, the deviant, and the poor—through the administration
of techniques of knowledge and power. Many of these influences are still with
us today and continue to shape social life. It is this relationship—between
knowledge and power—that is central to the operation of meticulous rituals.

At the same time, however, there is evidence that a new social order is emerging out of this older, modern one. This postmodern society, originating in developments since World War II, and more intensely since the early 1970s, is a culture characterized by fragmentation and uncertainty as many of the
once-taken-for-granted meanings, symbols, and institutions of modern life dissolve before our eyes. Time as well as social and geographical space are highly
compressed by rapidly changing computer and advanced technologies, information storage and retrieval, and scientific and medical knowledge. Ours is a culture deeply penetrated by commodities and consumer "lifestyles." In our day it
would seem that consumption rather than production has become the well-
spring of society, while highly bureaucratic (although increasingly "decentralized") state agencies attempt to order and regulate social life. What is "real" in
this culture is presented to us through the mass media in video imagery that has
become the primary source of our cultural knowledge. We are offered a nonstop
barrage of "crisis-level" social problems, leaving us wondering "what the world is
coming to." In turn, we are left cynically mistrusting each other and furthering
the disintegration of public life and discourse. This cultural hysteria creates a
fertile ground for those selling "science" and the seemingly innocent and "advanced" technological fixes that they claim will ease our fears. Under these conditions, we turn to increasingly more pervasive, rational, and predictable means
of surveillance and social control. In essence, we are seduced into believing that
subjecting ourselves to more and more meticulous rituals is an unfortunate but
necessary condition given the apparent tide of problems we face. The forgoing
conditions form what I will refer to simply as "the everyday life of the postmodern," and it is in this cultural context, I believe, that we continue to struggle with
problems and issues which arose during the early nineteenth century.

As an example of how our current disciplinary practices are a product of both
our historical past and our cultural present, let us consider an incident that took
place recently in my hometown. In this case, a school bus driver was accused of

physically restraining an unruly child. The driver was fired, and many debates took place in the local newspaper about the child's behavior on the bus, the reported good reputation of the driver, and about the way school district administrators (mis)handled the case. It was clear that no one trusted anyone's account of what had actually transpired on the bus that day. A few months later there was an announcement that each of the district's fleet of new buses would be equipped with a video camera "black box." The bus company claimed that, on any given day, just three video cameras would be rotated among all the district's buses and that, given the design of the boxes, neither the students nor the drivers would know when their bus was equipped with a camera. The bus company's manager stated that the use of the cameras would "help to improve student discipline" as well as ensure that the drivers follow "proper procedures."

Now, the principle behind the rotating camera is not new; it originates with a design by Jeremy Bentham dating from 1791 called the Panopticon, a central guard tower inside a prison or reformatory. The tower was designed in such a way that prisoners were never quite sure whether a guard was present or not and would have to assume that they were being watched. The inmates, in effect, watched themselves, internalizing, if you will, the watchful gaze of the keeper. It was a simple, even elegant, solution to the problem of disciplining people in an enclosed space—a dilemma brought about with the birth of the asylum, the modern "solution" to criminal behavior, madness, poverty, and the like. The evolution of this idea two hundred years later—and applied in a postmodern context—produces a flexible design, routinely applied in the everyday life of schoolchildren and their adult supervisors, none of whom apparently are trusted to act responsibly. Inexpensive video technology—and our willingness to define schoolchildren's behavior on a bus as being so problematic that it warrants "objective" surveillance rather than personal monitoring—makes the use of this new form of social control possible. Curious about what people thought of the cameras, I spoke with friends and others in the community about the new policy. Most seemed shocked at the idea at first, but then, in resignation, many would concede that it was probably a "good idea" for the "safety" of everyone involved. I see the new disciplinary techniques, then, both as a product of important, long-term processes set in motion more than two centuries ago and as shaped by a newly emerging cultural context.

Let me make a few things clear from the outset. I am *neither* a technological determinist nor a neo-Luddite. I do not believe that technology "drives" social life or that it is inherently "bad." I do assume, however, that technologies are *social* products, created and implemented within a complex matrix of cultural, political, and economic influences. In this book I attempt to uncover those influences as they relate to the actual workings of disciplinary power, its daily practices, rituals, and minute procedures, and how those workings are often bound up with the use of new technologies. Moreover, I am *not* suggesting that there is no need for social control in our society or that shoplifting, drug abuse, and violent crime are not real problems with real victims. Of course they are. Having lived in Los Angeles for nearly a decade, I have witnessed firsthand the crime, violence, and chronic social problems that seem to define the hard edge of U.S. urban life. But the issues I am raising are of broader, sociological concern and have to do with the "big picture" of where we are going as a culture and with the balance of power, if you will, in that larger society. In other words, I want to look at the evolution of surveillance as not simply a judicial matter but as an entry point to understanding our changing attitude and practice toward social control in general.

I want to first dispel any notion that the last two hundred or so years of "reforming" justice practice has unequivocally produced a system that is more "just" or more "humane" than the brutal, public punishment that came before it. Therefore, I want to challenge the idea that, simply put, we keep building a better mousetrap. Rather, I want to argue that the modern attempt to transform, mold, shape, and "rehabilitate" the criminal, the deviant, and the poor in the name of more effective and even progressive social policy may, in fact, be seen as a more general model for the rational ordering of the entire society. That is, I am concerned here with a process, set in motion in the early nineteenth century, whereby the enforcement of ever-finer distinctions between what is "acceptable" and "unacceptable" behavior has become part of all our daily lives, and not just the lives of those who break the law. Ultimately, I will show how we are indeed building a culture of surveillance when we infuse daily life with practices that constantly assess our behavior, judge our performance, account for our whereabouts, and challenge our personal integrity by assuming that we are guilty until proven innocent.

Let us consider another contemporary example. I find it remarkable how quickly people will agree to give up their constitutional right to freedom of movement in order to stop what some claim to be rampant drunk-driving behavior. We accept this, despite the evidence that so-called "sobriety checkpoints" apprehend very few excessive drinkers.[7] Supporters of these bodily based surveillance ceremonies contend that "if you have nothing to hide, you have nothing to fear." Yet we know from experience that unbridled police powers are likely to present a serious challenge to individual liberties. Obviously, even one person injured or killed by a drunk driver is a tragedy, but it might be argued that creating a police state to thwart the behavior could be an even greater catastrophe. As Supreme Court Justice John Paul Stevens declared in his dissenting opinion on the legality of such roadblocks, "Unfortunately the Court is transfixed by the wrong symbol—the illusory prospect of punishing countless intoxicated motorists—when it should keep its eyes on the road plainly marked by the Constitution."[8] Why not focus our efforts on education and safety programs (funded by the businesses that profit from the sale of alcohol)?

Next, consider the proliferation of metal detectors and bodily searches, not simply at airports but also in schools, courthouses, dance clubs, and the like, to thwart the possession of weapons. (Ironically, at the same time, a majority of states has passed laws that *permit* people to carry concealed weapons.) Rather than seriously confront the issue of the widespread availability of guns in our society (in this case, a "right" that is arguably not protected under the Constitution's Second Amendment concerning a "well regulated Militia," and not permitted in any other "developed" country), we subject all citizens to this kind of daily surveillance and monitoring.[9] This, it seems, may be the most fundamental question raised by this book: Are we, in our attempts to preserve our freedom and security, entrapping ourselves in our own solutions? Before we can debate such questions, however, I need to explain more fully the origins of my perspective on the changing nature of discipline and social control. I begin chapter 2 by focusing on the work of the late French philosopher Michel Foucault (1926–1984). It is from Foucault, a pioneering social theorist, that I take the idea to concentrate on the small, seemingly benign rituals at the intersection of power, knowledge, and the body. In his strikingly original book, *Discipline and Punish*, Foucault presented a political history of two basic forms of discipline: the physical torture associated with the "Age of the Sovereign" and, later, the emergence of the asylum, a product of modernity.[10] Building on Foucault's analysis, I chart the evolution of disciplinary practices and surveillance techniques from the invention of the asylum on, and, by taking up where Foucault left off, I hope to extend his study of modern social control into the postmodern era.

As I have noted in this chapter, postmodern surveillance practices have four characteristics:

1. They are increasingly technology-based, methodical, automatic, and sometimes anonymously applied, and they usually generate a permanent record as evidence.
2. Many new techniques target and treat the body as an object that can be watched, assessed, and manipulated.
3. The new techniques are often local, operating in our everyday lives.
4. Local or not, they manage to bring wide-ranging populations, not just the official "deviant," under scrutiny.

These characteristics form a descriptive type for what I am calling meticulous rituals of power. The central purpose of the next three chapters is to use this classification scheme to identify and examine these cultural practices and the locations where they take place. In these chapters, I sometimes draw on examples from, and move back and forth between, the official justice system and our everyday postmodern life. In chapter 3, I focus on new forms of surveillance that systematically watch and monitor our bodies and behaviors; I show how our communities, homes, schools, and workplaces are increasingly infused with meticulous rituals and surveillance ceremonies. In chapter 4, I turn my attention to practices that treat the body itself as the site and source of evidence and knowledge or, alternatively, that attempt to take control of the body through the use of various technologies. In chapter 5, I address the emergence of the Internet and examine, among other things, "dataveillance" capabilities of the network that facilitate the collection and exchange of information about individuals, monitor the activities of users on the network (at work, school, or home), as well as the extraordinary voyeuristic and exhibitionist activities emerging on the World Wide Web. Finally, in chapter 6, I return to considering the important questions I have raised in this introduction about these contemporary developments, assess their consequences, and consider what the future may hold.

A NOTE ON SOURCES

This book was written as an essay-argument rather than as a typical academic monograph. Fitting this style, it is filled with anecdotal evidence, journalistic accounts, and my own interviews and observations of contemporary surveillance practices. I use this pastiche of material as my primary data for several reasons. First, like many sociologists, I see culture as inconsistent, contradictory, and complex; it simply defies the more linear, "cause and effect" models associated with more "scientific" inquiry. Does this mean that I do not need evidence to support my claims? Hardly. It simply means that my objective is, as Diana Crane puts it, "to interpret a wide range of materials in order to identify what might be described as an underlying 'gestalt.' "[11] Therefore, I take *recorded* culture to be both a window into society and a legitimate source for the interpretation of social meaning.

Second, despite the proliferation of new books on privacy issues, few, it seems to me, offer an account of how ordinary people experience, live with, and may actually contribute to the new surveillance practices.[12] Sociology is sometimes referred to as "slow journalism" since it often takes quite some time to conduct formal studies, collect data, and publish findings. By citing the work of professionals in print and other media, I hope to bring together current developments reflected in the lived experiences of ordinary people and the power of sociological theory and analysis.[13] And third, while I recount the stories of individuals in my narrative, I also reference broader trends by citing, for example, government reports and data, pertinent legal cases, changes to federal and state laws, the results of national opinion polls, industry-wide trends and assessments, and relevant scholarship and debate. These I believe bolster my claims and lend substantial credence to my arguments.

Finally, readers will notice my frequent use of quotation marks on words and phrases without necessarily citing sources. Their use in this way is both stylistic and substantive. Some of the marks simply reference everyday colloquialisms. Yet others are intended to alert the reader to the socially constructed nature of language and to suggest that meanings are inherently unstable and potentially contested. Expressions such as "substance abuse," "dysfunctional family," and "learning disability" are labels created by those in positions of authority or those who claim professional expertise. I do not necessarily agree with the meanings evoked by this language nor do I wish to speak to their validity.

2

⤿

The Scaffold, the Penitentiary, and Beyond

In the colony of Virginia during the 1760s, the theft of a hog would bring twenty-five lashes well laid on at the publick whipping post; for the second offense he was set two houres in the pillory and had both ears nailed ther to, at the end of the two hours to have the ears slit loose; for the third offence, death.[1]

Yet by the 1830s,

Within an atmosphere of repression, humiliation, and gloomy silence, the Auburn Penitentiary convict performed an incessantly monotonous round of activity. He arose at 5:15 and as soon as his cell was unlocked, he marched out holding three pieces of equipment: a night tub used for calls of nature; a can for drinking water; and a wooden food container. Holding this paraphernalia in his left hand, he laid his right hand on the shoulder of the felon who occupied the next cell and marched in lock-step across the court yard to his workshop.[2]

Here we have two very different forms of punishment. What happened to bring about this radical change? For years, legal scholars and historians advanced the idea that the "invention" of the modern penitentiary was a product of a deep, humanitarian impulse on the part of reformers, the public, and state officials. From this perspective, the ritualized torture on the public scaffold used in Europe and the whipping post favored in the United States were, quite suddenly, deemed barbaric and unenlightened, and, if one reads the rhetoric of the reformers of the nineteenth century, this theme is certainly evident. Yet, in recent years, some people have come to question this interpretation. One significant figure in that debate is Michel Foucault.

Foucault argued that while indeed the penal reformers of the eighteenth century may have set out to reduce the ferocity of punishment—along with its public spectacle—they did not necessarily aim to punish *less* but, rather, to punish *better*. In other words, their intent was to make punishment and the system of justice more efficient and effective. Punishment, under their plan, would be rationally organized and proportional to the crime; deterrence, rather than retribution, would be its central purpose. These ideas helped set in motion a series of "reforms" by which the "soul" as well as the body of the offender became the target of punishment. The perpetrator would now be sent away for years to the modern asylum, such as the Auburn penitentiary, to be subjected to an institutional regime that would isolate his mind and discipline his body. The staff would watch his every move, accumulate knowledge of the circumstances of his crime, his family background, and life history. It would break him of his bad habits and transform him into a model citizen. Punishment would succeed when the inmate had been "rehabilitated."

But Foucault, in a book entitled *Surveiller et punir: Naissance de la prison* and translated from the French as *Discipline and Punish: The Birth of the Prison*, questions the very notion that all this "rehabilitation" necessarily meant "progress" and the more "humane" treatment of the offender.[3] Indeed, we might want to ask ourselves: Is more or less physical pain the only yardstick of benevolence? Of suffering? Of human dignity? On what basis and with what values do we assess whether a deviant is treated more "humanely"? On what scale, for example, do we place ten lashes versus ten years in prison for a "three strikes and you're out" offense? I am not advocating a return to physical punishment but rather questioning the philosophical and ethical basis on which claims of "justice" and "humanity" have been asserted. Such claims can often appear quite contradictory. Take the case of the young American in Singapore in 1994 who was sentenced to six lashes from a rattan cane for vandalism. Following the sentence there were cries of brutality and "inhumane" treatment from U.S. officials. Curiously, at nearly that same time, a criminologist and longtime death penalty proponent in New York was calling for the substitution of lethal injection for the electric chair to carry out that state's recent return to executions. He claimed that the injections were a "painless and nonrepulsive way of doing justice."[4] This suggests that, for some, even a death sentence can be considered "humane" as long as it is "painless."

With the purported "march of progress," then, while it may be said that social control has, in some ways, become more "lenient," even "gentle," it may also be true that it has become more widespread and more invasive. What do I mean? Simply this: that changes begun in the early nineteenth century to make justice more "efficient" set in motion a process whereby the authority to judge an individual's behavior has been extended well beyond any legal offense committed.

Since that time, a complex machinery of organizations, institutions, and practices (e.g., a myriad of different kinds of jails, prisons, courts, probation and parole systems, halfway houses, community corrections programs, and the like) has been developing and is now part of the justice system. The result has been a proliferation of the number of crimes it is possible to commit as well as the number of "judges" to assess them. These judges are the armies of personnel who appear as "expert" authorities—probation officers, wardens, psychiatrists, social workers, criminologists, penologists, along with their diagnoses, assessments, evaluations, and classifications. In fact, rather than simply responding to a specific behavior or infraction, this kind of judgment goes beyond simply what someone has done and extends to the very core of who he or she is. In other words, this "power to punish," as Foucault called it, assesses something other than crimes alone. It judges what kinds of persons offenders are and whether they measure up to the kinds of persons society wants them to be. This book is not only about how this power to punish, and the making of ever-finer distinctions between what is "acceptable" and "unacceptable" behavior, has taken hold in the official justice system but also about how it has spread to communities, workplaces, schools, homes, and most spheres of social life. It is about, in essence, the enforcement of "normalcy" and the attempt to eliminate all social, physical, and psychological "irregularities."

Seen in this way, a man who stole a hog in the colony of Virginia was simply *punished* for his crime. No one expected him, as part of his penalty, to reflect on his inner self or to become a productive worker. No one really cared if he came from a "dysfunctional" family, if he had a "personality disorder," or if he was a good candidate for "rehabilitation." While there is little doubt that torturing the hog thief was a brutish act, there were limits to how much pain and punishment could be exacted on him without killing him (which, of course, effectively ended his punishment). His body was all he had to offer; it was all that the authorities could take from him. Yet, at some point, it was decided that the thief had more to give; it was not enough that he simply stop stealing hogs. Reformers, philosophers, jurists, and state officials began to argue that, with the right program, the criminal, the deviant, the delinquent, and even the poor could be "morally reformed"—*from the inside out*. Why did all this come about? Where did these influential people ever get the idea that, in the name of "doing good," they could change an individual's behavior by remaking the self, indeed, by "improving" the offender's "character" with "moral guidance"? What happened, I want to argue, was that forms of punishment and justice such as the public whipping post, like other "pre-modern" social practices, were swept away with the birth of the modern era. In order to understand the kind of disciplinary techniques we practice today, we need to understand them in historical context, and this demands that we interrogate the very meaning of modernity.

BIRTH OF THE MODERN

The roots of modernity lie in the post-Renaissance period from the mid-sixteenth century until about the early 1800s, a period often referred to as the Enlightenment. From this age came a fundamental break from medieval tradition and religious dogmas. Unfettered by such constraints, the idea emerged that autonomous, universal, human "reason," not simply God's laws, would bring certainty, hope, and progress to the world. Indeed, the Enlightenment is credited with giving birth to a near-utopian vision of a future in which human emancipation and "enlightened" thinking would prevail. As these ideas and practices took hold, more traditional forms of social, economic, and cultural life began to crumble under the weight of changes in economic organization, scientific experimentation, and the rise of democratic states and rational law.

This movement intensified and culminated in the birth of the modern era—for our purposes, from around the turn of the nineteenth century and continuing through the first half of the twentieth century. We can summarize the main themes and characteristics of modernity as follows:

- An increased rationalizing or calculating attitude toward social life based on notions of efficiency, predictability, control, and discipline, epitomized by the emergence of the factory and machine-based capitalism.
- The progressive differentiation of social life in the division of labor, specialization of occupation, and separation of the "public" and "private," "home" and "work" life.
- The rise of large-scale state and private organizations and bureaucracies as well as large, urban centers.
- The acceleration or "compression" of time-space relations—a fast-paced world that is made "smaller" by emerging modes of transportation and communication.
- The rise of a relatively large middle and professional class with its own self-interest, sensibilities, and culture.
- The development of the "human sciences" such as psychology, psychiatry, sociology, criminology, demography, statistics, and public health.
- The institutionalization of the belief in progress, driven by the idea that scientific knowledge, objective reasoning, and technology could harness nature and change social life and human existence for the better.

Modernity's achievements were considerable. It gave birth to democratic movements in the West that increased personal freedoms and liberties for most, including (eventually) minorities, women, and the propertyless classes. Governments regulated social relations and put in place rational systems of law, justice, monetary exchange, schooling, and social welfare systems. Driven by the dynamic and technology-based system of capitalism, transportation, communication, and utility systems proliferated, while literacy expanded and the standard of living increased as consumer goods became readily available. Scientific experimentation, medical discoveries, and public health and sanitation movements helped wipe out diseases and reduce various forms of human suffering.

Yet modernity has always had its detractors. Karl Marx (1818–1883) wrote about the devastating poverty, exploitation, and alienation that he saw in nineteenth-century capitalism. The French sociologist Emile Durkheim (1858–1917) considered how geographic and class mobility and the loss of tradition in culture were likely to produce a feeling of anomie, or normlessness, on the part of many. The German social scientist Max Weber (1864–1920) offered the view that modernity's distinctive "formal rationality"—as epitomized in large, bureaucratic organizations—represented an "iron cage" that would ultimately entrap us. And, an even darker view is found in the writings of anti-Enlightenment philosopher Friedrich Nietzsche (1844–1900).

Nietzsche offered a direct challenge to the optimistic worldview of the Enlightenment and the so-called advances of modernity. For Nietzsche, this period's "progress," the discovery of absolute "Truths," and its scientific and technical "innovation" were more about what he called the "Will to Power": the human drive to dominate nature and the environment. While Nietzsche praised the critical spirit of the Enlightenment, he disputed those who claimed to have discovered universal moral codes and systems of reason, since he believed that given the diversity of human nature, such codes could not apply to everyone. This meant that individuals asserting law-like standards must necessarily place themselves—morally, socially, and culturally—above others, thereby dominating them. From a Nietzschean perspective, the history of recent human experience is not a simple procession of higher universal morals and higher standards of reason. Rather, driven by the desire for some ultimate "Truth" and knowledge, humans have produced one system of domination after the other. (As it was once put, we "progressed" in the twentieth century, for example, from "the slingshot to the megaton bomb.") In this view, knowledge cannot be separated from power. The ideological system of Enlightenment reason, rationality, and progress is seen as just that: another ideology, another interpretation of reality, advanced by one group over others, rather than some ultimate, final, "Truth."

For Nietzsche, then, as well as for Weber and, later, for Foucault, the post-Enlightenment period is one of increasing domination masked in a guise of emancipation and humanitarianism. As one writer put it, "Awakening in the classical world like a sleeping giant, reason finds chaos and disorder everywhere and embarks on a rational ordering of the social, attempting to classify and regulate all forms of experience."[5] Foucault suggests that rather than a utopian dream of freedom, late-eighteenth-century politicians, philosophers, and jurists offered a blueprint for a military model of society in which discipline and self-control would become a central organizing theme. Uniform precision, bodily discipline, rigid hierarchies, and "the drill" designed to mold and shape the body would become techniques of social control that could easily be adapted beyond the military camps and hospitals where these techniques were discovered and perfected. The modern individual was born, according to Foucault, into a sea of regulations, petty rules and subrules, and fussy inspections, a world where the supervision of the smallest fragments of life and of the body takes place in the context of the school, the barracks, the hospital, and the workshop.[6]

The experiences that Foucault saw as the most vulnerable to rationalization, scientific inquiry, and official scrutiny were madness, criminality, poverty, forms of deviance, and even sexuality. With Enlightenment zeal, late-eighteenth-century ideologues turned their attention from the control of nature to the manipulation of "man" by way of the emerging knowledge of the "human sciences." This movement is reflected in the early writings in penology and criminology, psychology, neurology, and demography. In other words, in new and important ways, human beings—our bodies, minds, and behaviors—became the *subject* of scientific inquiry and the *object* of its passions. The rise of the human sciences as a topic of inquiry is closely linked with the emergence of new "disciplinary technologies" designed to treat the human body *as an object* to be broken down, analyzed, and improved. This is a crucial turn of events. Rather than focusing on dominating the world around them, late-Enlightenment scholars turned the Will to Power on the human race. Rational and scientific knowledge and discourses (that is, systems of language overlapping with cultural practices), along with bureaucratic organizations, provided the means to classify, regulate, exclude, and even eliminate any human behavior deemed outside an increasingly narrow definition of "normal." Some would argue that, say, Nazi Germany or Stalinist Russia were, rather than some aberration in the course of human progress, a natural outcome of the rational, calculating mind of modernity. As Foucault once said, both regimes "used and extended mechanisms already present in most other societies. More than that: in spite of their own internal madness, they used to a large extent the ideas and the devices of our political rationality."[7]

So, it would seem that this is the historical context of how we in the West got the idea that we could, regardless of an individual's particular "defect," reconstruct a more idealized person if only he or she could be subjected to the right disciplinary regime.

CASTLES OF OUR CONSCIENCE

This mentality and the emergence of the modern disciplinary institution are nowhere more evident than in the United States.[8] In addition to their sudden revulsion to violence, what became clear to reformers in the late eighteenth and early nineteenth centuries was that the whipping post and the rack were a messy business and, increasingly, a political liability in postrevolutionary America. These inherited English criminal statutes were a constant reminder of monarchical political oppression, while those involving "cruel" sanctions were not applied consistently, making criminal justice arbitrary and ineffectual. In these early years, "a jury, squeezed between two distasteful choices, death or acquittal, often acquitted the guilty," according to Lawrence Friedman.[9] This kind of "jury lawlessness" sometimes provoked vigilante justice, endangering the establishment of rational-legal authority and, therefore, the political power of the new government. A more predictable, orderly, and democratic set of punishments was needed to support the new political regime. We see, then, the emergence of a new discourse of crime and new forms of punishment.[10]

Inspired by the writings of, among others, the influential Italian criminologist Cesare Beccaria and his new "science of man," *Homo criminalis*, people such as Dr. Benjamin Rush (1745–1813), who was a signer of the Declaration of Independence, set out to reinvent criminal justice practices. This new discourse on crime and punishment was celebrated in a now well-known set of principles:

1. Punishment must be consistent and not arbitrary.
2. Punishment should be a deterrent to future criminality.
3. There should be temporal modulation, since punishment can function only if it comes to an end.
4. Each crime and each penalty would be clearly laid out in a classification scheme.
5. The guilty should be only one of the targets of punishment, for punishment is directed above all at the potentially guilty.

The bodies of condemned offenders were now the property of society rather than of the king. Such ideas were infused with the notion of the social contract: that crime was an attack on society itself and that punishment should right the wrong done to the community and restore offenders to their proper places in it. Criminal justice would be rational, not emotional, according to the reformers. It would approach the mind and soul of the criminal and not just the body.

For a while, it was deemed that performing public works was the best treatment for the offender. In Philadelphia, for example, the application of the city's "wheelbarrow" law of 1786 put ragged, shaven-headed, chain-gang prisoners to work cleaning the streets under the watchful eye of armed guards. But the sight of these men became increasingly distasteful to the good citizens of the city as the convicts went about "begging and insulting the inhabitants, [and] collecting crowds of idle boys," and they became the sport of others who tormented the prisoners incessantly. The law of March 27, 1789, soon sequestered prisoners to conditions of more private punishment at the Walnut Street jail.[11] Here the prisoners were subjected to a "moral" regime of solitary confinement, hard labor, diet control, and bodily hygiene. Yet not long after it was built, conditions at the jail deteriorated; jail inspectors began pardoning prisoners to alleviate overcrowding, abuses and neglect were exposed, and serious riots took place. The result was unanimous condemnation of the Walnut Street jail. But rather than scrap the experiment with incarceration, authorities pressed on and called for the building of new, larger state penitentiaries. Undertaking the most ambitious public works program in Pennsylvania's history to date, the western and eastern facilities were erected by the laws of 1817 and 1821, marking the beginnings of Pennsylvania's prison "system." The situation was similar elsewhere, as other states increased their commitment to institutional punishment.[12]

This turn to rationally organized reformatory institutions and the new "science of man" influenced society's response to other behaviors as well. Before about 1825, the majority of poor and dependent people had been customarily cared for in noninstitutional ways. Those close to the center of town life might stay in their own homes with the help of the community, or they were placed with relatives, friends, or fellow church members. Those on the margins were "boarded" with townsfolk, with a widow perhaps, at a negotiated price. Later, communities made direct payments to people in their homes, while some able-bodied poor might be "auctioned off" to farmers and others and were put to work for their keep. Yet, after the 1820s, these apparently flexible and informal arrangements began to break down under the weight of expanded commercial development, the erosion of social cohesion in small towns, the attraction of wealth, and the increasing stratification of towns and villages. Townsfolk, particularly those of the middle and upper classes, became less willing to take in and board the increasing number of strangers and outsiders appearing in their area.

In New York, for example, an influential report by the secretary of state in 1824 estimated the total number of poor in New York to be 22,111 and the cost of providing for them to be close to $500,000. The report advocated the establishment of a system of county poorhouses modeled after the "House of Industry," which had been erected in Rensselaer County in 1820. The idea was that each inmate would work to his own ability as a means of stimulating industry and sharing the expense of his maintenance. These houses of employment would ideally be connected to a workhouse or penitentiary "for the reception and discipline of sturdy beggars and vagrants." Street beggary would be entirely prohibited. By 1835, almshouses appeared in fifty-one out of fifty-four state counties.

The principal advantages of the poorhouse seem clear. It isolated the dependent from the growing middle-class community that increasingly considered the pauper an idler and troublemaker. Rather than have the indigent scattered around town in private dwellings or, worse yet, begging on street corners, the almshouse centralized relief administration and provided for more effective surveillance of their activities by one overseer. However, before long, the "new" system of county indoor relief was itself in crisis. For what was hailed as the final solution to dependency revealed itself as yet another administrative, jurisdictional, and financial mess. In New York, annual reports from throughout the state to the legislature uncovered shocking abuse of inmates. Idleness was pervasive, especially in the larger houses. Economic depressions between 1837 and

1843, and later between 1857 and 1858, combined with the dramatic increase in immigration, placed an incredible burden on relief agencies. State governments, grappling to gain some rational control over the system and expenditures, began to create central administrative agencies to coordinate the activities of public charities. Massachusetts was the first to create a state board of charities in 1863. Later that year, New York established its board. By 1873 boards had been set up in Illinois, Pennsylvania, North Carolina, Rhode Island, Michigan, Wisconsin, Kansas, and Connecticut.

One important development that followed the establishment of these state boards was the process of classifying and segregating the population of the almshouses and moving inmates into facilities designated for their particular "defect." Reformers contended that the care and control function of the poorhouse could be enhanced if each class of dependent had its own particular needs addressed, since the mixing of such classes had created conditions which were detrimental to all. This "classification" movement attempted to extend administrative rationality and planning by isolating each particular class of deviants and dependents, not only to physically separate them from each other but also to gain more effective surveillance, observation, and control. Gender, age, and mental and physical capacities were the basis of boundaries among the new facilities, which prevented, through the restriction of both social and sexual contact, the procreation of the "defective classes." Once so isolated, each facility could engage in a more exacting process of distinguishing the degree of each class's "rehabilitative" potential. Whereas custodial care was all that could be expected for the very old, the very young, the infirm, or the completely helpless, others, including recalcitrant children, the healthy deviant, and the slightly feeble, could be educated and trained to labor both inside and, eventually, outside the institution.

The first group of dependents affected by the movement for separation was the insane. By 1881, there were six state hospitals for the acutely and chronically insane in New York, for example. Between 1850 and 1869, thirty-five new hospitals were opened in other states, and, by 1890, fifty-nine others came into existence, with the post-1870 hospitals increasingly larger in size. Children were similarly drawn away from the mixed almshouse where they were, for the most part, "badly fed, badly clothed, badly taken care of, and exposed to the degrading influence of those in immediate charge of them," according to reformer Louisa Lee Schuyler.[13] Specialized juvenile correction facilities—houses of refuge, reformatories, and training schools—expanded both the classification scheme and the system of care and control of dependent and troublesome children. Not only were children increasingly institutionalized in segregated facilities, but the legal mechanisms by which they got there changed as well. The juvenile court represented one more manifestation of the increasingly bureaucratic system of social control and the trend toward administrative reform and rationality. Within twenty-five years of the adoption of the first juvenile court legislation in Illinois in 1899, juvenile courts were established in every state but two. While perhaps more ceremonial than substantive at first, the juvenile court evolved to possess broad-sweeping jurisdiction over the lives of children under the age of sixteen. The court's ideological foundation rested on the notion of *parens patriae,* or parental care, and thus the legal institution was charged with protecting and providing for the needs of delinquent, dependent, and neglected youth.

The darker side of the reform story, however, was the regulation of family life by the state along with few alternatives to an institutional response to youthful misconduct. By 1940, juvenile courts in the United States handled 200,000 delinquency cases alone, not including the dependent and neglected—a rate of 10.5 per 1,000 of those between the ages of 10 and 17. By 1955, the corresponding figures were 431,000 cases with a rate of 21.4 per 1,000. In comparing figures from the U.S. Bureau of the Census for juvenile correctional facilities between 1923 and 1950, we see that these populations rose from 27,238 in 1923; to 30,496 in 1933; and to 40,880 by 1950. The corresponding rates per 100,000 of those in the population under age 18 were 65.7, 72.3, and 88.8, respectively.[14]

Specialized facilities were also developed for the "feebleminded" and the epileptic. "Mental defectives" were further classified as "teachable" or "unteachable." Concerned with the "hereditary factor" in the proliferation of crime, pauperism, and mental deficiency, reformers and state welfare administrators sought to isolate its source, which, according to one reformer, was "the unrestrained liberty allowed to vagrant and degraded women." They urged the creation of an institution for "vagrant and degraded" women, which, if not for reformation, could at least cut off the line of pauper descendants. In New York, the campaign resulted in 1887 in the House of Refuge for Women at Hudson, where "all females between the ages of fifteen and thirty years who had been convicted of petty larceny, habitual drunkenness, of being common prostitutes, frequenters of disorderly houses or houses of prostitution" were to be placed. Suitable employment was to be provided, which would encourage "habits of self supporting industry" and "mental and moral improvement." This facility was soon filled to capacity, and three other women's reformatories were erected in the state by the late 1890s.

So, according to the view I want to take here, the inventions of the penitentiary, the poorhouse, and the mental asylum were not *simply* chapters in a long humanitarian crusade. Driven by ideas having their origins in Enlightenment reason and progressive faith, a constellation of influential philosophers, jurists, reformers, and state authorities aided in the creation and *expansion* of a system of social control for modern society not possible in the pre-modern, classical age. Ironically then, it might be argued that, in the name of "humanity" and "emancipation," reformers created *more* formal social control, not less. Reformers, interested in punishing more effectively and more certainly, went beyond the surface of the skin, into the very heart and soul of the deviant. In doing so, they approached the criminal, the deviant, and the poor as objects to be manipulated, whereas just a short time before, the community had confronted the "impenitent sinner" as deserving of corporal punishment or, in the case of the poor, simply as a person who had been "reduced to want."

Under the authority of the state and "in the name of the people," these reformers—increasingly from middle and professional classes—asserted a new system of universal "moral" principles and a new discourse on crime and punishment, placing themselves as "experts" at the center of justice practice. Reflecting the central themes of modernity, disorderly and ill-defined forms of public torture and stigmatization ceremonies were replaced by rationally organized legal codes as well as reformatory institutions such as prisons, poorhouses, and asylums that this new social class would run and supervise. As part of their new program, rather than seek retribution, they removed punishment from public view and placed it behind the walls of the institution. The "dangerous rogue," sent away to places like Auburn, was subjected to a secular, military-like apparatus that would transform him (or a woman sent to a "House of Refuge") into a newly refined democratic subject: "A diligent, literate laborer. A moderate, self-interested citizen."[15] And, as I have shown, it was soon asserted that the poor could be made "industrious," the deviant turned from deviant ways, and the insane brought back to reason. Listen to these notions in the words of some of these early reformers:

> You take a child; you must not expect to make her, without care, and instruction and patience, a useful domestic. Encourage what you may find good in her, and in punishing her faults, consider how you should endeavor to correct those of your own children.
>
> —Boston Children's Aid Society, *Reminiscences of the Boston Female Orphan Asylum* (1844)

> To make a vagrant efficient is more praiseworthy than to make two blades of grass grow where one grew before.
>
> —E. Stagg Whitin, *Penal Servitude* (1912)

> Outside the walls a man must choose between work and idleness—between honesty and crime. Why not teach him these lessons before he comes out?
>
> —Thomas Mott Osborne, *Society and Prisons* (1916)

DISCIPLINE AS A TECHNIQUE

The modern era gave birth to a range of discourses, techniques, and practices that were designed to mold and shape the body as well as the mind. These practices involve a distinctly modern form of social and political constraint that Michel Foucault called "disciplinary power," a kind of power that is exercised as a technique rather than held as a commodity. This is a radical alternative to traditional sociological conceptions of power. Most theories assert that power lies in the hands of the "powerful" who control social resources, for example, the owners of capital or political elites. "Power" is often assumed to emanate— somewhat mysteriously—from these resources. Additionally, these theories often neglect to consider the relationship between power and knowledge, taking for granted that knowledge is either politically neutral or necessarily liberating. Such "resource" theories of power may be important in understanding, say, the perpetuation of social classes or other forms of material inequality. Unfortunately, they are often "reductionistic" in that they reduce all forms of social power to class domination or to the more "macrostructures" of the economy, political authority, or the state. In doing so, they may tell us very little about the "microlevel"—the concrete ways in which individuals, their bodies and behaviors, are controlled and shaped in everyday life. The exercise of discipline may augment, and may even be intimately bound up with, other forms of political, social, and economic power, but cannot be subsumed by them.

Disciplinary power is "bi-directional," not simply operating from the "top down," but circulating throughout the social body. That is, it does not necessarily flow directly from the highest levels of the government, or from ruling elites, and imposed on the masses, but may be developed and practiced by a wide range of people in a host of institutional sites. So rather than being concentrated in the hands of a few, disciplinary power appears nearly everywhere, dispersed and fragmented. In this view, *we are all involved and enmeshed within a matrix of power relations that are highly intentional and purposeful; arrangements that can be more or less unequal but are never simply one-directional.* Some examples: consider the proliferation of drug-testing programs in the workplace and the cases of Samuel Allen and Daryl Kenyon. Allen is a highly paid president of the international division of a large corporate sporting-goods store with more than ten thousand employees. Kenyon, on the other hand, works on the production line at a large office-furniture manufacturer. Despite their obvious differences in resources, status, and authority, both men were required to offer hair samples to be tested for drugs when they were hired. Both men even consent to this form of surveillance by endorsing the programs in their companies.[16] Or think of the police. While they can exercise considerable authority over the citizenry, they must, in order to function legitimately, discipline themselves with bureaucratic rules and regulations, a rigid hierarchy of command, and the close monitoring and evaluation of each other's actions.

The exercise of disciplinary power is often continuous, automatic, and anonymous (think of the surveillance video camera, for example). It is extensive and thorough, and it is capillary as well, meaning that it extends out to the remotest corners of society. It disciplines individuals efficiently and effectively, with the least amount of physical force, labor power, and expense. Knowledge, in Foucault's scheme, is intrinsic to the spread and proliferation of disciplinary power. Knowledge is not equal to power, nor is power the same as knowledge; each presupposes the other. Again, consider drug testing. Such tests are a disciplinary ritual that uses scientific knowledge *of* the body to derive knowledge *from* the body. This information is then used as the basis to judge and/or to take action against an individual. Without knowledge, power cannot be exercised without force; without the authority to punish, the knowledge is meaningless.

Finally, disciplinary power is often productive and not simply repressive. This is an important point. If disciplinary power operated in a despotic fashion, it would meet with far more resistance. Instead of dominating with force and oppression, proponents stress the obvious productive benefits from various disciplinary techniques, thus appeasing opposition. The techniques of disciplinary power are "corrective," and agents may employ rewards or privileges to accomplish the goal of modifying behavior. For example, supervision in a workshop may have been set up to avoid theft, but the knowledge gathered from the monitoring may also be used to enhance employees' skills and productivity. In such a case, workers are encouraged to use the company's surveillance system to their own advantage by becoming "better" workers. Suspected substance users are taught to use the company's random drug tests to keep themselves "clean," while "motivated" students are persuaded to utilize a teacher's tracking system to meet goals and complete their work.

It is during the modern era that, according to Foucault, a variety of these relatively modest disciplinary procedures were perfected by the doctors, wardens, and schoolmasters of the new institutions. It was these individuals who were the first to confront problems of managing large numbers of people in confined spaces. With the help of the knowledge of the emerging human sciences, these institutional administrators devised detailed, micromethods for the efficient supervision and surveillance of inmates, patients, and students in order to produce obedience and conformity. These methods include strict posture and machine-like movements such as in the "lockstep-and-silence" system; monotonous uniforms; the separation and classification of people by their crimes, diseases, and abilities; orderly lines of desks so one teacher can observe the entire room; and even the smallest architectural details, such as large dividers between bathroom stalls to prevent sexual misconduct.

The control of time and space was crucial in these institutions; every minute of every day and every activity of the inmates were monitored and scheduled. Enclosure permitted the division of internal space into an orderly grid where, as Foucault put it, "each individual has his own place; and each place its individual." It was in these closed, disciplinary organizations where, for the first time, people were treated as "cases" about which authorities attempted to build extensive dossiers including life histories, family backgrounds, and rehabilitative progress. There were also series of micropenalties established to scan conduct and ensure social control. Offenses such as lateness, absences, inattention, impoliteness, disobedience, poor attitude, and lack of cleanliness were subjected to light physical punishments, minor deprivations, and petty humiliations. By specifying the most minute details of every day, disciplinary power makes almost any behavior punishable and thus the object of attention, surveillance, and control.

Disciplinary power is further enhanced by the use of more general procedures such as "the examination." This is a ritualized knowledge-gathering activity in which case files are built out of the often-mundane details of people's lives and activities. Two key elements are used to build these files. One is "hierarchical observation" that involves surveillance, information collection, and analysis as a central organizing principal of the institution. Disciplining individuals through observation requires the delegation of supervision. Here individuals carry out the act of watching others while they themselves are being watched. The other is "normalizing judgments" that entail the assessment of an individual's activity set against some standard or ideal where all behavior lies between two poles, "good" and "bad," and can be judged—with small, graduated distinctions—along the continuum. Foucault argued that the goal of these procedures was to forge what he called "docile" bodies: mute, obedient individuals who have been subjected, transformed, and improved.

This notion of docility is very important to the ideas presented in this book, for it is the ultimate aim of most forms of social control. The opposite of docility is rebellious, wild, and disagreeable behavior. Robert Emerson and Sheldon Messinger refer to the "politics of trouble" when they point out that most behavior that comes to be labeled "deviant," problematic, or disagreeable originates with people causing "trouble" for others or by feeling troubled themselves.[17] No matter what its stated purpose—to "help," "cure," "punish," or "rehabilitate"—social control that is aimed at the juvenile delinquent, the unemployed, the mentally ill, the nursing-home resident, or the recalcitrant worker is intended to render that individual manageable, submissive, teachable, tractable, and pliable. The "politics of trouble" are echoed in the commands "Keep in line," "Don't talk back," "Eat your dinner," "Don't make noise," "Don't cause problems," "Work harder."

BENTHAM'S PANOPTICON

Amid the array of modern disciplinary practices, Foucault chose to highlight what he considered to be an exemplar in the operation of modern disciplinary technology: the Panopticon. In 1791, British utilitarian philosopher, economist, and jurist Jeremy Bentham (1748–1832) printed a collection of letters he had written under the long-winded yet informative title of *Panopticon; or, The Inspection-House: Containing the Idea of a New Principle of Construction Applicable to any Sort of Establishment, in Which Persons of any Description are to be Kept Under Inspection; and Particular to Penitentiary-Houses, Prisons, Poor-Houses, Lazarettos, Houses of Industry, Manufactories, Hospitals, Work-Houses, Mad-Houses, and Schools with A Plan of Management Adapted to the Principle.* The detailed architectural design for the Panopticon called for the construction of a building with a central tower that contained the "inspector's lodge." Around the lodge, in a circular form, was a set of peripheral cells with windows in the rear and front of each cell so that, in effect, the cell space was backlit. The prisoner (lunatic, schoolboy, or other inmate) could then be subjected to the constant observation of the person occupying the lodge. Bentham himself anticipated the "politics of trouble" when he emphasized that the goal of docility could be easily achieved with the Panopticon design, "[n]o matter how different or opposite the purpose: whether it be that of punishing the incorrigible, guarding the insane, reforming the vicious, confining the suspected, employing the idle, maintaining the helpless, curing the sick, [or] instructing the willing."

The Panopticon reversed the principles of the dungeon; it was about light and visibility rather than darkness and isolation. Yet the person under inspection would be kept in the dark, in another sense, as the lodge would be constructed with an elaborate Venetian-blind effect that Bentham called the "inspector's lantern": a sort of one-way mirror that masked the presence or absence of an observer. Bentham created this device because, according to his very efficient plans, the inspector would also function as the institution's bookkeeper. Yet if he performed this task, his lamp would give away his presence to the inmates. So, Bentham designed the lantern so that the only thing the inmates could see was a dark spot at the center of the aperture. With this scheme, the inmates may or may not be under constant surveillance; they just think or imagine that they are. As Bentham put it, they are "awed to silence by an invisible eye." The inmates have therefore internalized what Foucault called *le regard*, or the "gaze" of the authorities, and, in effect, they watch and render themselves docile. In this way, power operates without coercion, force, or violence, automatically and continuously, whether or not the tower is occupied at all. With this technology, Bentham created an all-seeing, all-knowing "God" that was, in reality, nothing more than a dark spot in the lantern. In Bentham's words, "in a Panopticon the inspector's back is never turned." And he asserted the productive benefits of his design for the "inspection-house" in the opening lines of his treatise: "Morals reformed—health preserved—industry invigorated—instruction diffused—public burdens lightened . . . —all by a simple idea in architecture!"[18]

While the design for the Panopticon was never adopted in its pure form, many of its principles were deployed, and it stimulated considerable discussion and new techniques for social control. But the fact that it had limited direct impact did not diminish its importance, Foucault argued. Its significance lay in the very idea that such a design was thought to be necessary or desirable at the time. The Panopticon remains both an important symbol of modern disciplinary technology and a basic principle on which many forms of contemporary surveillance operate (for example, the video cameras rotating among school buses that I mentioned in chapter 1).

THE "SWARMING OF DISCIPLINARY MECHANISMS"

Let me summarize Foucault's contribution to our understanding of modern social control. Influenced by a radical critique of Enlightenment reason, Foucault chose to study the relationships among experiences such as madness and criminality, the knowledge produced by the new "sciences of man," and the manner in which power was exercised on bodies and "souls" through meticulous rituals in institutions like asylums and penitentiaries. It was in those institutions that he saw the fullest realization of the military model of society emerging in the modern era. In other words, life in the penitentiary, reformatory, and poorhouses was conceived as an idealized version of a utopian, bourgeois society; a machinelike, disciplined culture, set on obedience, order, and uniformity. The shaping, molding, and construction of "docile bodies" would be accomplished through the use of various "disciplinary technologies." These techniques ranged from the "lockstep" to ritualistic examinations with their "hierarchical observations" designed to instill the gaze of authorities and produce self-control, and "normalizing judgments" that set the behavioral standards to be upheld.

In *Discipline and Punish*, Foucault set out the early modern origins of disciplinary power within the confines of closed, disciplinary institutions. Yet this is only the beginning, as he quite clearly anticipated postmodern developments. "While on the one hand," he states, "the disciplinary establishments increase, their mechanisms have a certain tendency to become 'de-institutionalized,' to emerge from the closed fortresses in which they once functioned and to circulate in the 'free' state; the massive, compact disciplines are broken down into flexible methods of control, which may be transferred and adapted."[19] He calls this the "swarming of disciplinary mechanisms." Here he means that disciplinary microtechniques that were developed in the institutions began to reach out from those organizations, linking up with other institutions and practices, creating a macroweb of social control. For example, schools begin to supervise the conduct of the parents as well as of the children, the hospital monitors not only the patients but the other inhabitants of the district, too, and relief officials "oversee" not just the poor but their entire extended families, as well. Remember, disciplinary power is capillary; it expands out, colonizes, and moves to the tiniest reaches of social life. Once this happens, we have a society where everyday life is increasingly filled with meticulous rituals of power involving surveillance, examinations, and knowledge-gathering activities. This creates, according to Foucault, "[a] subtle, graduated, carceral net, with compact institutions, but also separate and diffused methods," which he sees as far more effective than the "arbitrary, widespread, badly integrated" practices of the classical age.[20] We see, then, "an increasing ordering in all realms under the guise of improving the welfare of the individual and the population . . . this order reveals itself as a strategy, with no one directing it and everyone increasingly enmeshed in it, whose only end is the increase of power and order itself."[21]

In Foucault's account, the foundation of this kind of disciplinary society was in place in Europe as early as the seventeenth century. I believe that it has only been in the last half of the twentieth century, at least in the United States, that we are witnessing the historical movement from exceptional punishment—that is, the disciplining of a particular individual for committing a particular offense—to the generalized surveillance of us all. I want to argue here that the conditions that constituted modern social control practices are changing and that new disciplinary technologies and discourses are taking hold. In short, I believe we are witnessing the emergence of a new regime of social control—a regime that retains many of the modern themes and practices of the past, while, at the same time, is both a product and a reflection of contemporary postmodern culture. Therefore I believe there exists today an increasing tension between two practices of social control. As Foucault put it:

> At one extreme, the . . . enclosed institution, established on the edges of society . . . arresting evil, breaking communications, suspending time. At the other extreme . . . the discipline-mechanism: a functional mechanism that *must improve the exercise of power by making it lighter, more rapid, more effective, a design of subtle coercion for a society yet to come.* (Emphasis mine)[22]

THE POSTMODERN MOMENT

It seems clear that we have witnessed, in the post-World War II period (and more intensely since the early 1970s), significant changes in the organization of Western society and culture. Some social theorists think that these changes reflect an "exhaustion" of modernity and signal the beginning of a new, "postmodern" period of history. Most scholars would acknowledge that this transition is happening while many "modern" institutions and practices remain in place. Accordingly, I tend to agree with Fredric Jameson and others who argue that postmodernism is the "cultural face" of a more developed stage of capitalism.[23] Just what are these conditions that make up postmodernity? We best see the characteristics by comparing them with the dimensions of modernity I offered earlier; see table 2.1.

Table 2.1 Characteristics of Modernity and Postmodernity

Modernity	*Postmodernity*
Rationalization of social life epitomized by rigid predictability and control; the factory and machine-based capitalism (Fordism)	De-industrialization and globalization; "flexible" use of labor, manufacturing, organization, markets, products, organizational innovation, and service and "information economy" (post-Fordism)
Division of labor, specialization, and clear separation of the "public" and "private," gender roles, home and work life, and the like; relatively stable nation-state boundaries and hierarchy and colonialism	Blurring of boundaries; implosion of once taken-for-granted meanings, symbols, and institutions of modern life: work, marriage, family, health, sexuality, intimacy, gender, privacy, etc., often combined with a nostalgia for the past; shifting global boundaries and power centers and decolonialization
Rise of large-scale, centralized state and private organizations and bureaucracies as well as urban space	Increasing decentraliztion; e.g., public housing, community "corrections" and "policing," public schools, corporate divisions, and suburbanization
"Compression" of time-space relations; fast-paced world made "smaller" by new modes of transportation and communication	Intensified time-space compression creating intense disorientation and disruption in cultural and social life; a dominant video culture; the commodification of sexuality and desire and a celebration of consumer lifestyles
Large middle and professional class with its own self-interest, sensibilities, and culture; it becomes the dominant cultural definition culminating in the 1950s	Increasing challenges to middle-class, "nuclear family" from women, gays, ethnic and religious groups, as well as cultural diversity promoting the "politics of difference"
Rise of the "human sciences" modeled after the physical sciences aimed at "knowable man" through individuality, consciousness, and behavior	Collapse of "grand narratives" and a turn away from the scientific approach to society; rise of feminist, cultural studies agenda that takes gender, class, race, and ethnicity to be central to any analysis of society
Utopian belief in progress, driven by the idea that scientific knowledge, objective reason, and technology could harness nature and change social life and human existence for the better	Increasing skepticism about progress and of those who assert its possibility; criticism of scientific knowledge and rationality

As I indicated in chapter 1, ours is a culture deeply penetrated by commodities and consumer "lifestyles." Generated by corporate marketing strategies, from Eddie Bauer to J. Crew, from Infiniti automobiles to the latest "concept" in chain restaurants (the simulated "neighborhood grill and bar" set in a suburban strip mall with no neighborhood), companies sell us images of how we want to see ourselves as much as they market products. As Donald Lowe puts it, most of us "no longer consume commodities to satisfy relatively stable and specific needs, but to reconstruct ourselves in terms of the lifestyles associated with the consumption of certain commodities" (the T-shirt inscribed with "I shop, therefore I am" says it all).[24] The economic viability of America is now in the hands of our willingness to purchase these prized lifestyle insignias, where, for most of us, time spent in work has become little more than a means to fulfill what is now defined as our near-patriotic duty to consume. And when we do go to work, it may be to a "virtual" company that "flexibly" hires consultants and "temp" workers for its labor force, "outsources" its manufacturing needs, and changes its organizational structure like a chameleon.

Increasingly, time and social and geographical space are highly compressed by rapidly changing communication, computer technologies, and information storage and retrieval. We have, at the click of a mouse button, access to vast amounts of information, but may not have a clue about how to make sense of it. We can "surf" the virtual globe of the Internet but not know or seemingly care who sits on our own city council. And we may have a cable television network that can bring us unlimited entertainment, but we may find that, as the title of one Bruce Springsteen song suggests, there are "57 channels (and nothin' on)." Each day brings us startling scientific and medical knowledge that seems to do little to help us cope with life. As Vaclav Havel, the playwright and president of the Czech Republic, has stated:

[W]e find ourselves in a paradoxical situation. We enjoy all the achievements of modern civilization that have made our physical existence on this earth easier in so many important ways. Yet we do not know exactly what to do with ourselves, where to turn. The world of our experiences seems chaotic, disconnected, confusing. There appear to be no integrating forces, no unified meaning, and no true inner understanding of phenomena in our experience of the world. Experts can explain anything in the objective world to us, yet we understand our own lives less and less. In short, we live in the postmodern world, where everything is possible, and almost nothing is certain.[25]

This uncertainty is exacerbated by the blurring of boundaries between the once taken-for-granted meanings, symbols, and institutions of modern life such as work, marriage, family, health, sexuality, intimacy, gender, and privacy.[26] An underlying anxiety may be created from our increasing inability to distinguish "fact" from fiction and the "real" from the "simulation of the real." Some argue that the "language of the visual," or "videocy," is rapidly replacing modern forms of literacy based on oral and written traditions. Within the flood of images presented in the mass media—this "ecstasy of communication"—how do we separate "investigative journalism" from "docudramas," *Real Cops* from the latest "breaking news" story, or "live" CNN coverage of an international skirmish from a cable show about advanced weaponry?[27] In this context, authenticity begins to lose its anchoring points. Importantly, since such chaotic media have become our primary source of cultural knowledge, we often believe that we know and understand the world simply because we "saw it in the movies." This society, according to one theorist, only knows itself through its own reflection in the camera's eye and through experience that may be replaced by its visual representation. In this culture, we learn to identify with the simulated world of television more readily than we do with the "real" world around us. As Sherry Turkle puts it:

> The bar featured in the television series *Cheers* no doubt figures so prominently in the American imagination at least partly because most of us don't have a neighborhood place where 'everybody knows your name.' Instead, we identify with the place on the screen, and most recently have given it some life off the screen as well. Bars designed to look like the one on *Cheers* have sprung up all over the country, most poignantly in airports, our most anonymous of locales. Here, no one will know your name, but you can always buy a drink or a souvenir sweatshirt.[28]

Another theorist suggests that television/video has a unique ability to break down the distinction between "here and there, live and mediated, personal and public" and has thus severed the links between social and physical space. This leads to a sense of "placelessness."[29] I am not surprised, for example, when a white, suburban, middle-class, midwestern college student told me that he liked the film *Boyz N the Hood*. "Why?" I asked. He stated confidently, "Because it was like real life in South Central L.A." Yet he has never even been to South Central—never mind having lived there—and, in fact, has no frame of reference to compare the "real" to this fictional portrayal.

The media(ted) culture of postmodern society has a tremendous effect on our ability to make informed political and policy decisions. Video journalists, sensational talk-show hosts, and those behind slick marketing campaigns have become, according to Norman Denzin, the new "intellectuals" and "historians" who hold a near monopoly on the presentation and interpretation of politics, social issues, and problems. "They have turned news into entertainment and their commentary into instant analysis," says Denzin.[30] Every night, hours and hours of TV "news magazines" turn everyday life into a theatrical drama where the most compelling stories are those that recount lives filled with uncertainty and unpredictability. They point to the next burgeoning "crisis" that threatens to make you or me its latest victim: your daughter may be a drug user, your ex-husband a child molester, or your study partner a rapist. Meanwhile, as industry representatives readily admit, local TV "news" stations typically follow the adage, "if it bleeds, it leads," where seemingly every segment begins with the most grue-some murder and mayhem stories. Here broadcasts are often littered with the word "you," attempting to personalize the events and tragedies: "Imagine if it were *you* dropping *your* baby off at the sitter, only to have him killed." "If *you* were accidentally exposed to the HIV virus, would *you* want to be able to take a potent medicine to prevent getting AIDS?"[31] As one author of a book about fear in our society put it:

> Worry is the fear we manufacture, and those who choose to do it certainly have a wide range of dangers to dwell upon. Television in most major cities devotes up to forty hours a day to telling us about those who have fallen prey to some disaster and to exploring what calamities may be coming next. The local news anchor should begin each evening's broadcast by saying, "Welcome to the news; we're surprised you made it through another day. Here's what happened to those who didn't."[32]

My point is not to suggest that life's tragedies are simply illusions. Rather my argument is that what may actually be a relatively rare occurrence is easily sensa-tionalized into a widespread "social problem," creating a level of fear, anxiety, and mistrust that distorts our ability to make informed political decisions.[33] For example, despite the fact that the nation's violent crime rate fell for the seventh consecutive year in 1999, 56 percent of those polled in a national opinion survey thought that there was more crime in the United States than there was five years ago. When asked, "Generally speaking, would you say that most people can be trusted or that you can't be too careful in dealing with people?" the proportion of Americans saying that "most people can be trusted" has fallen precipitously, from 46 percent in 1972 to only 33 percent in 1994.[34] As a parent, I have found myself hesitating to leave my child at a city park, as I have had nightmares of his picture ending up on a milk carton. Yet, despite the reported thousands of missing children each year publicized by a Washington-based lobbying group, the number of kids taken by strangers is actually extremely small. While even one kidnapping is obviously a tragedy, most missing children either are teenage runaways or are snatched by a parent in a messy divorce. Look closely at the fear campaigns of organizations such as the *Partnership for a Drug-Free America* that ask you to pick out the "drug dealer" from a full-page newspaper ad of laughing, squeaky-clean, white, middle-class, pre-adolescents. As the "director of creative development" (I love that title!) for the group has stated about the ads, "They are not pretty. They are not nice. They are not polite. They are designed to disturb and upset people."[35] Or think of the sensational case of accusations of child molestation at a preschool that results in teachers throughout the country not even daring—or even being allowed—to give a child a hug. Do we challenge the politician who claims that homicidal teenage "superpredators" are stalking the streets of America, when, at the same time, 80 percent of the counties in the country did not register a single homicide by a juvenile?

As the new purveyors of "truth" have gone about constructing the "reality" of epidemic crime and drug use, the disintegration of the nuclear family, or the laziness of homeless men and "cheating" welfare mothers, they have helped create a nostalgia for the "good ol' days" (that likely never existed). This lamenting for an ideal past became the platform of the New Right as it captured political power in the1980s and continues to be espoused well into the late 1990s. A coalition of right-wing politicians and religious fundamentalists began to (re)construct their version of the ideal citizen who personified the sacred values of religion, hard work, health, and self-reliance. This agenda was aided by both "New Democrats" claiming to be tough on crime, drugs, and welfare "dependency," as well as "liberals" who were willing to use the power of the state to enforce programmatic solutions to these "new" social problems. We therefore began a far-reaching campaign to regulate not only the traditional crimes of person and property but also the behaviors, conditions, and "lifestyles" of substance (ab)use, alcohol consumption, "eating disorders," tobacco consumption, sexuality, sexual promiscuity and "deviance," teenage pregnancy, out-of-marriage births, domestic violence, child abuse, "dysfunctional" families, various psychological or psychiatric disorders, and other medical conditions such as "attention deficit disorder," and such diseases as AIDS.

And yet, we see, at the same time, a rejection of the practicality and effectiveness of modern institutions where "nothing works" and where "rehabilitation" is a waste of time and money. In our day, the prison has lost the capacity to summon images of moral redemption and discipline. Not only does the ideology of reformation no longer conceal the reality of daily life on the inside, but the gaze of television and the cinema has taken us inside the asylum, offering us a drama of hopelessness and chaos. As a result of this attempt to regulate and control more and more of social life—as well as our increasing pessimism about institutional reform—we have turned to new meticulous rituals of social control that are being integrated into preexisting modern institutions and practices. Rather than isolating the body from everyday life for surveillance and control, these new techniques impose a structure and accountability on an individual's behavior and "lifestyle" in the everyday. And these new methods are often premised on regulating, probing, or measuring the body's functions, processes, characteristics, or movements. In other words, more and more surveillance ceremonies are taking place in our daily lives, and these are often based on assessing evidence and gaining knowledge from our bodies.

"JUST SAY NO" AND GONZO JUSTICE

The essentials of America's contemporary moral panic are best illustrated by the almost obsessional focus of the "war on drugs" that was set in motion in the late 1980s. As has been pointed out, the "Reagan-Bush administrations . . . needed a way to redefine American social control policies in order to further their broader political aims . . . Substance abuse was the problem they decided upon."[36] Here we saw a public discourse that held the defective character of the individual drug user responsible for nearly all the ills of contemporary society and helped justify a new politics of repression. This political agenda was underwritten by strategically cutting federally sponsored community mental health programs while allocating massive funds for a growing "substance abuse" sector.[37] Restrictive plea bargaining and longer, determinate sentences for drug-related offenses soon overwhelmed the country's courts, jails, prisons, and probation and parole departments and sent authorities searching for new ways to control drug-arrest populations.[38] Within the swirl of the "crisis," our video culture brought us publicity stunts, or what David Altheide calls "gonzo justice," such as the Los Angeles Police Department's use of a "battering ram," mounted on a military tank, to crash into suspected (and sometimes mistaken) crack-cocaine houses.[39]

Yet while such media spectacles held public attention, authorities were quietly introducing new disciplinary techniques, administered through an evolving network of local, public and private substance abuse and "community corrections" bureaucracies, and in what I will describe in chapter 3 as "intensive supervision programs." Supported by state subsidies to local agencies, these programs are intended to divert prison-bound, nonviolent felons from state institutions (a tactic known as "deinstitutionalization"). Proponents argued that these individuals are "better off" in the community, since they are "free" to participate as "productive" members of society. Yet I contend that this movement has, in effect, inserted the power to judge and punish more deeply into the daily life of the community, "deinstitutionalizing" not so much the offender but the disciplinary procedures and mechanisms of the prison. Once individuals become enmeshed in these organizational webs, their bodies, behaviors, movements, and actions can be monitored and controlled through a structure of bureaucratic accountability and disciplinary technologies and rituals such as drug testing, electronic monitoring, curfews, "surprise" work visits, and the like.

Given the "intensity" of these kinds of programs, haven't we then moved the disciplinary mechanism of the prison—the "gaze" of authorities, the surveillance, the judgments, the case files—into the community?[40] And having done so, haven't we blurred the boundary between the modern penal institution and the everyday life of the postmodern? Politicians, the public, and even the "clients" may think that such programs are "better" than doing time in prison (which, of course, was supposed to be "better" than public torture), but, again, what standard is being used to make these claims? Foucault argued that the enclosure of institutions permitted the control of time and space that was essential for the effective and efficient application of disciplinary power. It created an orderly "grid" that placed each inmate in a visible square of light. I argue, and illustrate in the following chapters, that such a grid is being built in the community. Here, the exercise of power is local and decentralized, methodical, and nearly automatic, as it is set within a framework of bureaucratic rules and regulations. Computers and telecommunication devices evoke the gaze of the state, while the body is monitored for evidence of deviant activity. Remaining "in the community" also integrates the deviant into—some would say "puts them under the control of"—the primary role of consumption in the society. To argue then that the emergence of new disciplinary practices is rooted in the postmodern is not to suggest that "modern" institutions or practices we have inherited will disappear anytime soon. After all, we are still incarcerating people at an unprecedented rate. Rather than replacements, these new applications should be seen as extensions of disciplinary power that invest, colonize, and link up preexisting forms. I describe this process in more detail in chapter 3.

But what do programs for convicted felons have to do with the rest of us? I want to argue that there are certain consequences for our society and culture as a whole that stem from recent policies. Foucault tells us to look to judicial practice to observe changing attitudes about discipline, social control, and surveillance in other spheres of society. In studying modern social control he saw, for example, important similarities between the rational organization and monotonous routine of prison life and the shop floor of the new factories. Today, I argue, programs like "community corrections" tend to normalize the presence of formal social control in everyday life. Such a presence—even though initially targeting people in the justice system—raises our tolerance for social control and provides models for other institutions to emulate. When combined with the rampant fear and mistrust generated by the media, the consequence is that we are more willing to condone, even insist, that we adopt more and more disciplinary practices and surveillance ceremonies that soon become routine and commonplace. For example, drug screening had been well established in the community corrections system before the Supreme Court ruled that, even without probable cause, any student participating in public school athletics could be randomly tested. Likewise, with the emergence of community-based "electronic monitoring" of convicted felons, we also see that employers are tethering employees to "beepers" or monitoring their activities with video cameras, computer terminals, handheld data-entry tablets, or other forms of electronic surveillance leashes. While prisons have armed guards, metal detectors, and video surveillance cameras, so does the Sunrise Multiplex movie theater in Valley Stream, New York, and so does Mount View High School in West Virginia. These parallels are too significant to ignore.

Even prisons themselves "blend in" to everyday life as they are made indistinguishable from other community institutions. In Lockhart, Texas, a small factory no different from the others on Industrial Boulevard makes computer circuit boards and air conditioners. Its 138 "employees" are actually inmates doing time in the medium-security prison run by Wackenhut Corrections Corporation.[41] Other facilities are designed to simulate suburban, high-tech industrial parks and often are referred to as "campuses." In Los Angeles, neighborhood-based, privately run "microprisons" holding illegal immigrants look no different from the surrounding apartment complexes—both have locked gates and bars on the windows. Meanwhile, in downtown Los Angeles, the Metropolitan Detention Center appears to be just another skyscraper or luxury hotel to those who drive by it every day. In this facility, guards sport preppy blue blazers as they ride elevators from floor to floor. As one inmate told author Mike Davis, "Can you imagine the mind fuck of being locked up in a Holiday Inn?"[42] In fact, in California, where more money is now spent to keep people behind bars than is spent on higher education, some institutions are no longer called prisons at all; they have names such as "Vacaville Medical Facility."

So, in the chapters that follow, I draw on examples from and move back and forth between the official justice system and the everyday life of the postmodern. In doing so, am I suggesting that "everything is a prison"? No, of course not. I do, however, illustrate how the lines between these two spheres of social life are increasingly blurred by the use of new surveillance and disciplinary practices. I show how these new meticulous rituals of power are constituted by and indicative of conditions of postmodernity, and I employ the ideas and concepts developed by Michel Foucault and other postmodern theorists to help us understand these developments. In chapter 3, I focus on new forms of surveillance that systematically watch and monitor our bodies and behaviors. I show how our communities, homes, schools, and workplaces are increasingly infused with meticulous rituals and surveillance ceremonies.

3

⤳

The Gaze and Its Compulsions

Disneyland is presented as imaginary in order to make us believe that the rest is real, when in fact all of Los Angeles and the America surrounding it are no longer real, but of the order of hyperreal and of simulation.

—Jean Baudrillard[1]

Court TV: Watching the Real Life Drama of Justice . . . Just the reality of real reality television.

—Advertisement, *New York Times,* 11 June 1994

Steve L., a convicted sex offender who lives in Tampa, Florida, returned home from work one day at 3 P.M., as required by his probation. At 4:09 he left his house for 17 minutes. The signal from the small radio transmitter attached to his ankle could no longer reach a monitoring box in the kitchen. Twenty miles away, a Florida Department of Corrections computer checked his work and treatment schedule, found that his brief absence was unauthorized, and sent an alarm to an office printer. The computer then automatically telephoned his probation officer.

—*New York Times*[2]

Much like Disneyland, Steve L.'s experience of "doing time at home" is a patchwork of preceding eras and futuristic possibilities. His Disneyland is a virtual world where all values (order, authority, justice, discipline, freedom, consumption, work, self-help, etc.) are celebrated, simulated, and presented. It is a bit of what French social theorist Jean Baudrillard calls the "hyperreal." How so? Hyperreality occurs in a postmodern culture when there are seemingly no longer any "real," stable reference points. For example, while Steve L.'s "electronic monitoring" is judged by its proponents to simulate the confinement experience of the prison, in practice, this popular new disciplinary technique bears little relation to any reality. We are told that offenders are "free" to participate in everyday life, yet their movements are highly regulated, the random gaze creating anxiety and, yes, obedience and docility.[3] Is this real freedom or a simulation? Steve L. is permitted to live at home, but is it "home," or is it "prison"? Is he a "convict" or a "client"? Is his home "private" space or a simulation of the private that can come under the scrutiny of public authorities? These dichotomies no longer make any sense and have been blurred to the point of non-distinction. If it is, and at the same time is not, "home," "prison," "private," or "freedom," then what is it?

This jumble of ideas is evident when officials discuss just what "house arrest" means. One advocate calls the concept a "winner" because it enables a person to maintain "the semblance of a normal life—even hold a job" (in other words, a simulated "normal" life). Another is critical, since agencies often fail to provide clients with "the kind of counseling they need to re-enter society." But aren't they already in society? Apparently not, according to the Superior Court of Arizona. The court ruled that a person under house arrest may be prosecuted for "escape" for unauthorized leaves, just as a prisoner may be prosecuted for breaking out of prison.[4] So then, "house arrest," once an odd-sounding contradiction in terms, has become part of the discourse and practice of justice officials who have normalized this simulation as accepted public policy. A client's home is characterized in this new discourse as simply another "correctional setting." It becomes, then, a "virtual" prison.

Within the hyperreality of house arrest, clients are rendered docile not through isolation and transformation of their "souls" during their segregation from society but rather through the surveillance of their bodies during integration into everyday postmodern life. During the industrial age of the nineteenth century, the "prison" (i.e., social segregation) and punishment were premised on the denial of "freedom" (i.e., social integration) and on the production of "useful" bodies trained to labor. Yet the social, cultural, and economic conditions of late capitalism shatter this theorem. Today, "useful" bodies are primarily consuming ones, and everyday life is marked by our growing dependency on the commodities that signal our desired lifestyles. Therefore, if formal, coercive social control is increasingly tied to social integration rather than to segregation, then "freedom" becomes simply that which can create, like the anklet device, the simulation of freedom.

SPIDERMAN MEETS ROBO COP

The brainchild of a New Mexico judge (who, it is said, was inspired by the use of a similar device in a 1979 Spiderman comic book), electronically monitored home confinement, or EMHC, programs tethered, by the late 1990s, more than ten thousand individuals in nearly every state to central monitoring systems installed by community corrections officials.[5] "It's just a given that business is going to grow," says one stock analyst speaking of the corporations that produce the devices. "These are the companies working to solve a social problem of the 90s . . . They are going to help develop the industry and . . . the state-of-the-art equipment that is going to be necessary."[6]

This disciplinary technology has much in common with the past. Like Bentham's Panopticon, the anklet device permits near-constant surveillance of movement. With most systems, individuals cannot stray more than 150 feet or so from the monitoring box without triggering a violation. Random checks, day or night, bring the discretionary and one-dimensional gaze of authorities onto the clients; they never know when they may be called. One news article about these devices states that, "while confinement by monitor does not include bars, correction officials say the psychological loss of freedom should not be discounted." In order to "sharpen a convict's sense of confinement," officials often visit homes or workplaces unannounced, "even reciting the prisoner's every move the previous day" to make it clear to the client that he or she is being monitored. Speaking in perfect Panopticonese, one probation officer stated, "We want them to know we're watching even when they don't know we're watching." "In a way, monitors are better than prison 'cause you're still at home and all," states a Floridian spending two years with the device for an assault conviction. "But you got to ask someone permission to do everything, and I mean everything, man. You can't go nowhere without them knowing about it. And that way prison might be better 'cause you get it over with."[7] One system uses a monitoring video camera, instead of the pager-size anklet device. The *Visitel* camera is described by its manufacturer's agent this way: "The system is unique because there is a human connection that will talk with the offender. That person will ask the offender to smile, or turn his head, wave at the camera, or something like that to make sure it is the offender."[8] Indeed, this is the contemporary equivalent of the prisoner standing before the inspector's lodge.

But the ultimate application of this panoptic mechanism requires no agent at all. With this particular system, verifications are completed by the computer itself, programmed to dial at random times. "Hello," says the voice simulator, "This is a Community Control officer calling to verify that the person under our custody is at home. I will pause ten seconds for the person to come to the phone." The prisoner is then told to state his or her name and the time of day.

The system stores voice patterns in order to verify an offender's identity. The prisoner then puts the electronic anklet into a device that sends an electronic signal to the computer.[9] Whether triggering a spatial violation or offering one's voice to the machine, such decentralized control encourages "participatory monitoring" whereby those being watched become active "partners" in their own surveillance.[10]

Yet while Bentham's Panopticon was an archetype of modern discipline—and the anklet device a logical extension of it—this new technique is, at the same time, quintessentially postmodern in design and implementation. The cybernetic life-world and video technology of contemporary society permit a new partitioning—a new "grid" of power—that extends into the everyday, in and through the gaze of community corrections. This new grid comes about because the anklet device no longer requires the boundaries or the division of space through the architecture of a building. Indeed, this exercise of power can operate more freely, down to the trivial extremities and the remotest corners of everyday life, rather than be confined, like the offenders themselves, within walls of the modern asylum. Disciplinary power, then, has been deinstitutionalized and decentralized. Unlike the somewhat primitive panoptic tower that could practically view only a limited number of cells, the cybernetic machine is capable of creating an infinite number of confinements, as Foucault put it, "like so many cages, so many small theaters, in which each actor is alone, perfectly individualized and constantly visible."[11] This technological marvel alters the cost equation of prison construction and administration. We now have in our grasp an inexhaustible supply of inexpensive, disciplinary "space."

The modern, nineteenth-century asylum once stood as a grand monument of state power displayed for all to see. The anklet device adheres to new principles of postmodern disciplinary power. Rather than a grand public display, it is nearly invisible to all, save the offender, yet it functions with great economy, constantly and efficiently. It replaces the heaviness of the fortress with the simple, economic geometry of the semiconductor. As Foucault claimed, "The panoptic schema makes an apparatus of power more intense: it assures its economy (in material, in personnel, in time); it assures efficacy by its preventive character, its continuous functioning and its automatic mechanisms."[12] Compared with the cost of building prison beds and the expense of confinement—more than $25,000 per inmate per year—EMHC systems require a small initial investment, few personnel to administer, and cost only about $2,500 a year per "client" to operate. And rather than subject the body to a regimented system of institutional discipline and control, with EMHC the disciplinary technology is located on the body itself. As one inmate at a Midwestern state penitentiary told me, "It's like carrying the state around on your ankle. I'd rather do my time in here and have them leave me alone."

First used on so-called nonviolent felony offenders who were on parole from prison, the anklet devices began to proliferate in the mid-1990s. For example, in my county, the devices were primarily used on juvenile offenders, some as young as twelve, and on others who have been charged but had never been convicted of a crime. Interestingly, the central monitoring office of the computer company that contracted for the service was located somewhere in Texas, about a thousand miles away. These systems cannot track a client who strays outside the range on the monitor. Yet I was told by one justice official that the next generation of devices will be able to report the whereabouts of clients at all times, permitting police to quickly apprehend violators.

A COMMUNITY *OF* CORRECTIONS?

With the extended reach of such community-based programs, the authority to judge individuals goes far beyond the walls of the prison that may have formally held them or any notion of a modest punishment for an offense committed. Now the gaze and surveillance of authorities can go straight into an individual's home, school, or workplace and can evaluate, assess, and enforce, if necessary, the person's "progress" on the road to becoming a model citizen. This kind of power is, indeed, capillary, circulating freely, far below the central administration of the state to the tiniest corners of society, and exercised by low-level criminal justice bureaucrats and technicians armed with a new discourse of accountability and what are referred to by practitioners as "case-management devices."

Anyone who thinks that "doing time at home" is "easy time" knows little about these new programs. One official told me that being sentenced to community corrections programs was, in many ways, much "harder time" than sitting in a jail cell. For example, consider the intensive supervision programs (ISPs) now operating in many communities throughout the country. These are designed for adult, nonviolent felons so that they may, according to one report, "remain in the community while becoming responsible, accountable, and self-supporting." One ISP requires a minimum of four contacts per week between a client and an intensive supervision officer (ISO) during the first year in the program. During this time, the ISO is charged with directing daily job searches, verifying employment through the provision of pay stubs, initiating at least one monthly meeting with employers or training/education providers (not including unannounced visits), coordinating community service work (forty hours per week for those unemployed; five hours for those employed), collecting court-ordered restitution, initiating client curfews (enforced by means of electronic monitoring if deemed necessary), running weekly computerized record checks, and performing random drug and alcohol tests on all participants. After successfully completing the first eight months in the program with no "major violations," an offender may progress to less-intensive surveillance "at the discretion of the ISO."[13]

I spent some time talking with directors and intensive supervision staff of several community corrections programs, and I took a monitoring tour with one agency's "Surveillance Officer" (his official title). "Pete," a twenty-year veteran of law enforcement and military policing, is responsible for checking up on program clients (both juveniles and adults) on weekends and evenings. He does so by driving around the county, stopping in on clients at random times, making sure they are at home as scheduled, generally checking up on them, and performing drug and alcohol tests. (I discuss these techniques in more detail in chapter 4.) Pete records his findings on a clipboard, jotting down the results of the tests as well as noting that the client was "watching TV" or had a "friend visiting," and the like. Sometimes he would "double back" on a client, fifteen or twenty minutes after his first visit, in order to "keep 'em honest."

From the eyes of an outsider like myself, Pete's ritualized visits to a client's home—sometimes as late as 11:30 P.M.—had an absurd and unnerving quality. I kept trying to imagine what it would be like to have someone knock on my door this late at night for what amounts to a very personal inspection. Indeed, it seemed clear to me that, while not exactly a prison, an offender's home was indeed transformed into a "correctional setting" in terms of the loss of privacy and the institution-like rituals that occurred with Pete's arrival. Despite this, every client I observed greeted Pete in a friendly manner as he walked—without hesitation or invitation—into their homes. It was obvious that these people knew "the drill" of Pete's visits, just as they knew the rituals of alcohol and drug testing. His showing up seemed as normal to them as the arrival of the mail carrier. I was also struck by how much Pete knew about their lives—not only the typical things that were likely to be in their files but also the numerous details about their friends, their habits, their likes and dislikes, their medical and family histories, who among them were likely to be the "success stories" and who were likely to "screw up." And "screw up" they do. One measure of the difficulty of the program is, according to its director, the fact that 50 percent of adult clients fail to complete their contract with the court (this appears to be typical of other programs throughout the country). Given what he called the "intrusive" nature of the surveillance program—as he put it, "We're out there every night, weekends and holidays"—it seems it would be difficult not to "screw up."

Moreover, as one program director told me, once such programs are put in place, judges begin to assign what he considered to be "inappropriate" offenders to the program, such as "low-risk" misdemeanants, juveniles waiting for hearings, adults convicted of non-aggravated sex offenses, and the like. Previously, these people would have been released or would have done short jail time, had the program not been available. But once people are under the constant gaze of authorities, other infractions may be uncovered; files get thicker, and the minor offender becomes the known "drug user" or the kid with "serious problems." These people, of course, are deserving of even more surveillance, and so it goes. This process has the effect of "widening the net" of the justice system and drawing in people who might not otherwise have been there. Interestingly, after being told that an increasing number of "sex offenders" was being assigned to one program, I asked officials why someone convicted of sex crimes should be tested regularly for alcohol (a legal substance) and drug use. No one could give me a defensible answer, saying only that it was "part of the program." Once established, then, programs like intensive supervision become general disciplinary tools that are used to let certain individuals "know we're watching even when they don't know we're watching," whether that form of surveillance is "appropriate" for them or not.

Finally, Pete told me, with little hesitation, that the ISP was "obviously better than putting them away." He repeatedly stressed the "productive" and "self-training and discipline" capacities of the community corrections scheme throughout our conversations. When I asked him, for example, what he thought his clients felt about wearing an electronic anklet device, he said, "They appreciate that it's an option for them rather than prison." He went on to relate stories about clients who themselves had requested to be in the program, in order to "clean up" from drugs or to "stop running with the wrong crowd."

"INTERVENTION OPPORTUNITIES"

As I suggest in chapter 2, I see these new community-based forms of surveillance as an extension of the disciplinary power first deployed in closed institutions. Once lodged in the community, however, they begin to reach out, to invest, colonize, and link with other organizations and practices. This is clear when we see the blurring distinctions among the legal, justice, and social welfare functions of these programs. During one of my rounds with Pete the surveillance officer, for example, he received a cellular phone call from a police dispatcher (he is not a law enforcement officer) who asked him questions about, and later had him call, one of his clients concerning a domestic dispute at her house. For advocates and administrators, this is the "productive" aspect of "inter-agency cooperation," "information sharing," and "efficient service delivery." Yet it is also these very activities that produce a more finely woven, integrated network of social control.

Another community corrections program I looked at has, in addition to the ISP, nearly a dozen other programs that it administers (and will even contract out to neighboring counties) including domestic violence intervention, rape crisis, victim-witness assistance, homes for children "at risk," educational services for clients, and the family training program, or FTP. The stated goal of the FTP component is to prevent the incarceration of the adult offender by tracking not only the offender but family members as well. The program involves an in-home style of intervention. Yet, despite the best intentions of its practitioners, it is a model that, I argue, significantly facilitates and enhances the exercise of disciplinary power. With this view in mind, consider how proponents characterize their activities. A report from the community corrections agency describes the FTP this way:

> By improving the stability of the offender and his/her family, there is a much higher likelihood that the offender will be productive and avoid additional criminal behavior that would result in incarceration. This goal is obtained by physically working in the home and teaching new parenting skills and child management skills to parents who have exhibited weaknesses in these areas . . . This is accomplished by a therapist of the Family Training Program going into the home and providing intense therapy within the home setting. In addition to scheduled appointments, the therapist will make intermittent unannounced visits in order to gain a more realistic view of the family's interaction and the use of the new skills.[14]

In fact, the "home-based" and "family preservation" models have become the most popular forms of "service delivery" throughout what one could call the burgeoning penal/health/welfare complex. For example, some see the supposedly therapeutic agendas of community mental health programs this way:

> Practitioners constantly seek innovative ways to improve service delivery to high-risk children and families who are isolated and unlikely to seek help at an agency. Home-based practice is rapidly becoming an alternative to practice in office settings [providing for] . . . enhanced assessment and intervention opportunities.[15]

> Home visits [that] allow therapists . . . direct observation of a family in the natural environment of their home can bring into focus more quickly the significant dynamics in the family and can help guide treatment. Therapy moved into the home setting occurs in a heightened reality context that includes the possible participant-observer role of the therapist, more active involvement of family members, and the opportunity for immediate analysis of family members' actual behavior.[16]

These kinds of home-based models, then, provide the means by which caseworkers, therapists, and others extend the gaze of disciplinary power into the daily lives of clients. As "experts," they are charged with making normalizing judgments not only about their clients but also about their entire families. (Are they "functional" or "dysfunctional"? Are they "multi-problem"? Do they have "borderline" personalities? Are they "at-risk"? Do they have the correct "parenting skills"? Do they use drugs? Do the kids go to school?) And even if, as individuals, these well-intentioned, dedicated professionals do not want to become the "eyes of the law," they are compelled, *by law*, to report any illegal behavior they observe to the appropriate authorities. Or take the situation where social welfare officials are trying to decide whether a child should be "reintegrated" back into a home after the parents have been deemed "unfit." "This is when the team has to decide to let go," according to one social worker I talked to. (The "team" is made up of the core members of what is called a "wraparound" treatment model that brings in welfare caseworkers, individual and family therapists, agency lawyers, and a host of other professionals.) In this case, the previously "unfit" family must meet the standard of the supposedly more "functional" foster family the child may be living with. The possibility of "letting go" creates considerable anxiety on the part of the social worker because "[i]t's hard to extract the kid out of this great home and put him back in with borderlines." While most of us might be able to identify cases of, say, physical abuse, one has to wonder what criteria are used to determine who is "borderline" and who is not. Just where is the line between a "functional" versus an "unfit" family? Who gets to decide what "parenting skills" are appropriate, while other skills are not? The fact is, this is not a science but a series of socially constructed judgments. I wonder how many American families could survive the assessment and be labeled as living in a "great home" if our behaviors were constantly observed, scrutinized, and clinically diagnosed.

THE JUSTICE FISHBOWL

With community policing and corrections, neighborhood detention centers, offenders under arrest in their own homes, and the proliferation of in-home social welfare models, we see then the process whereby disciplinary power leaches into everyday life. To reiterate Foucault, this is the process whereby the "massive, compact disciplines—the jail, the prison, the poorhouse, and the mental hospital—are broken down into flexible methods of control, which may be transferred and adapted."[17]

The next logical step in "decentralizing" the penal/heath/welfare complex is to bring courts to the local level as well. One model—simply riddled with postmodern themes—that is being heralded as a prototype court of the future was opened in New York City's Times Square district. Supported and financed by private developers who have spent billions rehabilitating the seedy district into a tourist mecca, this specialized "boutique" court deals only with street hustlers, graffiti artists, prostitutes, and shoplifters who traditionally had been kicked by uptown courts too busy with felony cases. The court processes more than fifteen thousand of these so-called quality-of-life offenders a year. It is characterized as a "computer-driven laboratory," a "fishbowl" that puts a "judge under the same roof as city health workers, drug counselors, schoolteachers and nontraditional community service outlets." A Digital Equipment Corporation computer is at the center of the management information system. It acts, according to one writer who observed the court,

> as the receptor for an elaborate system of remote feeds which, when combined, create the equivalent of a three-inch court file that can be accessed from a single screen. The process usually begins with a beat cop issuing a complaint to an offender, complete with a date for him or her to appear in court. Copies of the complaints are sent to the Manhattan DA's office, which in turn faxes them to the court.

When the defendant arrives in the new courthouse, his presence is noted on large screens that hang in the entrance way like airport flight monitors, displaying the names of all those scheduled to appear that day . . . In addition, a dozen monitors jam the interior well of the courtroom . . . If all has worked, the faxed complaint from the DA's office has been scanned into the computer and can be pulled up from any of those monitors. Ditto the defendant's rap sheet, which gets fed into the data- base by an online hookup with the state's Division of Criminal Justice.

Before long, an interviewer approaches the defendant with a laundry list of queries: Does he or she have a drug habit, a home, a job? Each answer is typed into a lap- top computer and downloaded into the DEC machine . . . By now thousands of bits of information about a single defendant are swimming around the electronic file folder.[18]

As the man who designed the court says, "We know very little about the 100,000 people who come through this system. In three years, we're going to know a whole lot more."[19]

THE TRANSPARENT SOCIETY

If postmodern culture is characterized by an implosion of previously accepted boundaries, we see, as well, the disintegration of the barriers that once offered us some form of sanctuary. "Such a society," according to Ronald Corbett and Gary Marx, "is transparent and porous. Information leakage is rampant. Barriers and boundaries—distance, darkness, time, walls, windows, and even skin, which have been fundamental to our conceptions of privacy, liberty and individ- uality—give way."[20] This condition has been brought about by the emergence of what Marx calls the "new surveillance": an optical revolution engendered by a dizzying array of digitized, computer/video/telecommunication devices that have made watching and monitoring deftly penetrating yet seamless and hidden. In our post-Cold War world, certain government agencies and former defense con- tractors have found a lucrative market in the "security" business. With develop- ments in night-vision technology, auditory devices, and telecommunications monitoring, the state, as well as private organizations and individuals, has an ar- senal of surveillance gadgets at its disposal. In the next few sections I introduce some of them.

The video camera, for example, has fundamentally altered the nature of polic- ing as well as the entire U.S. justice system. Videocams, mounted on the dash- boards of patrol cars, have become a central feature in the daily lives of the po- lice and those they encounter. Activated automatically whenever an officer turns on the car's flashing lights, the devices are a "real asset to everyone involved," ac- cording to one law enforcement official. "Tapes can be played in court," states a news article, "to give jurors an unadulterated account of the crime. Instead of hearing disputed testimony about a drunk driver's impaired driving, for instance, jurors could see the car weaving. The footage also serves for unimpeachable evidence of evaluating deputies. Video of an officer's conduct—correct or incorrect—could be used in training."[21]

Indeed. On the evening of March 3, 1991, four Los Angeles police officers were secretly videotaped beating unarmed motorist Rodney King. The widespread dissemination of these images created a media spectacle that was turned against the police department and the city. So, in order to shed more light on the subject, law enforcement officials began to experiment with installing video cameras in police cars. The same device used to expose this atrocity would now "protect" both the officers and their suspects. "I think they have the ability to bring credibility back to law enforcement," states one law enforcement chief about the use of such cameras. "When you're on TV, you don't do bad things. The officer acts his best and the actions are documented." The camera does not discriminate; its gaze is both controlling and productive as it disciplines the conduct of both suspects and police. It provides an elegant solution to the question: "Who is guarding the guards?" demonstrating the role of "hierarchical observation" as each individual carries out the act of watching others while he or she is also being watched. The visual technology not only empowers the calculated gaze and watches and renders the suspect docile but, as Foucault put it, also "constantly supervises the very individuals who are entrusted with the task of supervising."[22]

Like other technologies, videocams are becoming so inexpensive and small they can be used almost anywhere. A "badge-size" camera or "personal video surveillance system" created by Semco Company of Carlsbad, California, sends the image back to the recording unit in the police car. The company says that the device is particularly useful in recording combative suspects and in dealing with false-arrest lawsuits. Video technology is currently used in documenting interrogations and confessions, undercover investigations, lineups, crime scenes and their re-enactment, the testimony of victims and witnesses and the physical condition of suspects during booking, lockups, and on and on. One interesting use of the videocam has been to link judges and defendants during preliminary hearings and other procedural steps in the justice system. Rather than take the time and incur the cost of transporting numerous offenders to the courthouse from correctional facilities, the participants merely view each other on a monitor— constituting a sort of efficient "virtual" habeas corpus, if you will. Just imagine yourself as a defendant, watching your own preliminary hearing on a video screen while the television in the game room blares reruns of a gritty "reality" justice show or has live coverage of today's "trial of the century." The process of "justice" becomes yet another videoscape in the day-to-day world of the postmodern.

In Contra Costa, California, the television is used in another way. Here, a county supervisor, the district attorney, and about a dozen custodial parents have gotten together to produce a public-access show they call "Costra County's

Deadbeat Parents." The show, playing on eleven cable systems in the area, is modeled after the national series *America's Most Wanted* and shows a picture of the malfeasant parent while an announcer narrates the person's height, weight, race, last known occupation, and number of minor children. Each month the show includes a new crop of "deadbeats" from the county's roster. If viewers identify one of the parents, they are asked to call the district attorney's office: "We hope you'll wake up and tap him on the shoulder and say, 'Hey pal, I'm tired of paying my taxes to support your kids.' "[23]

Like the videocams in the police cars, all this tape contributes plenty of grist for the "real" cop and justice shows and other media spectacles. In fact, after years of resisting the intrusion of the camera into the sacrosanct courtroom and police precinct, it seems that some authorities have embraced them as a public relations tool. For example, following the Rodney King beating, the Los Angeles Police Department turned to network TV to help put their officers in a better light. Broadcast in 120 markets nationwide, *LAPD: Life on the Beat* is in its fourth year on the air. Producers of the thirty-minute show, featuring video footage of officers supposedly going through their shift, claim that it is "the most accurate representation of law enforcement on television." Yet critics contend it is simply propaganda for the department.[24] Likewise, after several years of resistance, New York City permitted the cable channel Court TV to begin filming a series called *The System* in and around the 101st Precinct in Far Rockaway. Videocam operators ride along with police, film arrests and bookings, and follow defendants through trial "like a nonfiction version of the NBC drama *Law and Order*," according to one news article. But wait: Isn't *Law and Order* supposed to be a "reality" drama based on the "true" stories of the justice system? Then is the filming of *The System* a case of life imitating art that, itself, was supposed to be imitating life? An official from the police commissioner's office stated that the filming will "help to tell a less-sensational story about the lives of officers and the true nature of police work." It may also provide a way of keeping his eye on his officers in a department plagued by allegations of police brutality, corruption, and other illegal behavior.[25]

POWER SEEING

Although video technology and its gaze have become commonplace in the justice system, they appear downright primitive when compared with what may be on the horizon. For example, one headline reads, "New Scanners May Redefine Strip Search," and the article describes researchers at a federally financed laboratory who have developed a "holographic radar scanner" that can peer through clothing in order to see hidden objects. There are two prototypes: one is a walk-in booth that scans the entire body, while the other is a hand-held device aimed at specific body parts.[26] Meanwhile, the FBI is pushing for the widespread adoption of the

NCIC 2000 computer system that is being installed in some police cars. This system allows police not only to confirm outstanding arrest warrants but also to store and transmit photographic images and fingerprints for identification and matching.[27] Once these sources of identification are digitized, widespread and instant dissemination is possible. In Kansas in 1995, the legislature adopted a computerized system for placing ID pictures on driver's licenses, providing police with convenient and essentially open access to this information. A lobbyist for several state law enforcement associations said the change to the digitized system would "promote effective criminal investigations."[28] (By 1998, the states of Colorado, South Carolina, and Florida had all signed contracts to sell millions of the digitized driver's licenses photos to a private company that wanted to use them in a computerized check-cashing identification system. But all the states were forced to hastily cancel the deal amid a storm of citizen protest.[29])

State troopers who set up random safety inspections on interstate highways are being issued a new high-tech tool called an "Ion-Scanner." These portable devices, passed over the logbooks of long-haul truck drivers, are capable of identifying drug residue. A positive reading justifies "probable cause" for searching the vehicle.[30] In 1997, Maryland State Police deployed a prototype of their new "weapon" against so-called aggressive drivers: a $400,000 sport utility vehicle "bristling with high-tech equipment" such as lasers and video cameras. A decade ago, the use of license photography in Maryland to catch speeders was stopped by a complaining public. "But with the increase in road rage today, the public is fed up," claims one authority.[31] (Yet, as some have suggested, "road rage" may be little more than a media myth that has no basis in empirical evidence.[32]) And in the self-declared "war" against marijuana growers in the Pacific Northwest, National Guard units are already using military technology such as night-vision goggles to flush out growers. Aided by drug enforcement experts from the Pentagon, the National Guard has turned to using thermal imaging devices to sense the heat seeping from growing lamps in homes, attics, and barns.[33]

This may be only the beginning of the uses of military technology for domestic "crime fighting." Lessons are being learned from so-called postmodern wars like the conflict in Bosnia and other regions. In these instances, nation-states are replaced by fragmented militias where the lack of a central authority makes the conflict seemingly intractable. Live images of death and suffering are distributed worldwide and "sap whatever will or ability there may be to prosecute a devastating military campaign."[34] The role of groups like the United Nations becomes primarily one of "peacekeeping," and this necessitates intense "intelligence-gathering" and surveillance capabilities to monitor the parties involved. In Bosnia in 1996, for example, the U.S. military command post was called "Battlestar." Here is how one reporter described the installation:

> Basically, you have tiers set up, and each department and each unit has its representative there sitting in front of a laptop, and they're all facing what's essentially a

large console that has TV sets and computer monitors and a bridge, basically, where the generals sit. *And, I mean, it's just as wired as can be. They can see virtually anything they want to see . . .* And, they have devices that allow them to view live photos, say, from Apache helicopters that are out in the field. *It's probably the most surveilled landscape in the history of the world.*

There is a system called *"power-seeing,"* and what it allows is them to take satellite photographs that already exist and put them over maps and create, basically, 3-D layouts so that, in fact, before anybody actually went into Bosnia, people down to the company command level had actually practiced with power-seeing flying through the route they were going to take, and see things down to the scale of buildings and intersections and railroads. And, it's like a video game. You have a joystick and you can kind of weave your way through.

We went out on a night patrol, and a lot of people have global positioning satellite readers. So, they know exactly where they are. And, everybody, virtually, has one kind of night-vision goggle. And, it's a camera [as well] and you have two eye pieces. In the eye pieces you see kind of a green and white representation of the landscape. (Emphasis mine)[35]

I would not be surprised to find *"power-seeing"* technology being deployed in the coming years by police departments in South Central Los Angeles, Detroit, or Philadelphia. In fact, we may be witnessing the "militarization" of the nation's police forces, something that has serious constitutional implications. Since 1990, a program has been in place to facilitate the transfer of "surplus" military hardware to the law enforcement agencies, supposedly justified to "fight drugs." Yet since that time, the war on drugs clause has been dropped and more than $200 million in equipment—everything from bayonets, helicopters, armored vehicles and night-vision gear—has gone to police. "As long as it's not a cannon, they'll probably get it," according to the person who determines if the requested equipment is appropriate for the department.[36]

On another front, with considerable pressure from the Clinton administration and the FBI, the Senate voted unanimously to support the so-called wiretap bill of 1994. This bill forces phone companies to make their emerging digital networks accessible to law enforcement agencies. Currently, these agencies need a court order to "tap" a conventional copper-wire phone line. With the new digital networks, the FBI will be able to listen in on as many as 1 percent of all phone calls made in what is referred to as a "high-crime" geographical area, which could mean that law enforcement agencies might be monitoring hundreds, perhaps thousands of calls, whether or not there was any probable cause for listening in. In 1989, California passed a law targeting drug dealers that allows police to use wiretaps when all other investigative techniques have failed. Since then, law enforcement officials in the City of Angels have followed what Deputy Public Defender Kathy Quant calls a policy to "wiretap a lot, and to wiretap everybody." Quant charges that police in Los Angeles are using wiretaps as a first step, not a last resort as required by law—and that many thousands of people are being overheard improperly. One particular wiretap order allowed police to listen in on 350 different telephones for what turned out to be an unusually extended period. Prosecutors say that some of the taps lead them to drugs and drug money, but most of the taps seem to lead nowhere while grossly violating privacy. In one case, five public pay phones were tapped. Police listened to 131,000 conversations without making a single arrest.[37] With authorities having access to digital network software, monitoring someone's phone (or any other communication device connected to the network, such as a computer) will be quite simple. No need to climb telephone poles, no clicking and cracking on the line; in an age of fiber optics, cellular grids, and satellite uplinks, the word *wiretap* is a quaint reminder of a bygone era.[38]

While law enforcement personnel rave about the next generation of weapons in their war on crime, others contend that the technology is subject to abuse and is prone to error, making many of the new devices a threat to our constitutional rights. For example, several lawsuits have been filed against the use of patrol-car computer systems. When police arrested a man on U.S. Route 1 in New Jersey in early 1995, it was not because they observed him doing anything illegal. Rather, the officers simply decided to run his vehicle's license plate through their patrol-car computer. It told them that he had a suspended license. But in a case filed with the state courts, the man contends that the police singled him out arbitrarily—without reasonable suspicion, or probable cause—and that the resulting computer search of his record was illegal. Others have sued because they were arrested for outstanding warrants that had in fact been cleared but were never deleted by a clerk. A representative from one privacy group stated: "They [the police] should not be able to go out willy-nilly to investigate everyone on a whim or a hunch. I mean the British in 1776 were saying, 'We're trying to investigate illegal smuggling, and you only have to worry about it if you're guilty.' But they were investigating everyone's houses."[39]

"SMART" ROADS, "SMART" CARS, AND "SMART" CARDS

Meanwhile, as we look beyond the justice system itself we can see other practices and technologies being put in place in everyday life that may mimic these kinds of monitoring and surveillance capabilities. We are seeing, for example, the emergence of intelligent transportation systems, or "smart highways," that attempt to rationally regulate traffic flows, alert drivers to accident scenes and other tie-ups, and automatically collect tolls at access points. Some of these systems are already operating. In the Los Angeles area, video cameras mounted along freeways feed information to the central offices of the state's transportation department. The New York City Department of Transportation brags of its

Vehicular Traffic Control System. The DOT employs fifty-five cameras to watch over Manhattan's major arteries and a centralized Advanced Traffic Management to control all the cameras and traffic signals to avoid congestion in the city (a driver sitting in traffic in either of these cities has to wonder about the effectiveness of the scheme). In Florida, a system called E-pass on the Orlando-Orange County Expressway automatically deducts tolls from vehicles that have a transponder mounted under the front bumper. In Kansas, when a similar system was installed, highway authorities mailed out twelve thousand transponders in the first week. Users marveled at the new system. "I just can't believe how convenient it is," one man stated. "The arm swings up and away we go, and wave to everyone else waiting in line."[40] Getting ahead of the line, however, comes at the price of a little less privacy. These systems are capable of generating a data set of the time, date, and location of each toll collected. Currently, the U.S. Department of Transportation is working on a plan to have a national standard for the devices so that they would work on roads across the country. The dark side of the plan, as pointed out by Simson Garfinkel, writing in the *New York Times*, is that "it offers unprecedented opportunities to monitor the movements of drivers. It would create a bank of personal information that the government and private industry might have difficulty resisting."[41] He cites the case of auto insurance companies, for example, that might want to use the data to assess their relative risk of insuring someone based on the person's driving habits.

Another system is being proposed by the California Air Resources Board, the state's air-quality management and regulatory agency. A new law requires new cars, after 1996, to be equipped with a computer that monitors and informs the owner of possible emissions malfunctions. But in order to make sure that the clean air standard is maintained, the board wants those computers to be fitted with a transponder that could be read by a technician during biannual inspections. In addition, the board sees the devices as being capable of routinely monitoring compliance by installing roadside receivers that would quickly let authorities know if the vehicle was in violation. Identification of the owner from the vehicle plate number means that an inspection notice—or ticket—might soon arrive in the mail.[42] Of course, similar lessons were learned from the use of automatic cameras that have been employed for some years in the United States and Europe, whereby speeding motorists trigger a camera that takes a picture of their license plates and automatically issues them a citation.

Last year, more than ten thousand people bought General Motors cars with the *OnStar* global positioning satellite, or GPS, system installed. The equipment, referred to in the industry as "active tracking," can call a live operator who can give directions and other assistance; it can also automatically alert police if an air bag is deployed, remotely unlock the vehicle, and track its whereabouts. "Can your husband use *OnStar* to find out whether you really went out on a business call?" asks one reporter. "We will tell the police where a vehicle is but not just any individual," says GM's Jeffery Depew. "We do not want to be a national detective service."[43] Almost every major car manufacturer will be offering such systems in the next few years with overall sales of GPS equipment expected to top $8 billion by 2000. Teletrac of Kansas City specializes in management of vehicle fleets such as public utilities, cable companies, and bakeries. The system helps cut delivery times while dispatchers can instantly review and verify the exact whereabouts of trucks, their routes, and the specific time it took to complete a job. In Kansas, the state Highway Patrol has installed a GPS system to monitor the location of troopers. Some of the officers say privately that the monitoring will become a "management tool" and that the information may be used against them.[44]

Another interesting little data sponge making its way into our daily lives is the "smart card," a credit-card-sized plastic card with a computer chip embedded in it. The chip can either be a microprocessor with internal memory or a memory chip with non-programmable logic. These cards are being adopted in a variety of sectors including banking, health care, telephony, information technology, mass transit, and identification. In 1998, the smart card industry shipped more than one billion cards. Almost every small dish TV satellite receiver uses a smart card as its removable security element and subscription information source; there are over four million in the United States alone with millions more in Europe and Asia. Every French Visa debit card has a chip in it; in Germany, millions of banking cards have been issued with it. In Portugal and Singapore, the national banking networks have launched "electronic purse" projects. Various countries with national health care programs have deployed smart card systems, the largest in Germany where cards have been issued to every citizen. There are over one hundred countries worldwide that have reduced or eliminated the need for coins from the pay phone system by issuing smart cards.

The Smart Card Forum, an industry trade group, was created in 1993 to "promote the widespread acceptance of smart card technology in North America." The members seem keenly aware that consumers are suspicious of their little gadgets and offer some sensible advice on how business should use the technology. One statements reads, "The Smart Card Forum strongly believes that an understanding of the benefits that can be provided and how privacy can be protected by smart card technology will lead to greater consumer acceptance and a healthier business environment for the development of this technology . . . For smart card technology to be successful, it must be embraced by consumers and it must not be unnecessarily or unwisely regulated by policymakers." They go on to outline the following:

Guide To Responsible Consumer Information Practices
—Identify, recognize, and respect the privacy expectations of consumers and make applicable privacy guidelines available to them.

—Establish procedures to ensure that consumer data—information directly related to the consumer's use of the card—is as accurate, up to date, and complete as possible.

—Promptly honor requests from consumers for information the company has about them as a result of the consumers' use of their cards and provide a procedure for them to correct inaccurate personally identifiable information.

—Limit the use, collection, and retention of information about consumers to what is necessary to administer their accounts, provide superior service and offer consumers new opportunities.

—If personally identifiable consumer information is to be provided to unaffiliated third parties for marketing or similar purposes, inform the consumer of that purpose and provide the consumer the opportunity to decline (i.e. "opt out").

—Provide a means for consumers to remove their names from the company's telemarketing, online, mailing and other solicitation lists.

—Maintain appropriate security standards and procedures regarding access to personally identifiable consumer information.

—Implement policies and procedures to limit employee access to personally identifiable consumer information to a need-to-know basis.[45]

It seems that officials at my own university did not heed the Forum's suggestions when they issued "smart" student and staff identification cards two years ago. The cards were in fact dressed-up automatic teller machine (ATM) cards from a local bank. Not given any choice about our participation in the use of the cards, students and faculty lined up as if we were being booked at the local police station and had our computerized pictures taken by bank employees dressed in embossed bank-wear. Others harangued us with sales pitches about their bank's services, filling our hands with leaflets. When I raised questions about who would have access to the pictures, I was simply told they were property of the bank. Not long after, I began receiving solicitations in the mail from the bank as well as ones from several other businesses that were specially targeted at the university community and could be traced back to the bank and its database. Ironically, after the cards failed to work properly on campus buses, they were quickly renamed "dumb cards" and were vilified in the university newspaper.

These examples highlight a postmodern paradox: that the gaze is increasingly secured through the very products and services that we are seduced into consuming. Portable phones are easily listened in on, and inexpensive video technology ensures that cameras and their tapes abound; meanwhile, emerging computer networks make our activities and correspondence easier to monitor. Is this what David Lyon has called "pleasurable" social control?[46] Moreover, Lili Berko argues that the proliferation of devices also increases the "pool of watchers" and fundamentally changes our role in the surveillance gaze. "In this way," she states, "the postmodern panopticon moves beyond Bentham's model . . . to a postmodern model, in which individuals enjoy the possibility of becoming the owners and operators of the personal and professional seeing machines.[47] Two examples will illustrate. The disappearance of a child in California turned the Internet's twenty-million-plus worldwide users, 250 bulletin-board participants, and thousands of facsimile-machine owners into "watchers." One of the individuals involved suggested that the dissemination of the girl's image was "like a good virus: it proliferated." The case seems to have laid the groundwork for "lightning fast searches in the future. At some point, ordinary citizens linked by nothing but goodwill and a keyboard will be able to check nation-wide bulletin boards devoted to cases of missing children."[48] In a second case, the *New York Times* headline, "Thousands of Eyes for State Police," was explained by the subhead: "Florida asks cell phone users for help on the highways." "A lot of people want to get involved," said one officer, "and this is a good way to do it." Yet even the police see the possibility that too much surveillance might not be very practical. The officer concluded: "We just don't have the resources to handle the calls if they call for every minor little thing."[49]

A CULTURE OF VOYEURS

Few of us stop to think about just how often, on any given day, we are being monitored or filmed by cameras. But it's not simply a kind of one-way, Big Brother surveillance that is going on. As a society, we have become obsessed with the gaze of the videocam, not only because we perceive that it brings us "security" but also because we are fascinated by the visual representation of ourselves. We are today, very much, a culture of voyeurs. This "serious" and "playful" fascination with the camera's eye results, I argue, in the normalization of the gaze in everyday life. As videocams are used around the house to capture our foibles and to make us all stars on *America's Funniest Home Videos*, they make us more and more comfortable with, and even drawn to, the idea of being preserved on tape. The proliferation of video means that we can all be "on film," just like our cherished cultural icons of television and the cinema, so much so that a men's clothing store advertisement reads: "You are on a video camera an average of 10 times a day. Are you dressed for it?" A state of permanent visibility looms over us as cameras and their tapes encroach into everyday life.

Today, the ubiquitous video "security" camera stares blankly at us in apartment buildings, department and convenience stores, gas stations, libraries, parking garages, automated banking outlets, buses, and elevators. No matter where you live you are likely to encounter cameras; some places simply bristle with them. Following up on the work of some geographers who set about mapping the video surveillance presence on the streets of midtown Manhattan, the New York chapter of the American Civil Liberties Union extended the survey in the fall of 1998 to include the entire island. The survey found that 2,397 cameras are taping the public on the streets of Manhattan. Nearly two thousand of the cameras are of the stationary type, mounted in doorways and alcoves, above garage doors and affixed to the fronts or corners of buildings, rooftops of buildings, pointing down at the street, or on free-standing poles. Others are "rotational" or "globe" cameras that can zoom in on and follow subjects. Of the 2,397 cameras, approximately 2,100 are installed and controlled by private parties, with less than 300 put in place by public authorities. Some of the private cameras are "stand alone" systems while others, like the Citi-Group bank's video system, are tied to a centralized system that monitors every single branch in the city and its suburbs. The ACLU estimates that a quarter of a million New Yorkers pass these bank cameras every day.[50]

City officials in Baltimore have moved aggressively into the public surveillance arena. The effort has been spearheaded and funded by a private group called the Downtown Partnership of Baltimore that has brought together city and private funds to "promote downtown businesses." More than two hundred video cameras have been installed, monitoring nearly every street corner in the city's downtown district. The videotaping began near the popular Lexington Market, which is reported to have been "plagued by crime and loiterers" according to one news article.[51] The cameras are mounted on traffic-signal posts and will be monitored sixteen hours a day by police, who are stationed in kiosk-style substations positioned throughout the area. According to Police Commissioner Thomas Frazier, the ninety-six-hour-long tapes will be destroyed unless police or prosecutors decide that a crime may have been committed. The tapes, the commissioner assured the public, would never be handed over to any private investigators. Dismissing questions about the cameras being an infringement on a citizen's constitutional rights, he claimed, "It's not an invasion of anybody's privacy. It's filming what you can already see."[52] Massachusetts officials have made similar claims about their plan to put videocams at traffic intersections to catch violators. "People say, 'Gee, this is Big Brother. This is 1984,'" said one legislator. "No, this is 1996."[53]

Interestingly, it was Great Britain that seemed to get the ball rolling with systematic public video monitoring. In 1986 in the moderately sized market town of King's Lynn, owners of an industrial park set up just three cameras in order to counteract a rash of burglaries. After two years, the problem "virtually disappeared" according to the owners. Local officials were so enamored with the cameras that they went on to install Great Britain's most sophisticated urban security system, known as closed-circuit television, or CCTV. Forty-five cameras monitor a community center, seventeen car parks, and the streets in both an industrial park and a housing complex. The cameras feed a central monitoring station that operates twenty-four hours a day, has twenty-two video screens, and provides a direct link to local police who permit the images to be sent to their station. The cameras can scan areas and zoom in on activity at the operator's will. (A more sophisticated system with personal identification capabilities in use in East London is discussed in the next chapter.)

On one U.S. television program about the use of the cameras in King's Lynn, the reporter asked an operator if he had ever used the cameras to "watch and follow pretty women or to get the plate number off their cars." He blushed and said "No," but, when the reporter persisted, he admitted that he had in fact done this. The manufacturer of CCTV contends that, within five years, "Every town in Britain will have a similar system." Today, Great Britain leads the world in the use of public surveillance cameras. It appears that most people in King's Lynn have accepted the idea of being on camera. Some say it makes them feel "secure." And on one "productive" note, a local radio station relies on images from the cameras to tell people driving into town where they can find parking spaces.

Much like the nineteenth-century advocates of a more rational system of justice, the police in King's Lynn think that the cameras provide more efficient and more effective social control. They cite, for example, the case of children playing on their bikes in a car park when one decides to write graffiti on a wall. Alerted by the cameras, the police arrive, confront the juvenile, and make him clean up the wall. This way, the police claim, "the whole incident—crime, detection, and restoration—was over in less than five minutes, and dealt with informally, without the child having to be taken to the police station." Moreover, like the all-seeing, all-knowing "god" of the Panopticon, the mere presence of the camera's gaze appears to have the power to expedite "justice." Police say that the tapes from the system are rarely needed in court because "most people who are caught on tape confess as soon as they are told of the tape's existence, without even seeing it."[54]

Ironically, while the tapes may turn out to be "rarely needed" for the justice function they are supposed to serve, they are being gobbled up by the public as voyeuristic entertainment. Seeing a potential market for the tapes, one enterprising young man decided to purchase footage from insurance companies, security firms, and local governmental authorities. "Caught on Tape" and the sequel "Really Caught on Tape" contain snippets of things like a man being beaten during a store robbery, supposed drug dealers bashing each other with pipes, office workers having sex in a storeroom, and one woman (described on the tape as a "shoplifter") disrobing in a department store dressing room. The producer of the tapes claims that they were created as a form of protest against the surveillance cameras, but he admits they are making him some money. "We sold 60,000 in the first morning," he said, and they have ordered another 125,000 copies of the sequel. "When it comes down to video journalism—and that is what we claim to be—we're total hypocrites."[55]

So while we are watched and monitored ourselves, we are also called to join in on the watching. Programs such as *America's Most Wanted* call on the public to "join the force," as it were, and to provide information about criminals on the loose. Mimicking this style, a TV station in Kansas City, Missouri (no doubt like other local stations across the country), regularly runs "real" surveillance footage in its popular "Crime Stoppers" segment, calling on the public to provide information about incidents. (When no videotape is available, they simply offer a "re-enactment" of the crime with actors and props, dramatizing its threat.) A favorite of the recent spate of tabloid news and entertainment television programs such as *Hard Copy*, for example, are segments like "Caught on Tape" that depict an array of behaviors or circumstances observed by the camera, including illegal activities that have been taped by law enforcement agencies. One recent show included tape—supposedly from infrared night cameras—of "bandits" crossing over the U.S. border from Mexico into El Paso, Texas. Finally, the Kansas City TV station mentioned earlier also has cameras set up around the "neighborhood" (in fact, a rather large metropolitan area involving several cities) to monitor the weather throughout its viewing area (and, you can bet, to catch any other story that happens to be played out in front of the camera's eye). "Let's just pop on over to the Plaza," chimes the effervescent weather person, "and see what's happening out there."

Of course, if this kind of watching lacks the "real," voyeuristic experience you seem to crave, you can always pick up a gadget or two and start spying on your own. The Sharper Image, for example—a perennial favorite amongst the gizmo-obsessed—will sell you night-vision binoculars for a few hundred dollars. Their two-page, all-black background, magazine spread tells it all without saying a word: the right-hand page has a small text box claiming how helpful the optics may be in identifying intruders or locating your lost dog. On the opposite page is a grainy, phosphorus image of a near naked couple embracing, the view framed by the casing of a window. Then there are the increasingly popular and inexpensive "pinhole" video cameras. Jeff Hall, vice president of Gadgets By Design, a Lansing, Michigan–based company that makes surveillance equipment, says, "We've put them in light fixtures, computers and VCRs." A basic pinhole video-cam costs $129, according to Hall. Most of the company's sales come from businesses that want to keep track of their stock or watch their employees (see next section). "If you wanted to put a camcorder in the back room, it's hard to do that inconspicuously," he says. "We have to get smaller and smaller to stay one step ahead of the bad guys." If there's no light to see by, then an infrared camera shaped like a long nightstick called *Searchcam* can be poked into small openings such as heat vents, doorways and windowsills. A New York company called Electronic Security Products sells wearable cameras disguised as brooches, pens and eyeglasses. "They're used for recording video one-on-one," says company president Avi Gilor. A wire runs from the camera to a transmitter concealed in a pocket.[56]

Our obsession with the gaze of the videocam leads to some amazing behavior and ironic contradictions. Take the two cases of teenagers—perhaps the first true video generation—who went about, seemingly illogically, filming their own deviant activities. In one instance, a group of kids drove around Los Angeles's San Fernando Valley and, over the course of several nights, made tapes of themselves smashing car windows with baseball bats and shooting bikers and pedestrians with an air rifle. In another case, a sixteen-year-old in Omaha had his friend videotape his premeditated assault on a younger student in the halls of their high school. Both tapes, of course, were then used as legal evidence against the adolescents. Like the Los Angeles incident, a version of the Omaha tape was played over and over again in the national media, the significance of the event taking on epic proportions. As one Associated Press story put it, "The attack in a high school lasted less than thirty seconds, but as a symbol of teen violence it will be around much longer."[57] At Heidelberg College in Ohio, a football player and a wrestler were arrested and expelled from school after being accused of videotaping themselves raping an unconscious woman and then showing the tape to other students. "They were proud of it," said Sarah Smith, an eighteen-year-old freshman from Canton.[58]

Expecting parents planning to capture the birth of their child with a video camera may be in for a surprise. It seems that "doctors, hospitals, and insurance companies—realizing that today's family keepsake can lead to tomorrow's million-dollar verdict—are banning some video cameras during births." One insurer of twenty thousand doctors in California claims, "The person who is doing the filming is not going to stop when something goes wrong. When either there is a problem with the mother or the baby, all of this is going to be on film." Doctors, then, are attempting to use their professional power to hide themselves from the eye of the camera. An obstetrician from Tulsa claims, "Our concern is this could be one more tool used by plaintiffs' attorneys to put the worst face on something. You have to try to explain enough away as it is."[59]

Authorities recently installed cameras at the county treasurer's office in my hometown; they were apparently concerned about the possibility of confrontations with irate taxpayers. One employee, who had been there twenty-seven years, could not remember one situation that had ever gotten out of hand but still claimed, "It's an added feeling of safety." The county treasurer herself said, "I feel more comfortable with them on." Ironically, not long after they began filming themselves and the daily line of bored but hardly hostile taxpayers, burglars broke into the building one night through a basement door and stole, among other things, several thousand dollars of the treasurer's own money that she kept in a file drawer. The video cameras were useless, since they were routinely shut off at night.[60]

WE HEAR YOU

While video cameras proliferate, a growing number of retail stores in the United States are adding audio surveillance technologies to their arsenal of "security" measures. Dunkin' Donuts, for example, is reported to use such listening technology in its stores. A security systems company representative in the state of Massachusetts claims that more than three hundred of the outlets in that state have audio monitoring on the premises. My local newspaper ran a hometown-style article recently about a friendly group of retirees who meet at a local franchise every morning for several hours of coffee and political banter. I wonder if they are aware that they are being taped? A Dunkin' Donuts corporate spokesperson asserts that the systems are there to increase security and to keep employees "on their toes," not to listen in on customers. Yet the CEO of Louroe Electronics of Van Nuys, California, a manufacturer of the devices, claims that his system can pick up conversations as far as thirty feet away. "Unfortunately," he argues, "this is going to be the future until we get to the point of minimal crime in this country. Until then, store owners are going to have to have these devices to protect their employees and their customers."[61]

Far from the local donut shop, in 1997, Lucianne Goldberg, a staunchly Republican literary agent, encouraged Linda Tripp to tape her conversations with her friend and ex-White House intern Monica Lewinsky.[62] "I said, 'What if anybody doesn't believe you, what proof do you have?' And she said, 'I don't have anything.' I said, 'Why don't you just put a simple recording device on your phone and tape your phone calls?' She thought that was kind of sleazy and I assured her, it was my mistake, that it was perfectly legal, because in New York and all but nine states it is legal. She finally agreed with me that this was the only way to protect herself, so she started taping."[63] It seems, however, that to most people, taping the intimate secrets of a friend constituted a serious betrayal, and Ms. Tripp was later pilloried in public opinion polls and the media.

Yet it is becoming increasingly common, for example, for lawyers to secretly tape-record conversations with clients, witnesses or the opposing counsel. Attorneys who use this tactic claim that they need the data as insurance against witnesses who might recant a story or fellow bar members who might welsh on a deal. Yet some professional ethics committees have argued that the taping is clearly deceptive and thus unethical. One committee member has stated that the practice "discourages people from looking at lawyers as people who can be trusted and who are to some extent above the more shifty, shady proclivities of other professions." Apparently for some, not high enough above. Recently, the New York County Lawyers' Association arrived at the extraordinary conclusion that such recording was not unethical as long as one party to the conversation—the person doing the taping—"consented" to it. Likewise, thirty-nine other states, including New York, allow taping in these "consenting" situations. Besides, proponents say, the technology has become so easy to use and the practice is so widespread that people should simply assume it is being done; thus it is not deception at all. "Perhaps in the past," one ethics committee member stated, "secret recordings were considered monovalent because extraordinary steps and elaborate devices were required . . . Today, recording a telephone conversation may be accomplished by the touch of a button, and we do not believe that such an act, in and of itself, is unethical."[64]

In the cultural context of messy divorces, child custody disputes, and sexual harassment lawsuits, the notion of "watching what you say" is taking on a whole new meaning. Indeed, inexpensive computer technology is making recording a telephone conversation quite simple. With the ever-expanding use of voice mail systems, our conversations and messages are being constantly recorded and possibly stored. Many of the current generation of home computer systems have built-in voice mail answering machine devices that can record all incoming calls (whether answered or not) and have built-in *CallerID* functions and other kinds of "security tools." Since these devices, like many voice mail systems, store the recorded data in digital form, a record of conversations can easily be built, passed on to others, and even edited and changed. There have been several notorious instances where people's "private" voice mail messages have been posted on the Internet for millions to listen in on (for more on the Internet, see chapter 5). One Internet site collects audio recordings, charging people a fee to listen to them. "Eargasmic . . . for people who like to eavesdrop." The site is described as "an erotic site, which hosts sound files of people making love, made by eavesdroppers all over the world." The owner claims, "Everyone makes a sound while they are making love. These sounds are like a fingerprint, unique to everyone on this planet," and "All work on the site is ORIGINAL and AUTHENTIC." The site's FAQ page has the following:

Is eavesdropping illegal?
    In certain states and countries eavesdropping is not allowed. Please check your local law before recording audio.
How can I help you maintain this site?
    Have you got noisy neighbors, a couple visiting, or are you going to spend the night in a hotel or motel? Take your audio recorder and start taping the minute you hear a couple in action! Digitize the tape on your PC, and submit the file to us! We'll supply you with a password to get access to all the files.
How can I make my own recordings of people making love?
    There are two methods, and each of them requires a different planning. You can hide a tape recorder in the bedroom of your potential 'victims', or you can record sound through walls.
    Hiding a recorder is the best way to get good quality recordings, but chances are that people will find your equipment because of the noise the tape mechanism makes, or because you simply didn't hide the recorder well enough. If you get caught, people might file a complaint at the police station and you might end up in jail, so watch out . . .
    If you want to tape sounds at a motel or hotel, the only solution is to record the sound through a wall. This is probably a less illegal act, since you are only taping what can be heard in your room. Because your ear is much more sensitive to sound than most microphones, you will hear more than you will tape. Here are some hints to improve the sound quality of your recording:
    Buy ultra sensitive microphones . . . Use the Super Snooper Big Ear kit as an amplifier (sold by Tandy and Debco as a make-it-yourself kit or by Gadgets-Inc as an assembled kit).

My friends/neighbors don't make noise!

Too bad . . . it really takes some luck to make a good recording! Lots of people do not make noise at all when they make love. Others do it at very strange times, like eight in the morning or four in the afternoon, which makes it almost impossible for you to hear them if you are out working. Making hidden recordings truly is a full time job! But those who try hard enough, will eventually succeed.[65]

While U.S. law says little about video surveillance, audio surveillance is regulated by the 1984 Omnibus Crime Control Act, and arrests and prosecutions for eavesdropping are not uncommon. Ronald Kimble, America's biggest spy shop owner, served a five-month sentence in 1995 after being arrested on seventy counts of dealing in illegal wiretapping equipment. Kimble spent eleven years as an agent with the Drug Enforcement Agency before starting a chain of stores called The Spy Factory.

HOME SWEET HOME

Increasingly, U.S. households are awash with intruder alarms and devices, video cameras, private police forces, and fenced perimeters. Taking these security techniques to the next level, the fastest-growing residential communities in the nation are private, usually gated, fiefdoms where, at some, visitors are videotaped as they arrive. About twenty-eight million Americans live in an area governed by a private community association. Here the enforcement of "normalcy" is taken to new heights. These serene fortresses have a plethora of rules and regulations that govern everything from the color you can paint your house to the type of toys that can be left in your driveway. Developers and the residents appear obsessed with creating a perfect world, where all things are controlled and predictable. Here is how one journalist describes the latest model, a private suburban development near Seattle:

> There are no pesky doorbellers, be they politicians, or girl scouts, allowed inside this community . . . A random encounter is the last thing people here want. There is a new park, every blade of grass in shape—but for members only. Four private guards man the entrance gates twenty-four hours a day, keeping the nearly 500 residents of Bear Creek in a nearly crime free bubble. And should a dog try to stray outside its yard, the pet would be instantly zapped by an electronic monitor.[66]

It seems no coincidence, then, that the Walt Disney Company, the purveyors of fantasy theme parks, has entered the private residential development business. Its first complete city, south of Orlando, is called Celebration, and it is founded on postmodern simulation and a deep nostalgia for the past. "Celebration's planners envisioned a community reminiscent of the quaint villages that dot New England's landscape," says one journalist. "They wanted sidewalks and picket fences, a town not unrelated to Disney World's Main Street, USA, just a mile or so away. They wanted to bring back a way of life lost when suburbs appeared." "It's like an old time kind of place," says one resident. Ironically, clean, safe streets away from ethnically diverse urban centers was precisely the promise of the suburbs. Yet gated, privatized, insular, and highly controlled, planned communities such as this one may finally deliver on the fantasy. With the average price of a home in Celebration at nearly $400,000, you won't see "diversity" used as a selling point. As one resident puts it, "when I drive through those white picket fences I say whew and think I'm home and I don't have to go back out."[67]

Yet while our dwellings may bristle with security devices and gated communities attempt to keep out the less desirable, some of the scrutinizing that goes on in some U.S. homes is directed more at family members and others on the inside rather than at strangers lurking about outside. With the increased need for child care in the home, for example, parents must often rely on near strangers to look after their children. With a string of baby-sitter-from-hell movies in the cinema and on television, paranoia runs deep in the middle-class household. "We give peace of mind," claims the president of In-Home Nanny Surveillance, Inc., a New York City company that rents video equipment to people who want to monitor baby-sitters. He had the idea for the company when he and his working partner faced hiring a child care provider and realized that "at the end of the day, a simple referral was not enough." In business for a little over a year, he has installed dozens of cameras, but rarely has a customer discovered serious problems. "Most parents find things that are correctable. Like a nanny who smokes in the kitchen." The owner of Micro Video Products in California contends that the well-known trial of English au pair Louise Woodward for the death of an eight-month-old in her charge "got us up and running" and continues with more than twenty calls per week.[68] Other companies offer several models of video cameras that are disguised as smoke detectors, boom-box stereos, and (the best-selling item, at three or four a week at the Counter Spy Shop) a teddy bear with a camera eye that feeds a videocassette recorder. Another target for the monitoring cameras, the storeowners contend, are spouses who are convinced that their partners are "up to no good."[69]

Children and adolescents are particularly vulnerable to all kinds of surveillance ceremonies and techniques. It would seem that we are either frightened of other people's "dangerous" teenagers or scared of what might become of our own. For some parents, technology provides peace of mind. In addition to the cameras just mentioned, some parents turn to drug testing as a way of checking up on their adolescents (see chapter 4). Then there is a fascinating little device called the *Drive Right* responsible-driving monitor from Davis Instruments of California. The company's print advertisement shows a contented-looking white man sitting in a chair reading. The caption states: "His teen has the car. So how come he's not worried? *Drive Right* uses advanced computer technology to track speed and acceleration to provide you with detailed accounts of recent driving activity." The device is capable of calculating "maximum speed and time it is reached, the # of times acceleration/deceleration exceeded, first and last time the vehicle was moved, and the total time the vehicle was in motion." It also has a "tamper indicator and password protected settings," while "optional software connects *Drive Right* to your computer to create an ongoing database for each driver." In a year and a half, more than 130 suspicious parents have paid a Winchester, Virginia, company to bring in drug-sniffing dogs to scour their homes for drugs or weapons. "Let us come in, just like you'd hire a maid service or Chem-Lawn to fertilize your lawn," says Russ Ebersole, the owner of the business that provides the dog searches. "We can sweep through your home. [If there are] no indications, then man, can you rest easy."[70]

In order to monitor other "deviant" activities your child may be up to, you can always listen in on their conversations. Among the hottest-selling items in electronics stores these days are telephone-taping devices typically purchased by parents to monitor their kids' phone calls. Jacqueline Salmon, writing for the *Washington Post* suggests, "For some baby boomer mothers and fathers, who once ranted at their own parents to get out of their lives and who transformed illicit drug use into an entire culture, the notion of snooping on their children with dogs and hidden tape recorders is deeply troubling." She cites the example of June Gertig, a district lawyer, who struggled with the ethical dilemma over tape-recording the telephone calls of her teenage son, and was forced to weigh his right to privacy against her need to know about any drugs he was using. "I felt absolutely filthy," said Gertig, who noted with irony that she is a member of the American Civil Liberties Union. "It's the last thing we wanted to do—turn into the KGB in our own house."[71]

When teenagers try to step outside the trusting confines of home, they are likely to encounter other forms of social control. More than 150 U.S. cities now have curfews in place to restrict the movement of teenagers at night. Typically, they ban anyone under seventeen from being on the streets between the hours of 11 P.M. or midnight and 6 A.M. While instituting a curfew in Washington, D.C., recently, a law enforcement official stated: "Our interest is not to go out, pick up and harass children. What we want to do is take these children out of harm's way." But curfew violators are subjected to an "automatic disciplinary process in which a violator is taken to a Juvenile Curfew Center, where a parent or guardian is notified and the teenager is counseled." One fourteen-year-old youth complained, "They should catch the real criminals instead of trying to keep us in the house. I don't think it's fair."[72] If these techniques can't keep kids under control or "out of harm's way," there is always the option of locking them up. For most poor children and children of color, this means a trip to the local juvenile detention center. I attended the opening-day ceremony of a multimillion-dollar public regional facility of this kind in my hometown. Here, the emphasis seemed to be on impressing visitors that taxpayers had gotten their money's worth. We were treated to a tour that focused on high-tech gadgets like the automatic door-locking system, surveillance cameras, and the listening devices installed in the inmates' rooms. Little attention was paid to kids or their problems, however. Indeed, a representative of the Chamber of Commerce, which hosted the event, praised local politicians for bringing much-needed dollars and jobs to the city.

Of course, if you are a white, middle-class teenager, you may find yourself shipped off to a psychiatric hospital or chemical dependency unit. During the last hundred years or so, behaviors which were once seen as instances of immorality or evil—such as drunkenness, drug use, sexual promiscuity, delinquency, and the like—have come to be reinterpreted as symptoms of sickness or disease.[73] Furthermore, increasing numbers and types of deviant behaviors are being treated in those institutions designed for the ill—hospitals and clinics—and with the sorts of psychological therapies deemed suitable to those who are seen as *in* trouble, rather than as *causing* trouble.

Running away, incorrigibility, minor theft, and other forms of teenage "acting out" are increasingly classified through psychiatric diagnoses such as "personality disorders" and "adjustment reaction to adolescence." As I like to say, I don't know anyone who *didn't* have an adjustment reaction to adolescence! In some of my previous research, I found that there was a dramatic increase in the 1980s in the use of private psychiatric facilities to control misbehaving youth.[74] Most of us have seen the commercials for these hospitals on TV. In most cases, they are likely profit-making operations owned by a large medical corporation and provide care and control of misbehaving or disturbed adolescents (and sometimes children) in return for third-party insurance money. Typically, kids are committed to these facilities as "voluntary" patients—after being checked in by their parents—and have no legal rights whatsoever. And, equally common, they are declared "cured" and released as soon as their parents' insurance coverage runs out.

SCHOOL DAZE, SCHOOL GAZE

If kids can't be trusted to act responsibly at home, they get even less a benefit of the doubt at school. In urban and rural schools alike, the country's educational institutions are quickly becoming security fortresses where increasing numbers of children are subjected to daily surveillance rituals. Of course, this trend, already in place in the early 1990s, has only accelerated in the wake of the awful shootings in Kentucky, Oregon, and Colorado. In 1993, the federal government got involved, passing the Safe Schools Act, which allocates $175 million for metal detectors, security guards, and violence prevention programs. At the local level, some changes have been striking. For instance, after one incident with a gun at a rural West Virginia high school that left one student wounded, outraged parents demanded the resignation of the principal and forced the school to institute new security measures. Within weeks, video cameras were installed to watch kids on their buses, follow them through the hallways, and monitor their classroom behavior. They are shuttled through metal detectors and X-ray scanners operated by security guards while drug-sniffing dogs search their lockers and cars. As one journalist observed the scene, "At a guard shack outside Mount View High School, three teenagers who had been unruly on a school bus stopped for inspection recently. The guard wrote down their names and ran a hand-held metal detector over each. The youths turned on command and raised their hands over their heads." One young woman at the school, a fifteen-year-old, stated, "It feels like a prison in here. The older kids don't care because they've gotten use to it. But the younger ones like me are coming from schools where you're still playing with blocks."[75] At the new $51 million so-called postmodern high school in South Brunswick, New Jersey, where kids carry their books through the halls in clear plastic bags since administrators banned backpacks, one senior philosophically said, "I look out the window and see a cop car, and that doesn't make me feel safe. All the police and all the hall monitors and locked doors can't stop everything that can happen."[76]

Like the young woman who compared her school to a prison, my then nine-year-old son echoed a similar sentiment when he came home from school one day to tell me that they had issued all the kids ID cards with bar codes on them. These devices are used in the cafeteria to tally up their biweekly bill and in the library to keep track of books and materials a child has checked out. I dropped by my son's school one day only to find him and his classmates in a silent, orderly line waiting to eat lunch, their bar-code "badges" dangling from their shirt pockets. It gave me a shudder. At the end of the cafeteria line, personnel stand with a portable computer scanning the cards and then the items that the children have selected. One staff member excitedly described the wonderful advantages of the cards: "This way we know, and can tell you *exactly* what items your child had for lunch, at *exactly* what time, on *exactly* what day!" "Gee," I said. "I guess my son will think twice about trying to sneak a chocolate milk past me again."

I have no doubt that some enterprising school administrator will get the idea to have bar-code scanners mounted at the entrances to the school to automatically take attendance and monitor the children's whereabouts. In fact, such a system may not be far off in one school district. "Just as they need a PIN number to withdraw money from an automatic teller machine," claims one journalist, "some Florida parents must now use secret passwords when picking their children up from school. No password. No kid." Officials claim that the system was initiated in response to a case in which a woman who had lost custody of her niece lied to the school staff and fled with the child. One Boca Raton elementary school principal stated, "Everyone is so paranoid when someone comes to the office to pick up a child." Many schools in the area maintain what are apparently called "hot files"—thick dossiers on students who have been involved in custody battles or who are under state care because of abuse or neglect.[77]

My hometown school district was one of hundreds across the country to rotate a set of videocams throughout the district's fleet of buses. One school bus driver claims that the cameras produced a "noticeable change" in helping her control behavior such as the dreaded "occasional slapping match." "They'd say, 'You didn't see me.' 'Yes, I did, and the camera taped it. Do we need to play the tape?' That was the end of it. I didn't have any more problems for the rest of the year." The director of the district's buses says, "I think it's just the idea that you're being watched that helps control the behavior a little bit." The children then are, like the inmates under the gaze of Bentham's Panopticon, "awed to silence by an invisible eye." [78]

Nationally, this trend has "just gone wild," states John Fox, a former auto mechanic whose Texas-based company sells the camcorders and manufactures the boxes designed to hold them. "Every school in the United States has this problem, and it's a lack of discipline," according to the less-than-disinterested and questionably authoritative Mr. Fox. "We give the driver a set of eyes and the kids are dumbfounded." Interestingly, Fox, who used to work on school buses for the Texas town, got the idea for the cameras when he was pulled over by a state trooper who videotaped him driving erratically. Fox was not charged with any wrongdoing but was so enamored with the technology that he thought, "Why can't we do that with our buses?" Meanwhile a Greenville, South Carolina, school transportation supervisor is sold on the system. "It has made a real big difference in behavior. We had one bus where people were fighting all the time. I couldn't keep drivers on that route. I put in our first camera there, and it was immediate relief, like the next day."[79]

If one reads the headlines, watches the television news, or listens to some politicians, one would conclude that our schools are decidedly dangerous places to be. In Lawrence, Kansas, for example, a school board member called for the formation of a district-wide "safety committee," claiming that we needed to be "pro-active" when it came to school security. (This was the same board member who, during her election campaign, circulated an advertisement claiming that the top ten problems reported in schools in the 1940s were things like chewing gum in class and smoking, while in the 1990s the main problems were assault, robbery, and rape. This widely cited "study" was subsequently shown to be apocryphal, according to the *New York Times*.) But like desperately ill people seeking a "miracle cure," this level of "pro-active" fear and suspicion can leave officials vulnerable to purveyors of "snake oil."

In one extraordinary instance, police and school authorities across the country were recently duped by a South Carolina company selling the $995 *Quadro Tracker*. This small handheld device was alleged to contain an "indicator, conductor, and oscillator" in order to detect "molecules, static electricity, and magnetic fields." It could, purportedly, "detect drugs hidden in air tight containers, a bomb inside a building from the outside, or a criminal suspect from 15 miles away." Touting it like some kind of cartoon decoder ring, the company claimed that you simply insert "detector" cards into the machine for whatever substance one is trying to uncover. When officials at several national laboratories finally got around to testing the device, they found inside "some plastic and a sheet of paper." The FBI has declared the device a fraud and is investigating the company. One school official from a Kansas City suburb who had been convinced by a demonstration by the company to purchase the product said, "We went after this in good faith . . . with a genuine interest in trying to keep our campuses safe. And with the state of today's technology, even things that seem hard to believe, we think they can actually do these things. I'm really disappointed."[80]

A more serious post-Columbine technological "solution" is being proposed by the federal Bureau of Alcohol, Tobacco and Firearms. The agency is working with a "threat-evaluation" company to develop a computer program to help school authorities identify potentially violent students. In December of 1999, a national pilot program, known as Mosaic-2000, began testing at more than twenty schools in the country "confidentially vetting and rating potentially violent students on a scale of 1 to 10." "I see this as being a useful tool," says Steve Dackin, principal of Reynoldsburg High School in Ohio. The Mosaic program is based on a series of questions about a child's behavior developed from case histories of people who have turned violent. It was designed by Gavin de Becker, Inc., a private software company. For about a decade, the company has been creating "risk-assessment" programs for special law enforcement situations such as threats of domestic violence, the safety of the Supreme Court, and the governors of eleven states. The school violence assessment program offers a database of questions culled from case histories "by 200 experts in law enforcement, psychiatry and other areas. A variety of concerns beyond alarming talk or behavior will be included, from the availability of guns to a youngster's abuse of dogs and cats. The questions allow a range of answers, from a student who has 'no known gun possession,' for example, to one who has 'friends with gun access.'" The company has not determined the overall cost of the program, but one state attorney general described it as "very affordable" at less than $10,000 per school.

But the Ohio chapter of the American Civil Liberties Union (ACLU) has called the program a "technological Band-Aid" driven by profiteering in parental fears. "We are understandably hesitant about any program designed to classify students or anyone else in society as potentially dangerous based on supposedly credible data fed into a black box," said Raymond Vasvari, legislative director of the Ohio ACLU.[81] Since administrators and teachers will be answering the questions with the students in absentia, one wonders how accurate the data for the forty questions asked can be. Would school personnel know, for example, if a student has experienced victimization by peers in the last eighteen months? It is not likely that even the most insightful school principal or staff member on campuses with hundreds of kids is going to know who is or is not being teased and tormented. Will certain young people who are simply "different" be singled out as being "dangerous"? The Mosaic software has all the makings of Foucault's examination, the ritualized knowledge-gathering activities in which case files are built out of the mundane details of people's lives. It contains normalizing judgments created by experts that attempt to assess an individual's behavior against some standard and judge them—with small, graduated distinctions—along a continuum, in this case, between docile and dangerous.

In the end, we have to ask ourselves, is all this "security" and surveillance of our children really called for? In one of the final reports issued by the U.S. Office of Technology Assessment (it was shut down by a conservative, budget-cutting Congress in November of 1995), the agency concluded that children were in far greater danger off school grounds than in schools and on buses. The study's findings contradict the impression of schoolyard "war zones" that many seem to have. The director of the report stated, "We're convinced that a lot of national policy was driven not by actual data, but by fears. Any child getting shot at school is a terrible thing, and we don't want to imply that it's not. But we feel that children are in a safer environment than they would be out of school." "Schools Are Relatively Safe, U.S. Study Says," reads the less-than-sensational story as it was reported in the *New York Times*—on the bottom of page 20, next to the international weather report.[82]

NO. 2 PENCILS

But beyond the meticulous rituals children are subjected to as they move to and about school, we can't forget the classroom itself. For Foucault, the modern school represented a system of uninterrupted examination. While the stated purpose of the institution is to *disseminate* knowledge to the students, it has long been involved in ritualized knowledge-*gathering* about them. Case files are built out of a series of hierarchical observations and normalizing judgments. With increased measuring and testing, we make finer and finer gradients that distinguish one student from another. While the testers claim that they are simply better able to measure a child's innate abilities, one can argue that the tests themselves "create" the very thing they purport to measure. For example, before there were IQ tests, one wonders whether there was anything like what we consider today to be "intelligence." Before the tests, we looked at two people and said that both seemed "kinda smart" or maybe that one was "not so bright." Once they take an IQ test, however, we can claim that one is 9, 12, or 25 points "more intelligent" than the other.[83]

From the earliest grades, the process of sorting kids into categories begins, and their educational "careers" and identities begin to take hold. The smallest details of their performance, from penmanship to their ability to sit still, are measured and evaluated. After a battery of standardized tests little Peter or Annie becomes the "slow learner," or it is decided that she has a "learning disability" or that he is "gifted" or maybe "just average." In one account by a family friend, this single mother was told that her daughter was "having problems" in the second grade. This prompted a meeting with the school's "intervention team"—a group of very well-trained and well-intentioned professionals including the child's teacher, the principal, the school counselor, the district psychologist, a learning disabilities teacher, and a teacher of gifted children. The bad news was that the child's tests indicated that she had a "learning disability." The good news, however, was that she was also "gifted" (something that they would not have "discovered" if she had not been tested). This meant that the child was assigned an IEP, or individual education plan, which is an even more detailed set of criteria and goals that are monitored and measured throughout the year.

An amazing example of this mentality and the whole system of the examination—with its case files, hierarchical observation, and normalizing judgments—is being used by a teacher at one school in our district. She uses bar-code scanning to "revolutionize tracking a student's progress." The system, called *Learner Profile*, is used to build a database about an individual's academic and behavioral performance. Each category, from the smallest detail such as capitalization skills or listening skills, can be assigned bar codes with a scale of performance for each classification (e.g., "no understanding," "basic knowledge," or "mastery"). "Following the capitalization example," a journalist covering the story writes, "a teacher reads a student paper, scans the student's bar code, . . . Beep! the category, capitalization . . . Beep! . . . and says the student shows a basic understanding . . . Beep!" And, of course, "if students are interacting while she is grading, she can pause in the middle and scan in a behavior field." The teacher thinks that the information collected will be more "comprehensive" than a standard grade card that "tells us so little." She would also like to see "self-motivated students use the system, setting goals and tracking their own progress." Here, once more, those under surveillance are encouraged to use the system to monitor themselves. Asked about the distracting nature of the incessant beeping noise—but perhaps more telling about this new meticulous ritual itself—the teacher said, "I've found that they get used to it pretty quickly."[84]

Another computer software system goes even a step further, putting everyone in the classroom under the gaze. Designed by researchers at my own university, the system is intended to place a child's classroom behavior in context and "help explain why children act the way they do." The software, run on a laptop computer, is used by an "outside observer" such as a school psychologist to systematize or "impose a discipline" on observations of the classroom environment. The software "helps the psychologist silently tabulate, every fifteen seconds, the teacher's behavior, the activity of the moment, the teaching materials at hand, and the configuration of the class—students working alone, one on one, in small groups." Despite the fact that one of the developers claims that, potentially, "everything can go wrong" (such as that "people can take this, and in the worst case, use it to evaluate teachers under review"), thirteen school districts in Kansas, six in other states, and three in foreign countries are using the evaluation system.[85]

"ORDER AND CONTROL ARE EVERYTHING IN THIS BUSINESS"

"This is a controlled environment," states Ron Edens, owner of Electronic Banking System, Inc. His company processes paperwork and donations for companies and charities that choose to "outsource" their clerical tasks. Following is how one journalist described a visit to Edens's facility, an operation that may be the most extraordinary application of Jeremy Bentham's "Inspection-House" I have ever come across.

> Inside, long lines of women sit at spartan desks, slitting envelopes, sorting contents and filling out "control cards" that record how many letters they have opened and how long it has taken them. Workers here, in "the cage," must process three envelopes a minute. Nearby, other women tap keyboards, keeping pace with a quota that demands 8,500 strokes an hour. The room is silent. Talking is forbidden. The windows are covered.

> In his office upstairs, Mr. Edens sits before a TV monitor that flashes images from eight cameras posted through the plant. "There's a little bit of Sneaky Pete to it," he says, using a remote control to zoom in on a document atop a worker's desk. "I can basically read that and figure out how someone's day is going." "We maintain a lot of control," he says. "Order and control are everything in this business."

> But tight observation also helps EBS monitor productivity and weed out workers who don't keep up. "There's multiple uses," Mr. Edens says of surveillance. His desk is covered with computer printouts recording the precise toll of keystrokes tapped by each data-entry worker. He also keeps a day-to-day tally of errors.

> The work floor itself resembles an enormous classroom in the throes of exam period. Desks point toward the front, where a manager keeps watch from a raised platform that workers call . . . "the birdhouse." Other supervisors are positioned toward the back of the room. "If you want to watch someone," Mr. Edens explains, "it's easier from behind because they don't know you're watching." There also is a black globe hanging from the ceiling, in which cameras are positioned. His labor strategy is simple: "We don't ask these people to think—the machines think for them," Mr. Edens says. "They don't have to make any decisions."[86]

Extreme example? Or a sign of the times? Interestingly, Mr. Edens's company is located in an old New England garment factory where generations of young women toiled over weaving machines and were paid according to how many pieces they could produce in an hour. Today, the great-granddaughters of those women struggle to make a living in what is now an "electronic sweatshop" of the twenty-first-century "service economy," processing the financial paper of a consumer society and being remotely watched and monitored by the all-seeing, all-knowing foreman, Mr. Edens.

Surveillance and control have been central features of the world of work ever since people were hired to labor for someone else. As Karl Marx pointed out, nineteenth-century capitalism gave birth to the central problem of modern management: how to get workers to convert their potential labor power to labor done. In the two-hundred-fifty-odd years since then, we have seen countless "solutions" to this dilemma, from starvation and outright coercion, to company unions and Ford's "five dollars a day," to work teams and the latest prescription from this week's best-selling management guru.

Yet, machines and technology have, in the last hundred years or so, played an important role in keeping industrial workers "on task," controlled, and docile, thus reducing the need for supervision. This strategy was epitomized in the late nineteenth century by the emergence and evolution of the assembly line, which brought both the production process and the workers together in a centralized system. But with the "deindustrialization" of the nation, the rise of the service industry and the "information age," the "downsizing" and decentralizing of corporations, and the move toward more "flexible" use of labor, a new class of white-collar and service workers presented a fresh challenge for management. The result has been dramatic changes in the quality and quantity of watching and monitoring in the workplace and of those workers not tied to offices and desks. Workers who are increasingly using computers and other data-processing and communication technologies find that these devices become the very tools that management uses to monitor and control their movements, behavior (what they can say, write, and do in the workplace), and productivity.

For example, at first, the "personal" computer offered us an advanced, individualized tool for doing creative work. It spawned a whole generation of "hackers" and others that celebrated such machines and their liberating potential. But corporate America was, ultimately, not interested in workers' autonomy and liberation. It wanted the productivity gains the machines offered over a typewriter, calculator, or big mainframe computer, but it also wanted to eliminate the need for constant personalized supervision. In today's workplace, the friendly sounding "personal" computer is no longer personal at all; it has been transformed into a "workstation" connected to a local area network. Those spending their days at one of these terminals are increasingly vulnerable to managers who can use the network's operating software to peek at an employee's screen in real time, scan data files and e-mail at will, tabulate keystroke speed and accuracy, overwrite passwords, and even seize control of a remote workstation.

In a study done by the computer magazine *MacWorld*, 22 percent of business executives surveyed said that they had rifled through employees' electronic and voice mail and files. Based on this and other findings, the magazine estimates that as many as twenty million Americans may be subject to electronic monitoring through their computers on the job. With a few well-publicized harassment lawsuits against companies based on computer e-mail, many are arming themselves with sophisticated surveillance tools and monitoring employee e-mail, raising questions about the proper balance between employee privacy and an employer's need to know. While some believe that employers have a right, if not an obligation, to investigate specific complaints of computer-borne harassment, others think that firms are overreacting. In 1999, the share of major U.S. firms that checks employee e-mail messages jumped to 27 percent from 15 percent in 1997, and overall electronic monitoring of communications and performance increased to 45 percent from 35 percent, according to an annual survey by the American Management Association. (Additional forms of watching and listening, including video cameras, brought the total engaged electronic monitoring and surveillance to 67 percent in 1999, up from 63 percent in 1997.)[87]

To date, the U.S. Supreme Court has yet to hear an e-mail privacy case. Yet lower courts have generally upheld the rights of employers to use surveillance. Federal law prohibits employers from listening in on employees' private telephone conversations, but "there's absolutely no protection when it comes to electronic communications on computers," says Jeremy Gruber, an attorney with the American Civil Liberties Union's Workplace Rights Project. Employers at private-sector companies, Gruber contends, "can rifle through your e-mail, computer files and Web-browsing history at will—and in most cases don't even have to let you know they're doing it." Fully one-fifth of the companies surveyed in the American Management Association study cited above did not tell employees they were being watched. Gruber says, "Under current law, if I were an employee I would be extremely hesitant to do any kind of personal business at work."[88]

With billions of electronic mail messages flying through cyberspace every day, few people, it seems, give much thought to how public they really are. This kind of correspondence is openly available to network administrators and others along the line, while so-called deleted mail is often stored on system backup tapes for quite some time. Some examples: In late 1999, a security breach produced by a group of hackers laid bare some fifty million of Microsoft's Hotmail e-mail accounts. The hooligans set up a Web site that permitted anyone to log in to any Hotmail account without requiring a password. In a recent case in New Jersey, a man sued for divorce based on evidence that his wife was having a "virtual affair" with a man she had met on America Online. Evidence presented included dozens of e-mail messages the husband obtained from the couple's own computer, which had stored the copies.[89] In a more high-profile case, Independent Counsel Kenneth Starr's investigation of President Clinton turned to e-mail for evidence. Footnotes in his report include such phrases as "document recovered from Ms. Lewinsky's home computer," "e-mail retrieved from Catherine Davis's computer" and "deleted file from Ms. Lewinsky's home computer." "Recovering files that were deleted from a computer directory is a trivial process," says Joel R. Reidenberg, a professor at the Fordham University School of Law in New York who specializes in privacy issues.[90]

Even those in corporate boardrooms can have their correspondence scrutinized. In a stunning irony, it was, after all, the e-mail of Microsoft Chairman Bill Gates that flatly contradicted his sworn deposition testimony with regard to the Federal government's anti-trust suit against Microsoft. Like Nixon being thwarted by his own tapes, e-mail is, as Foucault said, a "machine in which everyone [is] caught, those who exercise power, just as much as those over whom it is exercised."[91] The Microsoft case has sent shivers down the spine of corporate America, and e-mail is increasingly being treated as the "real truth" of the hearts and minds of executives and CEOs alike. For example, employees at Amazon.com, the Internet bookseller, were issued a directive from senior management instructing employees to purge e-mail messages that were no longer required for business or not subject to legal records requirements. This Amazon "document retention" policy is referred to as "Sweep and Keep." "In the past, message-retention policies have been primarily designed for disk space management," says Jim Browning, a senior research analyst at the Gartner Group, a consulting firm. "The new question is how quickly should e-mail be deleted to prevent it from becoming a danger to the organization?" The consulting firm suggests policies that help employees understand what is now "appropriate business language." For example, in the new electronic workplace: "You talk about 'fair competition'; you don't talk about 'slaughtering' them. No warfare language. That way you have fewer messages you have to worry about in the files." Unlike policies prohibiting abusive or harassing electronic messages, the new rules attempt to suppress common forms of expression. As one observer put it, "And when such exchanges must take place in writing, the prevailing philosophy would have them expunged as quickly and ruthlessly as possible."[92]

For years, so-called futurists have been predicting that the "information age" and its associated technologies will free us from the drudgery of long commutes and the confines of the office. Today, the ideas of "telecommuting" and the "virtual office" are heralded as the means whereby we will find a new generation of happy, productive workers, who labor when and where they want. But this rosy picture has some thorns in it. While the scenario may be true for elite managers and some independent professionals, does anyone seriously think that this kind of flexibility and unsupervised work will be offered to the average worker? While the "virtual office" may not have walls—much like the "virtual prison" of house arrest has no bars—for many of the thirty million traveling businesspeople, the so-called road warriors, new telecommunications devices are becoming "electronic leashes" that keep them "wired" in and monitored. Corporate "downsizing" (i.e., massive layoffs) and decentralization, emerging global markets that demand instant availability, and a drive to boost productivity have created demand for the more flexible use of labor. The results are that people have an anxious preoccupation with work, that they are working more hours, and that the lines between home and work life are blurring as corporations use the emerging technologies to harness workers' productivity.

Take the case of American Express travel agent Kathy Jones, who works out of her home in Vineland, New Jersey, more than an hour's drive from the central office in Trenton. Customers' calls are routed directly to the computer in the corner of her dining room. "It's skilled work," her supervisor told one journalist. "It can take years to do it well." But just to make sure that the "skilled" worker is doing it well, Jones's boss can, with a touch of a key on her own computer, look at what her agents are typing on their computers. By hitting a button on her telephone, she can listen in on any of those agents' conversations as well. But rather than calling this technology a surveillance device, management contends that it's a "learning tool." "[I]t's not used to say, 'Hey, you know, we watch what you do.' It's basically used for training purposes to say, you know, 'Looks like you have some trouble in that area. Let me get you into a class, or get you, you know, something you need to assist you with that.'" Kathy Jones seems to agree about the productive benefits of being watched and doesn't seem to mind the monitoring: "If they see you doing something on the screen that they think you can do a quicker way, they can tell you—they can advise you of it. They can even tell you ways to talk to people, or they can tell you ways to do things quicker to end your call quicker, so it's pretty helpful."[93]

Recording workers' conversations are increasingly a part of the daily life of telephone operators, the "customer assistant" representatives of financial organizations, and the "sales associates" of catalog merchandisers. Many such organizations have decided that their employees—despite their "team spirit" and job titles that proclaim "we're a big happy family"—can't be trusted to conduct business properly and need to have their calls monitored. "This call is being monitored," announces the recording, "to ensure your prompt and courteous service." Since both sides of the conversation are recorded, it would seem that these businesses don't have confidence in their customers' integrity either. With recordings, if a "dispute" or a complaint arises—from a customer or an employee—managers have the "truth" in hand.

The legions of customer-service representatives throughout the country face the kind of grueling surveilled and rationalized workplaces once reserved for life on factory assembly lines. Take the third-party contractual firm in Carrollton, Texas, that handles calls for Microsoft Network. One worker, who, in an interview refused to use his real name, reports that he liked helping people solve their computer problems and thought he would enjoy the work. But he complained, "Whereas our trainers had encouraged us to take as long as necessary to solve each caller's problem, our manager pressured us to constantly finish each call as quickly as possible," he says. Managers there, as in many other offices, had the technology to monitor worker productivity: they timed each call representatives received, then computed average times. They monitored "idle mode" or the time when workers weren't on the phone with customers but were not signed off duty. Break and training time counted as idle time, as did listening to voice mail messages. "The clock ruled us," the former representative remembers. "As technology grows more sophisticated, there will be more ways to monitor people, and so it becomes more important to safeguard them against unreasonable use of these devices," says Candice Johnson, spokesperson for the Communications Workers of America union. Johnson cites customer-service centers such as the one run by the Bell Atlantic telephone company where employees were not given enough time to help customers and were monitored minute by minute by multiple supervisors. Some even had to key in special codes to be excused. As one rep put it, "Getting reports which tell you how many times you used the restroom and for how long is dehumanizing." Another worker, Jeb Bianco, employed by a temp firm providing interim staff to Symantec software in Eugene, Oregon, echoes the experience: "Everything you do is timed—the time you're on a call, the time you place a call on hold, the time you're waiting for the next call." Every two weeks workers were given a printout of their daily performance, expected to keep calls to four minutes apiece on average, no matter how many questions the customer had. The goal was for each rep to handle one hundred calls in an eight-hour shift.[94]

Another example of the post-Fordist shift in the workplace was the tactic by some large corporations to move away from sprawling suburban headquarters to large "cubicle" warehouses. Here, sales staff check in periodically and are assigned an "office" where they can plug their laptop computers into a network, make some phone calls, and then go back out on the road—no pictures of the spouse and kids on the desks, no time for chatting around the water cooler. With the decline of organized labor and a political movement aimed at dismantling workers' rights and privacies, the "virtual office" may take on an entirely different connotation in the future.

But it's not just office workers who are vulnerable to such monitoring. The computer and other kinds of new telecommunication devices are transforming jobs throughout the entire occupational structure. Here are some examples:

Fran is a meter reader in California. A few years back, I encountered her darting across my backyard. I went out to greet her, curious about the small black box she held in her hand. I began to ask her how the device worked, but she said, "Gotta keep going. You can walk along though." As we moved down the street at a clipped pace, Fran told me about the mini computer she was holding. It had recently replaced the pen and clipboard she used for more than five years to keep track of electricity consumption in the neighborhood. I asked why she was nearly running between houses, and she said, "Since this thing has a built-in clock, my supervisor can now calculate how long it takes me to do a house and how many I can do in an hour. We have an average we have to keep up, and I'm behind. See ya."

I'm at a rest stop off I-29 somewhere in South Dakota talking with Arnie who is standing next to his eighteen-wheel rig owned by one of the nation's largest trucking firms. "Hey, I hear you got a computer in your truck." "Goddam right," he says somewhat disgusted. Arnie's computer is part of an advanced satellite communication system that permits the corporate headquarters in Phoenix to know exactly where his truck is, within 1,000 yards, at any moment, day or night. The computer monitors his driving performance—average speed, idle time, fuel consumption—as well as the miles he has covered, and it will transmit to him instructions about where he is to pick up his next load. "I have to keep that truck as close to 58 mph as I can," he says, "otherwise they'll bust me." He is not worried about state troopers; he is talking about the company.

"I get twenty beeps a weekend," complains Peter Hart, a former equipment supervisor at an electronics plant in Freemont, California. Hart says that his job required him to be available to the company and other employees by pager and phone twenty-four-hours a day, seven days a week. He decided to quit his job, he says, after pagers, cell phones, and e-mail took over his life.[95]

Just look around. Restaurant workers are wearing vibrating beepers that literally prod them through their shift. Bookstore clerks are donning wireless headsets so they can stock shelves and answer phones and queries at the same time. Delivery people, auto-rental check-in clerks, parking-meter readers, and a host of others are carrying data-entry computers that not only make them work "more efficiently" but also keep tabs on their movements and/or keep track of their productivity. Businesses are increasingly installing "card-key" entry doors that record the activity at that access point. Since an individual's card is unique, the door can actually tally who went through each door at what time, giving administrators a record of movement in the facility. For example, employees at the San Carlos Apache Gold Casino in San Carlos, Arizona, use "smart cards" as part of a security system called *Traquer* that is integrated with the casino's pre-existing access/egress system. The *Traquer* system takes a digital picture of the employee and stores it on the smart card chip, which is then imported directly into the existing access control software.

Interestingly, at the elite, cutting-edge, high-tech research center of the Xerox Corporation called the PARC Computer Science Lab, designers have turned the tools of their trade on themselves. A local computer engineer has invented what he calls the "Active Badge": a very small pager-like device that emits an infrared signal every fifteen seconds. Detectors scattered throughout the facility receive the signals and feed them to the lab's local area network, telling the computer the whereabouts of any staff member at any time. This information is, of course, accessible at any workstation. Olivetti Corporation is now marketing a similar device to "insurance companies, hospitals, and other large institutions with an interest in the whereabouts of key personnel or patients."[96]

TESTING YOUR INTEGRITY

If overt monitoring of employees through computers, video cameras, data-entry tablets, beepers, and the like weren't enough, it is likely that your employer began building a "case file" on you before you were even offered the job. In the face of what employers claim is a rising tide of lawsuits, stringent hiring and firing regulations, drug use and alleged criminal activity in the workplace, corporations are increasingly turning to pre-employment background checks to screen applicants. These investigations can include a criminal records search; access to driver's-license, credit, and workers' compensation histories; and verification of educational and professional credentials, along with personal interviews with references. Of course, these kinds of extensive background checks are becoming easy to complete as more and more computerized databases come online and as those who control them are in the business of selling the information. Larry Craft of Datacheck Company advises employers to compare data from each record. "If an employer finds an applicant has several convictions for possessing drug paraphernalia, the employer might look at the credit report to see if the person has trouble paying their bills."[97]

Assuming you survive this kind of scrutiny, you may find yourself confronted with a pre-employment "integrity test" (a favorite substitute for the lie detector which was outlawed for most pre-employment situations back in 1988; I discuss the lie detector and the drug test in chapter 4, which focuses on surveillance and the body). Written integrity tests are used, supposedly, to measure a person's level of "honesty or dishonesty." Typically, testers will pose a set of questions that may come right out and ask whether you have committed various offenses (Have you ever stolen products from your place of employment?), or see what you would do under certain circumstances (If you saw a coworker taking money from the cash register would you report it to your supervisor?), or more subtly assess a person's values and attitudes (Do you agree with the idea of once a thief always a thief?). Estimates are that nearly three million of these tests are administered each year in thousands of workplaces across the country.

Finally, an estimated two million employees every year are required to take written "personality tests" that probe into aspects of their lives such as hygiene habits, sexuality, and family relationships. The 1990 Americans with Disabilities Act put some limits on the use of tests designed to reveal a physical or mental impairment. Yet, in 1998, the American Management Association reported a "definite upward movement, especially in personality measurements (28% this year compared with 19% in 1997)" in its annual survey of member organizations. They go on to point out that

> Recruiting is ever more expensive in the current tight labor market, with a concomi-
> tant increase in the cost of a wrong choice when hiring an applicant or promoting an
> employee. As is true of all forms of testing, larger organizations are more likely to en-

gage in psychological measurement than smaller ones, although the variations are not dramatic: psychological measurements are performed by 39% of firms grossing less than $10 million annually, compared with 54% of billion-dollar companies.[98]

OK, now let's assume that you clear the background check; pass the integrity and psychological tests, the drug test, as well as the physical; and are offered a position. Once you are on the job, your supervisor is likely to add to your file through an ongoing monitoring and evaluation process made infinitely more systematic and thorough than ever before with the use of new kinds of inexpensive computer software. For example, KnowledgePoint software claims that its *Performance Now!* package is so "remarkable" that it "actually writes your employee reviews!"

> You rate each employee on a scale of 1–5 and *Performance Now!* generates clean natural text that recognizes strong points and addresses areas where improvement is needed. But that's not all; *Performance Now!* interactive advice alerts you when your ratings need to be backed up by concrete examples. A built in Employee Log helps you track examples of day-to-day problems and accomplishments throughout the review period. Increase productivity, raise morale, and protect your business against expensive wrongful termination suits.

Other packages include *Employee Appraiser*, which its publisher claims is being used in thirty thousand corporations nationwide. This program consists of

> more than 600 professionally written paragraphs that you can use in your own review documents. It includes a coaching advisor that offers motivational ideas and solutions to everyday performance issues. The Language Scan feature ensures you have said the right thing in the right way.

And then there is the *WorkWise Employee File* that

> helps you document performance, attendance trends, and benefits more easily than ever . . . *WorkWise* lets you audit and maintain employee records (even with on-screen photos!) . . . Supervisors can make notes "on the fly" and higher management can be assured that employee documentation is maintained consistently and reliably.

Much like the bar-code system being used to keep track of the smallest details about students' behavior, software can subject workers to minute measurements of performance; evidence can be documented and tabulated, and penalties can be meted out when necessary. And like the teacher who would like to see the "self-motivated students use the system, setting goals and tracking their own progress," the makers of this software believe that the feedback provided to workers will increase their "productivity" and raise their "morale." Interestingly, these software programs generate a kind of simulated evaluation; only the appearance of a "real," thorough appraisal is needed to create the necessary knowledge base. Just plug in the numbers and the program produces the sterile, legally safe text necessary to maintain the illusion of rigor.

Now, one could argue that if you are doing your job and "keeping your nose clean," why should you care about what's in your file? How you do your job, your performance, is what matters, right? But what exactly does "performance" mean? On the scale between doing the minimal amount of work required and failing to adequately do your job (grounds for firing), there is a vast gray area where you may find yourself defined as a "problem employee." In fact, your boss may have just taken a business-consulting seminar entitled "How to Legally Fire Employees with Attitude Problems: A Step-by-Step Guide." This brochure states:

Are You Stuck with Problem Employees Like These?
—Susan seems to work in only two speeds—slow and stop. She performs the minimum amount of work required, complains weekly about her workload, and rushes out of the office at five o'clock on the dot every day. She makes her deadlines but you have to push her constantly. Can you dismiss her for being a *foot-dragger*?
—Tom is sharp as a tack and performs like gang-busters. The only problem is he thinks he knows everything. He always insists on doing things his way . . . openly criticizes anyone who disagrees with him, including you . . . and locks horns with coworkers every week. You've counseled Tom about his abrasive attitude but he says that you're the one with a problem, not him. Can you terminate Tom for being so *cocky*?
—Lisa has been whining since the day she was transferred into your department. She moans about company policies, her paycheck, her health, and everything else under the sun. And when you counsel Lisa about her negative attitude, she complains to your boss about you. Lisa is really driving you up the wall and her negative attitude is starting to rub off on others. Can you legally fire Lisa for being a *whiner*?
As a manager, you know only too well how these kinds of employees can kill morale, add dead weight to your department, and make your job a miserable chore. But can you fire workers with bad attitudes and still legally protect yourself? The answer is YES, you can. After you attend this one-day seminar and learn the skills and techniques you need to turn an employee's poor attitude into a concrete reason for termination, you'll be able to fire problem employees legally, safely, and confidently . . .
Attend this seminar and you'll learn exactly what it takes to build your case against employees with attitude problems. You'll learn how to expertly document negative attitudes and take disciplinary action quickly and effectively . . . You discover how to dismiss a worker whose personality grates on everyone's nerves . . . how to legally protect yourself when conducting a termination session . . . what to do when an employee tries to intimidate you physically . . . and more . . .
Take the Stress Out of Firing—If you're like most managers and supervisors, you know how to fire for theft, tardiness and absenteeism, but you're not so sure how to fire for attitude . . . Come to this invaluable six-hour course and learn the tips, strategies and guidelines you need to terminate employees with poor attitudes confidently and painlessly.

Finally, if on-the-job monitoring and surveillance are not achieved by the computer you use, the beeper on your belt, or the periodic review of your computerized "employee file," they may just be provided by your coworker in the next cubicle. "Like a lot of people who transfer to new jobs in another state," writes Ellen Schultz of the *Wall Street Journal*, "Lewis Hubble was glad to quickly make a new friend at work." However, Schultz goes on the say:

> Within weeks of his arrival at the Manteno, Ill., distribution center for giant retailer Kmart Corp., Mr. Hubble, a 29-year veteran of the company, and his new friend Al were having lunch, and the occasional beer after work . . . What Mr. Hubble didn't know was that Al was part of a married team of investigators Kmart hired to pose as employees. Over a period of seven months, the two operatives befriended co-workers such as Mr. Hubble and wrote reports about conversations in the workplace, at employees' homes, at parties and at a Hardee's restaurant. A note about conversations at the American Legion Hall included the number of pitchers of beer ordered by each employee.[99]

When the spying was later exposed by employees, it was determined that the team had reported to management things about financial and domestic problems, drinking behavior, sexual preferences, rumors about employees' sexual affairs and interoffice romances, as well as noting that one worker had "shopped at Wal-Mart."

Ironically, as workers have brought lawsuits against employers for violating the legal notion of a "reasonable expectation of privacy," some employers have adopted the strategy of informing workers, up front, that they should not expect any privacy in the first place. Indeed, some court decisions have held that employers can be found liable for invasions of privacy only if they have given their workers an expectation of privacy. "You do not want them to have a reasonable expectation of privacy," states one attorney who represents management exclusively. Instead, he said, employees should "realize if they come to the place of work, the employer is going to be opening up anything, any time, any place."[100]

PSYCHOGRAPHICS

The importance of our role as consumers in late capitalism is told in the story of how much energy goes into monitoring and tracking our buying habits, "lifestyle" choices, and financial stature. As I noted earlier, new forms of watching may be created through the very products and services we are seduced into purchasing, such as cellular phones, computers, and video cameras. Yet there is an extraordinary amount of ritualized surveillance and monitoring taking place in our most mundane consumer activities—from our preferences in breakfast cereal, the type of pain relief we take, or the magazines we read. Today, amazing amounts of personal, comprehensive information are collected and stored in both private-sector and governmental databases, offering easy access to this wealth of knowledge. This is quite a switch from a few hundred years ago. Think about it. Before the rise of modern, bureaucratic organizations and their knowledge-gathering activities, the only people "known" in society were elites—heroes, villains, royalty, heads of state, and religious leaders. Everyday folks were ignored, in their day (and by historians), in part because there were few sources of information about them and, without a mass market for goods, there was no rationale for collecting the data. But now it seems just the opposite. Today, those who have social power and wealth may use these resources to insulate and shield themselves from scrutiny as best they can while the rest of us are simply issued yet another account number.

In a marketplace overflowing with goods and services, the most effective and efficient way for sellers to bring order to this chaos—to increase their "targetability" as it is called—is by gathering up all the bits and pieces of our lives and reassembling them into highly individualized consumer profiles and portfolios. Indeed, the use of basic "demographic" data for mass marketing has given way to a finer mesh of personality profiling and market segmentation known by those in the trade as "psychographics" (examining attributes related to how a person thinks, feels, and behaves). As one marketing company pitches it,

> If you find today's marketplace turbulent, complex, and highly competitive, tomorrow's will be even more so. The most profitable strategic directions stem from comprehensive and integrated views of your most profitable customers and what they value about your products and services. Psychographics and advanced analytics give today's marketers the clear actionable insights and applications they need to be successful.

Of course, this schema, like other constellations of power/knowledge, has its roots in the rise of the human sciences and as such is designed to treat human beings as "objects" to be broken down, analyzed, and acted upon. Psychological studies are used to assess a wide range of behaviors, tastes, and preferences.[101] Other social science techniques and methods are put to use in surveying, interviewing, and focus group studies. Given its highly specialized nature, the plan depends entirely on the supervision and surveillance of the smallest fragments of daily life. While this kind of surveillance is clearly on the "soft side" of our spectrum of control, it should not be discounted as trivial. The use of computerized information storage and retrieval, and, I would argue, their intersection with the knowledge of the human sciences, prompts Oscar Gandy to suggests that this kind of "cybernetic" capitalism "increases the ability of organized interests, whether they are selling shoes, toothpaste, or political platforms, *to identify, isolate, and communicate differentially with individuals, in order to increase their influence* over how consumers make selections among these options"(emphasis mine).[102]

Some scholars go as far as to suggest that our participation in mass consumer culture has become a primary means of social integration and, in the broadest sense, social control in postmodern society. Like the shift from the brutal treatment of the offender in the classical age to the "gentle way" to punish in the modern era, social control, the argument goes, subtlety moves from the older panoptic and coercive forms of repression of, say, the factory, to the quiet seduction of the consumer market. Here any political discontent or social malfeasance is quickly absorbed into the stupefying complacency of the dominant consumer culture. Zygmunt Bauman declares, for example, that consumer conduct is moving "into the position of, simultaneously, the cognitive and moral focus of life, the integrative bond of society, and the focus of systemic management." Echoing Bauman, David Lyon adds, "Consuming, not working, becomes the hub around which the life-world rotates. Pleasure, once seen as the enemy of capitalist industriousness, now performs an indispensable role."[103]

Yet I would argue that, in practice, the seduction and pleasure of consuming are made possible only with the obsessive "data mining" of our personal lives as well as the use of surveillance ceremonies such as shoplifting systems, surveillance cameras, and other gadgets to keep an eye on us while we are at it. The old panoptic model, I argue, has been more fully integrated into the new consumption model. My point was nicely illustrated in a recent television commercial created by IBM to sell its new business strategy tagged as, "Know more, Sell more: IBM Business Intelligence." On the television screen we see a view of a food store through the somewhat distorted fish-eye effect of a panning video surveillance camera, as if we are looking through the camera. Two clerks appear on the screen in front of a display case:

Clerk 1:	"Smell this stuff."
Clerk 2:	"Ewwwwe."
Clerk 1:	"It's green, it stinks, and it's . . . eight bucks!"
Clerk 1:	"Marty" (both clerks waving their arms towards the video camera lens; the camera continues to pan slowly back and forth). "Marty. Hey Marty . . . Who buys this stuff? It stinks."
Marty:	"Well Fletcher, the people who buy that stinky cheese also buy (keyboard typing) 92% of the miniature vegetables we sell" (more typing). "Wow, look at the margins on miniature vegetables."
Clerk 1:	"How can he know that?"
Clerk 2:	"He's making it up."
Marty:	"No, I'm not."

The closing caption reads: "Solutions for a Small Planet."

Direct marketing campaigns accounted for $750 billion in business in 1998 and, in order to produce those sales, the direct marketing industry keeps a keen eye on everyday folks and their habits—a form of "dataveillance," if you will. These data are extremely valuable, both to anyone trying to sell something and to the data profiteers who broker data. Companies such as Donnelly Marketing and R. L. Polk and Company keep the equivalent of dossiers on over 90 percent of American households. Marketers can purchase more than twelve thousand types of specialized mailing lists that take the notion of "niche marketing" to new heights. As one journalist put it, any manufacturer can purchase a listing of, say, "every suburban male BMW owner under 25 who previously owned a Honda. With a few more links in the chain, it's possible to know which of those Beemer boys are young white Republican heterosexuals who earn more than $150,000, groove on hip-hop, and would like their leather jackets cut long and modeled by Derek Jeeter."[104] The "target marketing" subsidiary of the TRW credit bureau sells data about the heads of households of eighty-seven million Americans, including their age, weight, height, ethnicity, net worth, and financial status (some of these data are gleaned from the driver's license records that are public information in twenty states). The *Behavior Bank* can offer subscribers data about more than twenty-eight million households divided into one hundred different "lifestyles" based on the types of investments they have, their hobbies, and the kinds of vacations they take. Meanwhile, the *Information America* database contains the phone numbers, addresses, dwelling type, estimated age, and average income for seventy million Americans. Another database, called *Assets*, contains the property records of nearly everyone in the country, while other sources can tell someone what high school you attended and whether you have ever filed a lawsuit, filed for bankruptcy, or had a lien on your property.

Corporate information banks are filled, organized, and sold off in a variety of interesting ways. When we call toll-free consumer help numbers we may not be getting much of a bargain, as these numbers are often linked to now-common *CallerID* systems. I recently dialed a customer "care" center of a national appliance company and, in addition to being told by a recording that my call might be monitored for "quality assurance purposes," I was also informed that *CallerID* may also be employed to "maximize" service. Other companies use *Caller ID* to sort out and identify "worthy" (i.e., the most profitable) customers who get preferential treatment by service representatives. In one account,

> [on] computer screens at First Union telephone-service centers, calling customers are identified with green, yellow or red signals. Green means profitable, so be nice and give them a break. Yellow means marginally profitable, so negotiate firmly with the customer. Red means loser (unprofitable), so waste little time and offer no breaks. NationsBank has its own version, as did Barnett Banks before it was bought. At Sanwa Bank California, when customers dial (888) GO-SANWA and enter their account number, the computer shows they are ranked as A, B or C and are treated accordingly.[105]

Southwestern Bell Corporation offers a service to businesses called *Caller Intelidata*. This product packages standard *CallerID* information such as the date and time of each call and the caller's name, address, and zip code with information compiled by Equifax, Inc., a national credit reporting and information service. These additional data include income, "lifestyle," education, neighborhood, and other personal information.[106] Meanwhile, when the *Wall Street Journal* reported that the Blockbuster Video chain was preparing to sell mailing lists of its customers, arranged by the types of movies they had rented, customers and consumer groups made it known that they were not pleased with the idea. Several days after the story broke, the company's chairman announced that the executive who had disclosed the plan had "misspoke."[107]

In an "information economy," personal data becomes such a valuable commodity that companies are willing to resort to a variety of schemes, gimmicks, and giveaways to collect it. For years now, product "registration cards" have warned us to fill out the "personal information" section, seemingly under threat of voiding our warranty. Corporations regularly collect data about customers through mail-in coupons and rebate forms. (The magazine *Consumer Reports* once covered this story with the headline "Smile—You're on Corporate Camera.")[108] Magazine sweepstakes regularly cajole people into offering themselves up to company data scavengers. Recently, corporate giant PepsiCo offered free beepers to teenagers, then paged a quarter million kids with ads and a message to call corporate headquarters to win more stuff. This strategy reflects a trend of trying to build "brand loyalty" at early ages where, for example, sport shoe manufacturers give away products to inner-city kids, hoping that the next Michael Jordan cash cow will stick with their shoes. This kind of "relationship marketing" seeks to build life-long name recognition and customer loyalty through schemes such as frequent-flier programs, renewable leasing, and high-profile customer-service campaigns.

A kind of consumer version of an electronically monitored home confinement anklet device has been developed by The PreTesting Company. The device is embedded in a watch and it records and tallies signals encoded in the sound tracks of radio and TV commercials. "The future Neilsen families who wear this timepiece will give marketers unheard-of accuracy about who tunes in to what. The same device will also detect signals from a chip inserted into the spines of magazines, conveying how long a reader spends perusing a publication."[109]

The General Accounting Office estimates that there are more than nine hundred federal government data sets containing personal information that are shared with other government organizations as well as with corporations and private groups. As these kinds of data become available, politicians, policymakers, and run-of-the-mill agency managers come up with new and innovative ways of using the data (and, likely, in ways that the data were never intended to be used). For example, the federal Family Support Act of 1988 mandates that states put "online" data about so-called deadbeat parents who do not make their child-support payments. These data can then be cross-referenced with other state agencies. Once this is done, welfare workers can use information from driver's license records, or even applications for hunting licenses, to track down offending parents. Or take the issue of illegal immigration. A few years back, a presidential commission chaired by former representative Barbara Jordan, a longtime advocate of constitutional rights, concluded that the problem of immigration could be addressed with computers. Jordan's commission advocated the use of a computerized national registry based on Social Security numbers. Critics charged that such a program would amount to the equivalent of a national identification card.[110]

"WILL THAT BE ON YOUR CREDIT CARD TODAY?"

While advocates of privacy and immigrants' rights decry the move toward a national identification card, it seems clear to me that the vast majority of us carry around the functional equivalent of one right now. It's called a credit card. Credit cards function as a form of identification (increasingly they have our pictures on them and, very soon, are likely to have our fingerprints or other information embedded in them). A credit card is a certificate of financial worth and an increasingly necessary key—as well as a leash—to a vast electronic financial network. You can't rent a car without one, but the police can also check your records to trace your whereabouts. As financial institutions and corporations nudge us down the road to a "cashless" society under the spell of "fast" and "convenient" service, they are building for themselves unprecedented access to our daily habits and routines. With every electronic purchase or transaction, we leave an electronic "paper trail" of our activities that can be used to build a profile of our habits and tastes and even our movements and patterns of behavior.

For example, many grocery stores, gas stations, and convenience stores are increasingly encouraging customers to use checking-account cards (ATM cards) and credit cards at "the point of purchase." In the case of grocery stores, paying with one of these cards instantly connects you to the computerized inventory of the store, which, of course, reflects the transactions of the bar-code scanner at the checkout counter. This way, a record is created of what you bought, when you bought it, and how you paid for it. These data can then be used by the store or sold to marketing firms to build a detailed portrait of your buying habits. Marketing firms are then able to sort you by your perceived value in the marketplace, and can ensure precise target marketing, making you susceptible to particular campaigns. (Even shoppers who pay by check can be tracked. Put in place to thwart the passing of bad checks, computerized checkout systems currently used in many national chain stores compile data about check writers, including their spending habits.) If you pay cash, the transaction cannot be linked to you personally.

In 1996, a major U.S. bank offered a glimpse of the "cashless" future at the Olympic Village in Atlanta, as athletes were all issued "debit" cards, and no cash was accepted in the facilities. A British bank has begun a similar experiment in a small enclave in London where local merchants and all others previously handling cash are using electronic debit "smart cards." The consumer culture and the cashless society are due to come online as soon as the giant cable television and media conglomerates deliver on their promise to turn the nation's TV sets into "interactive" communication devices. Once every household is "wired" into these vast networks, the television will be become our primary source for new forms of multimedia entertainment, shopping for goods and services, and financial transactions. According to its promoters, the system is all about consumer choice and convenience: We will be able through our TVs to choose the programming we want to watch, when we want to watch it; to receive information about and see demonstrations of products, as well as order them instantly; and to pay our bills and make other financial arrangements. But by doing so, these and other corporations will have unprecedented access to our viewing habits, our buying preferences and choices, and our financial status as potential consumers. In other words, someone will be keeping track of just about every aspect of our daily lives in postmodern America.

4

❦

Bodily Intrusions

Revolutionize Your Drug Testing Simply and Economically. On Site. In Sight. On Time. Anytime.

—*OnTrack,* Drug Testing Kit

I'm out on patrol with a community corrections surveillance officer. At 10:45 P.M. we pull into the driveway of a modest suburban house. "Pete" walks up, rings the doorbell, and, a minute or so later, a sleepy twenty-eight-year-old male answers in his nightclothes. Pete slips an alcohol scanner pipette to his face, the client breathes into the tube, Pete takes his reading, says "good night," and walks back to the car to record his findings.

—Field notes, Staples, 19 April 1995

Tests of eyesight, skill and intelligence hardly prepares [a citizen] for Government demands to submit to the extraction of blood, to excrete under supervision, or to have these bodily fluids tested for the physiological and psychological secrets they may contain.

—Supreme Court Justices Marshall and Blackman on drug testing and individual Fourth Amendment rights

In *Discipline and Punish,* Foucault begins his history of Western social control by recounting, in gruesome detail, the torture and execution of a man on the scaffold in Paris in 1757 who has been accused of trying to assassinate the king. Foucault argues that this "carnival of atrocity," this public theater, was a political

93

ritual, a symbol of the excessive power of the sovereign invoked against anyone who challenged his authority. As the prisoner was tortured, he was forced to confess and thereby set the seal of "truth" on the already-established, secret proceedings of the magistrates. The confession was an act of the criminal playing the role of responsible, speaking subject. The disciplinary technique of public torture, then, was an elaborate display of power and knowledge, inscribed on the body.

But as I have argued, coinciding with the rise of the modern nation-state, a new form of political power took hold. With Enlightenment zeal, late-eighteenth- and early-nineteenth-century philosophers, jurists, reformers, and state authorities asserted a new discourse on crime and punishment that placed themselves as "experts" at the center of the practice of justice. The body of the condemned man was now the property of society rather than that of the king. Here we see the gradual disappearance of public torture and the rise of rationally organized reformatory institutions. Within this new political regime, punishment was no longer aimed at destroying the body, but rather was intended to discipline it, to rehabilitate it, through meticulous rituals of power. As I have shown, this disciplinary power is advanced through the use of procedures such as the gaze, the examination, hierarchical observation, and normalizing judgments. With this modernist agenda of "rehabilitation," criminals would be understood and known in their individuality—through biography, observation, and behavioral analysis—with the ultimate aim being the transformation of their "soul." Punishment would no longer breed terror and exact a public confession; it would produce deterrence and private penance.

Now, while the king could reduce an offender's body to dust or the modern asylum could watch it or train it, I want to argue that, today, there is a proliferation of postmodern surveillance and disciplinary technologies that are founded on deriving knowledge *from* the body. The modern regime of rehabilitation was premised, at least in part, on the idea of an appeal to the criminal's conscience, to what may "enlighten him from within," so that he (or she) might adhere to the social contract. Yet clearly, any behavior modification on the criminal's part was at the mercy of what we might call the individual's "privileged access" to his or her inner self. In other words, criminals had to accept their own "rehabilitation"—their new identities if you will—and change their ways accordingly. But this ideology of rehabilitation demanded considerable trust on the part of authorities to believe that the offender was, in fact, "a new man," and not simply on his "best behavior" while in custody.

I argue that these modern ideas and practices regarding power, knowledge, and the body are changing rapidly. New developments in science, technology, and medical knowledge are making the human body infinitely more accessible to official scrutiny and assessment. The legacy of the Enlightenment continues to foster and support our almost obsessive use of both the physical and the human and clinical sciences to treat human beings as "objects" to be analyzed rather than as speaking "subjects." Every day we are told that researchers at universities, private foundations, and corporations have "unlocked the door" to something new about our bodies, minds, and behaviors. Yet such studies and discoveries—while they may disclose a cure for cancer or are often carried out under the guise of "intellectual curiosity" and for the "good" of human advancement—are, nonetheless, directly and indirectly contributing to the creation and use of new techniques for observing, manipulating, and controlling our bodies. This means that the ability of organizations to monitor, judge, or regulate our actions and behaviors through our bodies is being significantly enhanced. And while we see some of the most blatant examples of this phenomenon in the official justice system, we also see them at work in schools, workplaces, and other community settings.

Once put in place, these new techniques reduce the need to trust offenders to "mend their ways" or for suspects to "speak the truth," as in confessing to the use of drugs, to being at the scene of a crime, or even to having "deviant desires." Rather, it is individuals' objectified bodies that will "tell us what we need to know" and "who they really are," as in such categories as "known drug user," "sexual predator," or someone with a "personality disorder." In other words, it is no longer considered effective or efficient to simply gaze at the body—or to train it in hopes of rendering it docile—rather, we must surveil its inner evidence and secrets. I call this a "pornography of the self" because it is an obscene gaze that attempts to lay bare an individual's "true" identity. In fact, it would seem that organizations inside and outside the penal/health/welfare complex possess a raft of new devices intended to derive knowledge—or impose a form of accountability on individuals—through their bodies. And it is the social, cultural, and economic logics of late capitalism that are making this pornography of the self possible.

THE POLITICS OF "SUBSTANCE ABUSE"

This new relationship among power, knowledge, and the body is pointedly displayed in the practice of drug and alcohol testing. Meshing well with the rhetoric of a war on drugs that blamed the defective character of the abuser for the country's drug problem, individual testing has become the "weapon of choice" to confront the suspected drug user. Estimates are that more than fifteen million Americans were tested in 1998—up more than 50 percent from five years before—at a cost of $600 million. SmithKline Beecham Clinical Laboratories performed 300,000 in 1987; in 1999 it did 5.5 million. The most common location for testing appears to be the workplace, where the vast majority of the tests are used in pre-employment screening rather than on current employees. However, in certain occupational categories, drug and alcohol tests can take place under conditions of "reasonable cause" (or suspicion), after an accident, before treatment, and randomly, as during pre-employment. In 1994, the

American Management Association (AMA) reported that drug testing in the private sector has increased 305 percent since 1987, the year the association first began conducting the survey. Much of this testing was spurred on by President Ronald Reagan's 1986 Executive Order 12564 stating that all federal employees may be tested for drugs; subsequent testing was mandated for specific occupations by the Department of Transportation and the Department of Defense. According to the latest AMA survey of major U.S. corporations, 89.8 percent of manufacturing companies tested their employees in 1993; and 30.6 percent tested periodically or at random. In the transportation sector, 87.5 percent of workers were tested for drugs, and these companies reported the highest rate of periodic or random testing, at 75 percent.[1] Today, it seems that the most common response to news reports of a plane crash, train derailment, or construction accident is: Were the individuals involved tested for drugs before or after the accident? And with the defeat of almost every civil suit brought against testing—most recently the court decision that permits the testing of public school athletes—these numbers are expected to grow.

Currently, the most common drug-testing procedure involves a two-part analysis of a bodily fluid (typically, urine) to determine whether traces of drugs are present. The first part, a screening test, involves a relatively simple and inexpensive analysis using thin-layer chromatography. Under most circumstances, if the sample tests positive for drugs, a more sophisticated and more accurate confirmation test employing GC/MS (gas chromatography/mass spectrometry) is performed to verify the presence of the "abused substance." In addition to urine analysis, the testing of hair samples is expanding rapidly these days. The leading tester of hair samples, Psychometrics Corporation of Cambridge, Massachusetts, claims that more than five hundred U.S. corporations have turned to this method. Advocates argue that such tests "give employers a bigger and clearer picture of drug use than urine analysis can provide." This is because, when someone ingests a drug, the drug is circulated in the bloodstream, and traces of it remain in hair follicles. Since hair grows at a rate of about one and a half inches a month, this method provides "a 90 day profile of drug use." In contrast, drug traces in urine disappear in three or four days.[2]

The simplicity and efficiency of the screening technology make the use of drug-testing programs quite compelling in the world of community corrections and substance abuse programs as well as in schools, workplaces, and even homes. The commonly used urine analysis (UA) screening device consists of little more than a small plastic testing well where the body sample and reagents are mixed and the results are indicated. One manufacturer's advertising card reads:

> The Assay designed to dramatically change your drug testing capabilities . . .
> Fast setup with results in approximately three minutes.
> Convenient to perform on the spot, at any location.

Simple procedure requires virtually no technical training—anyone can perform the test in just four simple steps.
Economical testing with no equipment—a test kit and pipette are all you need.
Clear, objective, easy-to-read "yes" or "no" results.
Reliable—proven in clinical studies.[3]

I see drug testing, much like the electronic monitoring device, as an extraordinary example of a postmodern meticulous ritual of power. The local, capillary nature of a urine analysis is clear. Urine analyses can be administered effectively anywhere; an offender need not be institutionalized to be watched and monitored. It provides instant knowledge of an individual's behavior, and codes a complex set of activities into simple "yes" and "no" categories. The device is lightweight and efficient; there is little need to collect heavy dossiers or engage in long interrogations in search of evidence or a confession. And, again, since traces of most drugs (with the exception of marijuana) are present only for one to three days after use, random rather than scheduled testing is often justified. Random screening has the effect of making this form of surveillance operate "panoptically," since individuals never know when they might be tested. In the community corrections program I observed, drug testing was done fairly routinely in the office. A screening was also conducted in the home, on a surveillance tour, when it was requested by an individual's probation officer, or when Pete the surveillance officer decided to "pop them any time things don't look right." This was frequently the case with "John," a seventeen-year-old "heavy marijuana" user who had been caught "peeing dirty" quite often. "We can't seem to get it through his head to stay clean while he's on the program," Pete explained to me.

The drug test constitutes what Steven Nock calls an "ordeal" or a form of surveillance intended to divulge the "truth" and thereby establish or maintain a reputation.[4] But it is also a ceremony of bodily objectification, an examination, in Foucault's terms, and a disciplinary drill. Nock describes the ideal conditions under which the ritual should be performed. It is worth quoting at length, since it offers us a glimpse of the ceremonial quality of the test:

> The actual administration of the drug test is done in a controlled situation where the applicant or employee can be watched or listened to while urinating. A photo identification must be presented to verify that the individual taking the test is who she or he claims to be. To guard against possible adulteration of the urine (many methods exist to confound urine tests), they must be conducted in such a way to eliminate the possibility of adding something to the sample, substituting another person's urine, or substituting a sample obtained during a drug-free period. Elaborate preparations and precautions are required. To prevent the applicant from concealing test-confounding substances under the fingernails, for example, the administrator of the test must witness the applicant thoroughly wash the hands. "Unnecessary" garments that might conceal things must be removed. A number of forms must be filled out to verify the chain of custody of the urine sample as it finds its way through the testing process. Both the subject of the test and the person

monitoring it must fill out forms indicating that the test was, in fact, done at that time and place. The urine sample, itself, must be measured for temperature at the time of collection (to prevent the substitution of another person's urine). The sample is inspected also for color (to prevent the use of water). The urine must be kept in sight of both individuals throughout the entire process of preparing it for transmittal to the lab.[5]

During this meticulous ritual, the person being tested is forced to consent to the petty humiliation of the procedure and to the voyeuristic gaze of the tester, who must literally watch the person urinate. So while the person's "self" is embarrassed and ashamed, even, as Erving Goffman called it, "mortified," the body and its fluids, as the preceding description shows, are treated with extraordinary care. For it is the body that holds "truth," not the self. The examination is pass/fail, employing the normalizing judgment, in local terms, of being "clean" or "dirty." Moreover, the technique evokes the legitimacy of science and technical objectivity as it disassociates the client's surveillance from any particular individual. That is, it would appear that you are not really being tested by "the boss," supervisor, or your probation officer, but rather by the scientific "magic" of the test kit and the laboratory. Power is, therefore, seemingly exercised independently of the person who administers the procedure. As the maker of the testing kit described earlier states, the procedure is "useful in case-management because both you and your client can watch as results develop." Here again, those watched become "partners" in constituting the gaze upon themselves. And finally, the screening ceremony, performed enough times, becomes a disciplinary "drill." Like other surveillance ceremonies, we are at first apprehensive, unsure, and uncomfortable. But, much like the way we march through metal detectors at the airport, the test becomes routine and repetitive. Therefore, drug screening acclimates clients to accepting their own subjugation and encourages their general docility. They may even find themselves wanting to take the test since this becomes the only way they can prove they are indeed "clean."

Alternatively, of course, one can try to beat the test. Given the widespread use of drug-testing programs, there has been a proliferation of companies that will sell "clean" urine for purposes of substitution. F. Allan Hanson reports that people have attempted to alter their samples with salt, detergent, and other substances, while others have tried drinking large quantities of water or taking diuretics; in one reported case, university athletes were said to have consumed the urine of pregnant women, since they were led to believe that this would mask the evidence of steroids.[6]

Families are increasingly encouraged to use drug testing to check up on their kids' activities. The *Drug Alert* tester, for example, marketed by SherTest Corporation, is targeted at the potential drug user in the family. You simply wipe the surface of the skin with a piece of paper and then spray the paper with the product. A representative of the company was quoted as saying that the device is intended to enhance the love and care in the home: "It's about breaking down barriers of denial between parent and child."[7] Barringer Technologies, Inc., a company that makes particle detection devices for law enforcement, created a consumer division in March of 1995 that has sold "thousands" of similar $35 testing kits to parents. The leading tester of hair samples mentioned earlier, Psychometrics Corporation, introduced a service in mid-1995 designed for parents. The $75 kit even included instructions about how to cut the necessary sample. (The day after this product was introduced, the stock price of Psychometrics leaped from $3.00 per share to $10.50.)[8] Other products on the market claim to read the pupils of a person's eyes and the like.

If their parents aren't testing them, kids are increasingly being confronted with drug testing at school. Following the Supreme Court decision that upheld the monitoring of student athletes, schools across the country have expanded programs to include any extra-curricular activities. Delaware Valley High School in Pennsylvania tests every student who wants to join activities—from yearbook and chess club to sports and drama. "To test everybody just because they volunteer for something shows a basic lack of trust in students and families," says Sarah Casey, a seventeen-year-old senior who passed a drug test to participate in the environment club and the National Honor Society. "It's an invasion of privacy," says seventeen-year-old Jen Stangl, a senior who took the test to get a parking permit. "It was disgusting. I felt violated. They just presumed everyone was guilty."[9] Indeed, in the first two years of widespread drug-testing at the San Bernardino, California, school—one of the largest in the nation—only two students tested positive. Taking this one step further, however, Miami-Dade Public Schools launched a "voluntary" drug-testing program in 1998 for *all* high school students, requiring consent from both parents and students.

Drug testing has generated a considerable amount of litigation over the issue of privacy, but many rulings seem to follow the now-established "greater good" argument. This reasoning holds that there is a "greater good" for society established at the cost of minimal individual invasion of privacy. For example, in a case in the late 1980s the California Court of Appeals held that drug and alcohol testing of job applicants did not violate the right of privacy set forth in the California Constitution. Interestingly, the court stated:

> Common experience with the ever-increasing use of computers in contemporary society confirms that the amendment was needed and intended to safeguard individual privacy from intrusion by both private and governmental action. If the right of privacy is to exist as more than a memory or dream, the power of both public and private institutions to collect and preserve data about individual citizens must be subject to constitutional control.

But while the court concluded that collecting and testing of urine samples in this case intruded on the applicant's reasonable expectations of privacy, it decided, despite its spirited defense of personal privacy, that the "intrusiveness" of the drug screening was minimal. In most cases, the court claimed, applicants were required to take a pre-employment physical exam anyway, and in this case they were informed ahead of time that any job offer would be conditioned on consent to drug testing. Moreover, it was the court's opinion that the collection procedures were designed to minimize the intrusion into individual privacy (although this is not the opinion of people I talked with who have been tested). The court concluded that the applicants have a simple choice—either "consent to the limited invasion of their privacy resulting from the testing" or decline the test and the job.[10] To date, few states have enacted protective legislation against random testing, leaving private employers, in the vast majority of jurisdictions, to test anyone for any reason, or for no reason at all.

Lately, much of the credit for a reported decline in drug use has gone to testing programs. "Corporate programs make drug use more of a hassle and make it seem less socially acceptable" according to one drug program director; "There's no question they have driven down drug use." The evidence offered for this turnaround is that the tests themselves are uncovering decreased drug use. For example, in 1987, when Pfizer Pharmaceutical, Inc., started testing job applicants, 9.9 percent turned up positive. Last year, the company reported that the number had fallen to 3.2 percent of applicants. But, in fact, we do not know if such testing programs have anything to do with whether or not people choose to use drugs. The lower rate may simply reflect the kinds of individuals applying for these jobs. In arguments before the U.S. Supreme Court in the case regarding random testing of public school athletes, it was reported to the Court that the program in the Oregon high school named in the case found "two or three" positive drug tests in the five years it was in place. Justice Scalia asserted that this was evidence of the program's deterrent effect, while Justice Ginsburg claimed that one could just as easily read this as evidence that drugs were really not a problem in the first place.[11]

CLEAN AND SOBER

As I pointed out in chapter 3, our society has increasingly taken to "medicalizing" behaviors that were once seen as immoral or evil. (This phenomenon is often comically displayed on daytime TV talk shows and "tabloid" news programs.) It would seem that in our contemporary culture, where the medical model dominates, and the "sick" and "survivor" roles have become a national obsession, it is far more agreeable to be the "victim" of a disease than it is to be considered personally weak or sinful. At one time, for example, excessive drinkers were simply "drunks" who did not have the moral backbone to resist temptation. Today, these individuals are said to suffer from alcoholism, a purported medical "disease" or "addiction" that can, according to some, be "diagnosed" by family members, friends, counselors, and even judges in courts of law. Part of this transformation has been the result of medical research that suggests various underlying biological explanations for the phenomenon. But whatever physical "predisposition" there may be to abusing alcohol, drinking is primarily a behavioral activity that can be socially defined and constructed in many different ways. If we look cross-culturally and historically, we can see that what is defined as "problem" or "excessive" drinking varies widely from one setting to the next. Therefore, I would suggest that much of the contemporary definition of the situation comes both from today's "victim culture" and from the people who have an interest in framing alcohol (ab)use as a problem that only they themselves as "experts" can treat. Importantly, in this context, the expert response to and the control and treatment of alcoholics have been increasingly centered on the body and on a variety of therapeutic approaches. While "excessive" drinking has been medicalized, it has also been criminalized. The tolerance levels for blood alcohol—the legal definition of being "under the influence"—have been lowered, while penalties for drinking and driving, for underage consumption, and for public drunkenness have increased. Between 1981 and 1985, state legislatures passed more than five hundred laws regulating drinking and driving. The result has been the emergence of new devices designed to assess the body for evidence of alcohol use and an explosion of public and private agencies geared to controlling and treating the alcoholic.

The use of alcohol is often tested by such means as the commercially available *Alcoscan Saliva Test*, the *Final Call Breath Tester*, and others. Like drug-testing kits, these are quite simple portable devices that take little or no training to use. These devices are carried by law enforcement officials as they enable "field sobriety" checks on drivers, underage partygoers, and anyone else acting suspiciously. At my local Salvation Army shelter, all those looking for a bed at night are tested with a "breathalyzer." Anyone with a blood-alcohol content of more than .08 percent is turned away. Another increasingly popular device is a breathalyzer that is installed in a convicted drunk driver's vehicle. Here the machine must be breathed into each time the person attempts to start the car. If alcohol is detected, the device will render the starter inoperable. The "ignition interlock machine" will even start beeping periodically after the car is in motion, demanding another breath test to prevent the driver from drinking after the initial test. The computerized unit records the results of each test, which are routinely passed on to probation officers and judges to assess whether the client is "backsliding" into alcohol use. Another drinking monitor has been added to the house- arrest system, this one produced by Digital Products Corporation. With this device, random phone calls are breath-tested for the presence of alcohol. After calling back twice to verify a positive reading, the computer will automatically call a probation officer to the offender's home for more conventional testing.

In the community corrections program I observed, alcohol testing was used during all surveillance tours. You would hardly notice as Pete slipped the tester up to the offenders' mouths as he approached them, and they seemed quite ready for the tester to appear. Most of the clients I saw were "clean," but occasionally one would "slip up," like seventeen-year-old "Eric," who registered a .064 blood alcohol level. We drove by his house, and, although Pete said he was not supposed to be home from work until 9:00 P.M., his car was in the driveway, so Pete said we would "go ahead and catch 'em anyway." "Liar, liar, pants on fire," Pete says, getting back into the car. "Claims he is taking *Nyquil*. Yeah, right . . . Anyway, we tell them not to take such medication when they are on the program." Of course, all this running around the county that Pete has to do to test people for substance use is terribly inefficient and costly. He tells me that the next generation of electronic monitoring anklet devices will likely put him out of a job: they will automatically test for drugs and alcohol directly through the skin.

The enforcement of "no alcohol" under the community corrections "contract" underscores both the medicalizing and the criminalizing impact on what is, in fact, a legal substance (at least for the adults in the program). For some, it may be that program officials have decided that they have a drinking "problem," while for others, restricting alcohol is simply part of the overall project of transforming them into "productive members of society" (i.e., clean, sober, literate people who go to work and pay taxes). For those not in a community corrections program, the "road to recovery" may begin at a detoxification hospital, a rehabilitation or treatment center, a private counselor, or at the ever-present Alcoholics Anonymous (AA) meeting. While it's clear that many people have sought relief from these agencies and organizations on their own, increasingly, others may find that they have been ordered to participate in such programs under the threat of the criminal justice system. Here again, as I pointed out in chapter 3, we see a blurring of the distinction between legal/justice and medical/therapeutic practices and discourses.

For example, for a first conviction of "driving under the influence" (DUI) in the state of Kansas, the law calls for 48 hours of mandatory imprisonment, 100 hours of community service, mandatory completion of an alcohol education program, fines of $200 to $500, plus court costs and evaluation fees, and suspension of driving privileges for 30 days and restricted privileges for another 330 days. One community-based, for-profit treatment center is "certified by the City and District Court to provide court-ordered evaluation for DUI . . . Following evaluation, we are certified to provide the court-required ADSAP—Alcohol and Drug Safety Action Education Treatment Program." This "evaluation" involves personal interviews with a counselor and a series of written tests designed to assess how much treatment someone requires. So it would seem that the same agency that is charged with evaluating an individual's status as a potential "problem drinker" is also in a position to benefit from the services that person is required, by law, to participate in—and the services that the agency just so happens to provide for a fee.

Another interesting example is the case of courts ordering violators to attend AA meetings. Here we see the assumed highly effective nature of the twelve-step model as well as how a primarily therapeutic program that has existed outside the law gets colonized and linked to the system, thereby enhancing disciplinary power. As most of us are aware, the AA twelve-step program has been widely emulated. It has been adapted by the spouses and children of alcoholics—the so-called co-dependents and enablers—as well as the overeaters, the oversexed, and other assorted "excessive" personalities. But despite its popularity and significant anecdotal evidence, it has never been demonstrated, in any systematic evaluation, that AA "works." So not only are courts ordering people to participate in something they cannot say is effective, but, at a minimum, it brings into question the idea that this is anything like "self-help." In this context, the twelve-step program becomes a disciplinary technique that provides a monitoring, surveillance, and social control function for the state.

THE "TRUTH" MACHINE

The availability and proliferation of drug and alcohol testing relieve workplace supervisors, athletic-team coaches, justice officials, and others of the tedious task of interrogating suspects while ritualized, random testing may offer a significant deterrent effect. But what if we think someone has stolen money from the cash register, sold industrial secrets, or just simply isn't telling us what we want to hear? Deciding whether someone is lying has been the responsibility of another technology of bodily "truth," the polygraph. The idea behind this device dates back to Italian criminologist Cesare Lombroso (1836–1909) (who, incidentally, asserted that criminals are born with certain recognizable hereditary physical traits such as skull size). During the mid–nineteenth century, Lombroso began taking measurements of the blood pressure and pulse of suspects under interrogation. The technique was later "refined" in the United States; the first portable polygraph machine was developed in the 1920s and was used extensively in criminal investigation.[12] By 1987, one government agency estimated that as many as two million tests were being done each year in the United States. And, in a wonderful postmodern twist, one of the most popular television shows in Spain in the late 1990s was called *The Truth Machine*. Styled after a failed 1980s U.S. show starring F. Lee Bailey (one of the famous lawyers who defended O. J. Simpson), this successful ninety-minute drama subjected politicians, businesspeople, and celebrities who have been accused of assorted infractions to the test so they can attempt to prove their innocence. One show included American John Wayne Bobbitt, who, when asked whether he had beaten his wife that infamous night she cut off his penis, recorded "significant deception" on the test.

Like the drug test, the polygraph evokes an extraordinary ceremonial procedure. Most of us have watched the scene in the cinema at one time or another: A blood-pressure cuff, attached to a sphygmomanometer, is first wrapped around the suspect's upper arm. Then two tubes are wrapped around the person's upper and lower chest to measure any changes in respiration. Finally, two electrodes are placed on the index and second finger of one hand; these will assess any changes in the person's perspiration level. Data from these sensors are displayed to the examiner on a rotating paper chart, showing changes as spikes, peaks, and valleys, much like an earthquake monitor. The theory behind this is that, when a suspect is questioned about his or her activities, a "lie" will be detected by increases in blood pressure, respiration rate, and perspiration rate.

The polygraph, like the drug test, is a portable machine that can be set up anywhere. And here, once more, the remarkable power of science and objectivity is conjured up to authenticate the "true self." As Hanson claims, "Some polygraph examiners, in an effort to heighten subjects' perception of the test as a professional procedure, go so far as to wear a white coat, stethoscope dangling from the neck, and to spray the air of the examining room with ethyl alcohol."[13] Yet the lie detector is a charlatan's tool. Its use has never been shown to accurately discern truth telling from deception. In fact, as David Lykken put it in his comprehensive study of the history and practice of lie detection, "we have no definitive scientific evidence on which to base precise estimates of the lie detector's validity. But we have enough evidence to say that an innocent person has nearly a 50/50 chance of failing a lie detector test, much worse than in Russian Roulette." It seems that CIA agent Aldrich Ames was willing to take those odds when he played his own game of Russian Roulette. When asked about how he managed to pass several agency lie-detector tests during his years as a Soviet mole, he replied, "Well, they don't work." Indeed, even the U.S. Congress was so convinced of the fallibility of this technology that in 1987 it passed the Polygraph Protection Act of 1998, which outlawed the test in pre-employment situations. The statute defines lie-detector tests broadly to include polygraphs, deceptographs, voice stress analyzers, psychological stress evaluators, and similar devices. Yet despite this legislation, it is still perfectly legal for employers who suspect losses or sabotage to hire private security firms to test suspected workers and dismiss those who fail. And lie-detector results may be introduced as evidence in courts in about half of the states in the United States under certain circumstances.[14]

If the polygraph is indeed so seriously flawed, despite its "scientific" underpinnings, one could ask, why is it used at all? The lie detector functions quite nicely in most situations as a way of coercing confessions and as a general form of surveillance. It does so by creating the illusion that the truth can, in fact, be had. Yet the "truth machine" is all smoke and mirrors; it generates knowledge through the simulation of the objective power of science. Since most people are not aware of its flaws and do not know how to "trick" the machine, they are likely to be very intimidated by the process. Like the black spot of the inspector's lodge of the Panopticon, the lie detector leaves people uncertain about what it is capable of knowing. As one writer put it:

> If a subject believes that the ordeal works . . . there is strong incentive for the guilty to confess. The ritual aspect of the polygraph ordeal (the pretest interview, the connections of electrodes and straps to the body, the careful repetition of questions

over and over) . . . sensitizes subjects—it frightens them. It helps convince them that there is no hope in fooling the ordeal. It makes lying seem senseless.[15]

It is said that it is often the case that individuals subjected to this ceremony are so terrified by its purported ability to reveal their inner secrets that they confess to activities having nothing to do with the present questioning or, incredibly, to crimes they are, in fact, innocent of committing. The disciplinary ritual is, therefore, capable of "creating" the very phenomena it seeks to uncover. Used judiciously, lie detectors may encourage self-surveillance and function as a deterrent to acting or behaving "inappropriately." In a culture where "everyone is so paranoid," disciplinary ceremonies like the polygraph remain popular devices despite the laws that prohibit their use. For example, following on the heels of the case of Susan Smith—the South Carolina woman who rolled her car into a lake in 1995, drowning her two children strapped into their car seats—the Justice Department issued a 220-page guide for law enforcement officials investigating the cases of missing children. The report, written by the National Center for Missing and Exploited Children, claims that the police should assume that any child missing is in immediate danger and that they should search the home, even if the child has been reported missing from somewhere else, and they should quickly give the parents a polygraph test.

DEVICES AND DESIRES

Recent developments suggest that even our most intimate, private thoughts may be available for official scrutiny. Based on some of the same principles as the polygraph, that is, the measurement of the flow of blood to a limb, the plethysmograph, or "p-graph," is a narrow metal or rubber band that is placed around the penis of a male subject. The individual is then forced to watch visual displays of naked adults and children or, sometimes, to listen to audiotapes. The band, of course, measures variation in the circumference of the penis. The accompanying computer software enables the examiner to know which stimulant produced an arousal and the relative degree of the erection. Use of the p-graph has been a favorite technique among sex therapists for more then twenty years, and it is now commercially available and aggressively marketed by several manufacturers. The president of the leading producer of the devices, Farrall Industries, Inc., contends that the device is, indeed, capable of "accurately measuring sexual desire" but that it cannot determine whether someone has committed an offense or is likely to do so in the future. The p-graph is presently being used in over four hundred sex-offender treatment centers in forty states in the United States and in several countries around the world.

Yet the mechanism is, according to one article, "emerging from behind the locked doors of adult treatment centers and into the broader legal arena" and is turning up in sentencing and parole decisions, custody fights, and the like. For example, fathers are being subjected to p-graphs in child custody disputes as lawyers seek to prove that they are—or are not—likely to abuse their children. In a case in New York, a psychologist used the p-graph on a father whose parental rights the county was trying to terminate. He concluded from the test that the father "did not become sexually aroused by either male or female children." But an expert witness for the county disputed the findings on the ground that the test could not predict any potential behavior. At a hospital in Phoenix several years ago, boys as young as ten who were accused of abusing other children were tested with the p-graph. The law seems ill-equipped to deal with questions of privacy and rights since there are no regulations regarding the devices at this time. One therapist acknowledges that "a majority of people who undergo the assessment would prefer not to go through it. It's measuring the one thing left that is supposed to be private."[16]

In an extraordinary case in Maine, a police officer whose name was simply raised in a local sex-abuse case was told he had to submit to a p-graph as a condition of keeping his job. In a bizarre string of accusations, Officer Harrington was one of 170 other people, including a U.S. Senator, who were accused of sexual impropriety by four siblings. While no legal evidence was ever brought against him and he was never formally charged, the district attorney said he had "doubts about the man's character" and wanted "to be sure that the officer didn't have deviant thoughts that might lead to dangerous behavior." As Foucault put it, when one wishes to create a "case" out of the "healthy, normal and law-abiding adult, it is always by asking him how much of the child he has in him, what secret madness lies within him, what fundamental crime he has dreamt of committing."[17]

Harrington was ordered to see a sex therapist who requested that he take a sex-offender profile test as well as the p-graph. The written exam determined that Harrington's "personality profile" was supposedly similar to that of about 6 percent of sex offenders. He later refused to take the p-graph. Some in the town suggested that this was a sign of guilt, but some two thousand others began a petition drive to support him. Three years after he was accused, Officer Harrington still had not gotten his job back and was filing a federal lawsuit against the town.[18]

REGULATING SEX AND TESTING FOR AIDS

"Dangerous" sexual behavior may also be a factor when authorities confront a disease such as acquired immune deficiency syndrome, or AIDS. Currently, more than a million Americans are infected with the HIV virus that causes AIDS, and more than two hundred thousand died of AIDS-related illnesses in 1998. Estimates are that one in every ninety-three young men between the ages of twenty-seven and thirty-nine may be infected. Since AIDS first appeared in the male homosexual community in the United States (as opposed to the sexually active heterosexual population in Africa, for example), public health officials and politicians have had to involve themselves in what the *New York Times* called "The Indelicate Art of Telling Adults How to Have Sex."[19] What concerns health officials the most are public meeting places such as bars, bathhouses, and swingers clubs, where people go to have sex. While such places are legal, most fall under and are regulated by the health department. In most states, health codes prohibit a list of sexual acts from taking place in commercial facilities. Yet, medical experts argue that the crucial factor in AIDS transmission is not a matter of what kind of sex you have, but whether or not participants use a condom. So the question of just how much "regulation" is to take place pits public health protection against civil liberties and personal freedom. Advocates of protecting the public contend that "reasonable intervention" involves education and inspection of businesses to see whether violations are occurring. Civil libertarians, on the other hand, argue that the government, besides making information available, has no business, particularly at taxpayers' expense, telling adults how they should have sex.

But officials worry that the sex clubs—that have both homosexual and heterosexual patrons—are a particular danger because their customers tend to be young adults, men who have sex with men but who do not identify themselves as gay, and visitors from out of town who may not be aware of prevention practices. In most cities, club owners have the responsibility of making sure that "high-risk" sex does not occur in their clubs; some hire "monitors" who patrol the premises, while others require patrons to sign a written pledge to use condoms. In New York, in order to make sure the clubs are in compliance, a dozen health inspectors are trained to do "spot checks." They are assigned to look for monitors and to see that the business itself is watching customers. "Closed rooms and poor lighting would raise a red flag," according to one journalist.[20]

The AIDS epidemic has also brought about the thorny problem of mandatory testing for the disease and issues regarding the privacy of test results. The questions have arisen in a variety of settings. In the workplace, owners and managers fear the spread of diseases in their organizations and the potential for lawsuits against them. On the other side, workers, particularly those in "high-risk" occupations, fear contamination by the public they serve; while others, who may be contaminated themselves, worry about possible discrimination or losing their jobs or insurance if test results are made available. The case of four Floridians who claimed they contracted AIDS at their dentist's office brought calls for the testing of all health care workers. Later, medical, labor, and advocacy groups, along with the Centers for Disease Control, argued that such testing made little sense, since it is health care workers themselves who are more likely to be exposed to the disease from their patients. Olympic diver Greg Louganis spurred calls for mandatory testing of athletes when he announced that he had AIDS and that he had tested positive for HIV before the 1988 Olympic games. Louganis bled after cutting his head on a springboard during competition in the 1988 games. Others have called for mandatory testing of boxers as well as other athletes.

Some in the medical community and public health advocates have called for a law to compel pregnant women to be tested for the HIV virus and then, if they test positive, to be required to undergo Zidovudine (AZT) drug therapy to help save their unborn children. Proponents argue that pregnant women must be tested for venereal diseases and that there is no reliable means of preventing the transmission of the virus to the child. The New York state legislature passed legislation mandating HIV counseling for all pregnant women but stopped short of authorizing hospitals to test infants without their mothers' consent. The state's medical community came out against mandatory testing, arguing that more children's lives would be saved through testing with the mothers' consent. When a man facing twenty-four charges in the rapes of six women went on trial in California in 1993, his alleged victims were issued notices from county health officials that they might have been exposed to HIV. Health officials, however, would not reveal whether the man had tested positive or not, citing the state's confidentiality law, which protects the identity of people who test positive for HIV. In Nebraska, a U.S. Circuit Court held that a mandatory HIV testing program of a state agency serving the mentally retarded violated the employees' Fourth Amendment right against unreasonable search and seizure. This case challenged the constitutionality of the agency's chronic infectious disease policy, which required HIV and hepatitis B tests of all employees in positions involving direct contact with clients. Yet in another case, a federal district court upheld the permissibility of AIDS testing of a health care worker whose long-standing roommate was admitted to the hospital and diagnosed as having AIDS.

A disease like AIDS demonstrates how the body is becoming a contested terrain in the battle over questions of individual privacy and organizational demands, be they schools, hospitals, workplaces, or public health departments. The social control implications of the battle are clear, however. As Dorothy Nelkin and Laurence Tancredi state in their book *Dangerous Diagnostics*:

> Institutions must operate efficiently, controlling their workers, students, or patients in order to maintain economic viability. In some cases social controls are explicit, exercised through force; but more often institutions seek to control their constituents less by force than by symbolic manipulation. Sanctioned by scientific authority and implemented by medical professionals, biological tests are an effective means of such manipulation, for they imply that institutional decisions are implemented for the good of the individual. They are therefore a powerful tool in defining and shaping individual choices in ways that conform to institutional values.[21]

VIRTUAL IDENTIFICATION

Clearly, advanced capitalism is engendering rapid technological developments in the intersecting field of forensic, medical, and computer sciences that are creating new forms of body-based evidentiary and archival knowledge. For years fingerprints and dental records were used in criminal investigations and courtrooms. Today, not only have these sources of evidence become far more sophisticated and more proficient, but they also are creeping outside the bounds of the judicial system. For example, in 1990, the FBI began converting its forty million fingerprint cards and crime-history records into digitized files, creating a huge centralized computer database. This database includes not just the files on previously convicted criminals but also the prints of ordinary citizens who apply for federal jobs or special licenses. Law enforcement agencies in thirty-nine states, the District of Columbia, and some 350 towns are adopting optical-reader fingerprinting systems like those sold by such companies as Digital Biometrics, Inc., that will be linked to the centralized data sets. Even mobile scanners, used on the street, are not far off, according to one FBI official.[22] "We scan prints from all 10 fingers and initiate a search of the other known offenders to see if the person has been arrested before but under a different name," one police official said. "You cannot imagine the pleasure it gives you to go to that person arrested on a DWI and say, 'You want to tell us about that murder a few years ago?' "[23]

But such dramatic, "feel good" stories from the world of law enforcement conceal the more mundane encroachment of these kinds of techniques and databases in the public arena. California is now taking a computerized thumbprint of every person simply issued a driver's license. In many states now, if you try to cash a check at a bank where you do not have an account, you must now offer your thumbprint to a scanner and place another copy of it on the check. The Unisys Corporation markets a line of identification products it calls *BioWare*. The company advertises that its *BioWare* computer workstations

> can be configured to perform enrollment and verification, fraud investigation, card issuance, and/or administration functions. To ensure security of operations, operators can be assigned specific roles with access to the functions (and only the functions) required to perform their roles. Operator identity is verified through finger image identification.

> Unisys *BioWare* is your opportunity to capitalize on government concerns about fraud. You can use our platform to address the ID requirements of these large-scale public sector applications:
>
> | | |
> |---|---|
> | Social services | Inmate verification |
> | National identity | Fire arms licensing |
> | Driver licensing | Immigration control |
> | Voter registration | Patient verification |

Learn more about *BioIDentification* solutions for national identity and social serv-ices here. Or, check out how Unisys Information Services has successfully used the *BioWare* platform to develop personal identification solutions for the public sector.[24]

Likewise, I/O Software markets a fingerprint identification system called a "biometric terminal" which includes a Fingerprint Identification Unit manufac-tured by Sony. The unit is designed to read fingerprints in about .3 seconds and verify the identity of the person attached to the finger. The terminal includes a keypad, LCD screen, and optional smart card reader.

Los Angeles County was the first to begin taking fingerprint images of all wel-fare recipients; authorities expect the practice to be universal in a few years. The county's slogan for this program is "Fingerprints for better service," and it expects to save $18 million by preventing fraudulent claims over the next five years (minus the $10.8 million needed for staff and equipment). Yet a spokesperson for the U.S. Department of Health and Human Services asserts that there is no empiri-cal evidence that fingerprinting is an effective means of preventing welfare cheat-ing. So why invest all this money and create a new system of potential surveillance and social control? The head of New York State Social Services asserts that fin-gerprinting is mostly to negate the widespread feeling among the general public that they are "being taken" by "welfare cheats." "The public has the perception that the welfare system is rife with fraud," he said. "It is a wrong impression."[25] One has only to listen to the rhetoric of the latest political campaign or a so-called investigative news program to see how that misconception has been created.

In addition to traditional fingerprinting, biomedical information about indi-viduals is being derived from tissue typing, hair, blood, urine, and semen analy-sis, voice imprints, and the "reading" of eye pupils. (In Newport News, Virginia, last year, police arrested a man for "peeping" into an apartment after they lifted a "lip print" from a windowpane.) In 1998, there was $25 million in sales of "biometric identity" devices, and that figure is expected to double the next year. Currently being tested by Citi-Group and other banks is a gadget developed by Sensar, Inc., which enables automated teller machines (ATMs) to use the iris of the human eye to verify the identification of a user.[26] Sensar's Web page opens with "Welcome to Sensar: 'Opening a world of convenience in the blink of an eye'" and claims, "The matching probability of Iris Identification is greater than that of DNA testing. In fact, Iris Identification is the only form of personal electronic identification that has never granted a false acceptance."[27] Another company, Personnel Identification and Entry Access Control, has devised a new system of identification that is based on the measurement of the human hand. It has spent more than $2 million developing the machine with grants from the state of Ohio as well as from the U.S. Air Force. The president of the company, a medical physicist, said he is marketing the device to companies and other or-ganizations that want to restrict access to high-security areas.[28] The Department of Energy's Idaho National Engineering and Environmental Laboratory and Miragen, a biotechnology company, are developing a technique that can display a "bar code" of antibodies that is unique to each person.

A British firm, EDS Scicon of Surrey, has designed software for a computer-driven video system called *Sentinel* that can detect objects of a particular size stopping in the region on the camera (e.g., a human shape). It then automatically turns the camera on and records the movements of, say, everyone leaving a certain door of a building and indicates what direction each person is headed. As I pointed out in the previous chapter, Britain is a world leader in the use of CCTV in public places. One system currently in use in East London is unique, however. Not only does the system videotape people walking down the street or coming out of shops, but, using fractal processing, it is able to isolate, recognize, and identify an individual's facial characteristics and compare them with those stored in a database. The police claim that the database contains only the images of convicted criminals and suspected terrorists. Yet, as it has been pointed out, "an innocent person walking in public has no control over his own actions: who may record them and what the monitor may do with the tape. With the current ubiquity of cameras, the actual ends of individual tape becomes a moot point. The fear of being watched has already been instituted."[29]

Graphco Technologies, Inc., developer of security applications using biometric technology, released its *VoicePass* Speaker Verification technology for smart cards. *VoicePass* technology stores a user's specific voice characteristics in digitized form on a personalized smart card. The cardholder is granted access to the additional functions of the card only if the user's voice matches the pattern stored in the card.

IT'S IN THE GENES

A full page in the *New York Times* in 1999 is white and blank except for two sentences written across the middle: "Thank you for turning this page. We now have a sample of your DNA." The page is an advertisement for a so-called science fiction film called *Gattaca*. Yet in reality, in the earlier 1990s, the FBI initiated the Combined DNA Index System, or CODIS, a national DNA identification system. Kansas, for example, was selected to be part of the program, and, under a law passed by the state legislature in 1991, samples of blood and saliva from several thousand individuals with criminal records have been collected to date. As many as fifteen other states have joined in and collected thousands and thousands of samples. Later in 1999, the International Association of Police Chiefs urged Congress to require that DNA samples be taken from every person arrested in a crime. This evidence would then go into a FBI database and be made available to law enforcement agencies nationwide. Police, it seems, are now routinely collecting DNA evidence from crime scenes, from saliva on beer cans left behind by a burglar, from sweat on a baseball bat used in a beating, from blood on a bullet that passed through a suspect. In Florida, after seeing a rape suspect spit in the street, a St. Petersburg police officer grabbed some paper towel and, jumping out of his car, blotted the spittle and gained enough DNA evidence to make an arrest. A prosecutor in Wisconsin filed rape and kidnapping charges against a defendant who has no name. John Doe is known only by his DNA code, extracted from semen samples from three rapes, samples that have been tested after six years of storage in a police property room. "We know that one person raped these three women," said the prosecutor, Norman Gahn, assistant district attorney for Milwaukee County. "We just don't know who that person is. We will catch him." A warrant must identify the person to be arrested, and this one names "John Doe, unknown male with matching deoxyribonucleic acid profile."[30]

A central feature in the infamous O. J. Simpson murder trial was what has been commonly referred to as "genetic fingerprinting" (although courts prefer the less precise term "genetic profiling"). Here an individual's unique genetic material, DNA, which is found in all human cells, may be used as evidence of criminal involvement. As of January 1998, the Human Genome Project, an international effort by scientists to map the entire set of genes comprised by human DNA, had identified 6,909 of the approximately 100,000 human genes. At this rate, they will likely conclude the project as early as 2005. With this project, more will be known about the human body and how it functions than ever before. And much like drug-testing technology, genetic screening will become lighter and more effective, working its way into everyday life. For example, in 1999, Myriad Genetics, Inc., announced a patented technology for "cheaper, more efficient, less resource-intensive DNA diagnostic tests" using DNA on silicon wafers, or biochips. The company, based in Salt Lake City, is described as "a genomics company focused on the discovery and commercialization of genes involved in major common diseases including cancer, cardiovascular disease and central nervous system disorders." "This exciting technology paves the way to development of more highly automated analytical methods with resulting reductions in reagent and labor costs," said Gregory Critchfield, M.D., president of Myriad Genetic Laboratories, Inc., "Myriad's patented technology has the potential to provide a rapid diagnostic test at significantly reduced cost compared with current methods." For the three-month period ending December 31, 1998, genetic testing revenue increased for the company by 131 percent.[31]

In this context, genetic material will become increasingly important, perhaps a determining factor, in assessing an individual's predisposition to diseases and certain personality traits and their assumed links to behavioral patterns. Organizations such as workplaces, schools, hospitals, insurance companies, health and welfare agencies, courts, and those involved in law enforcement will all have increasing incentives to store and use this kind of information. As with many medical discoveries, knowledge, and tests, we seem ill-prepared as a society to deal with the social, legal, and ethical implications of DNA evidence. While the use of such material in the criminal justice system is taken as legitimate, its use in other spheres of life seems questionable. For example, genetic testing in the workplace can take the form of screening employees for susceptibility to disease or of monitoring employees to determine the extent of damage caused by workplace exposure to hazards. Once the data are available, individuals could be subject to genetic discrimination in employment based on test results. A worker's privacy could be undermined through the compilation, storage, and release of non-job-related, sensitive medical information. Finally, the fear of employment discrimination through employer's access to genetic records might discourage certain individuals from undergoing needed genetic testing.

Concerned about privacy with regard to genetic material, the American Civil Liberties Union produced a "Genetic Discrimination in the Workplace Fact Sheet" in 1998.

Myth: Genetic testing is an accurate way to predict disease.
Fact: While some genetic tests can accurately predict that an individual will develop a certain disease or condition (for example, Huntington's Disease or sickle cell anemia), even those tests often do not indicate when the individual will develop symptoms or how severe the symptoms will be.

Myth: Genetic tests are reliable and safe.
Fact: Currently the U.S. Food and Drug Administration (FDA) has declined to regulate genetic tests, despite the fact that many are commercially available and aggressively marketed by biotech firms. The absence of regulation means that there is no government oversight or quality control, and the accuracy and reliability of the tests are unproven.

Myth: Genetic testing is not really a serious workplace issue.
Fact: Genetic testing in the workplace is on the rise. In 1982 a federal government survey found that 1.6% of companies who responded were using genetic testing for employment purposes. In a similar survey conducted by the American Management Association in 1997, 6–10% of employers were found to be conducting genetic testing.

Myth: Certain work environments may hasten the onset of genetically based diseases, and genetic testing can protect employees who are "at risk."
Fact: Currently no one knows whether some work environments hasten the onset of genetic disease. According to the American Medical Association, "there is insufficient evidence to justify the use of any existing test for genetic susceptibility as a basis for employment decisions."

Myth: Federal laws like the Americans with Disabilities Act (ADA) protect employees from genetic discrimination in the workplace.
Fact: The extent of federal protection against genetic discrimination is unclear, and limited at best. The federal appeals courts are divided on the scope of protection of

the ADA, particularly for employees who have not yet manifested symptoms of illness. In any event, the ADA addresses workplace discrimination, but not privacy.

Myth: State employment discrimination laws protect workers against genetic discrimination.
Fact: Currently only 12 states have enacted laws that protect employees from genetic discrimination in the workplace; a handful of other states have legislation pending.

One example of the misuse of genetic information involved a social worker who had an exemplary record. Her employer fired her after finding out that she was at-risk for Huntington's disease. The information arose during an in-service training session about caring for persons with Huntington's disease. The social worker related that she had someone in her family with the disease. Prior to the in-service she was given three promotions and outstanding performance reviews. Subsequently, she received a poor review and her supervisor was unable to give her examples of why her performance was considered poor. Shortly thereafter, she was fired. A co-worker told her that the employer was afraid she would develop Huntington's disease.[32]

In 1993, the federal government's Task Force on Genetic Information and Insurance concluded that the rapid expansion of predictive genetic testing would result in an explosion of information about genetic health risks and that risk underwriting should not determine access to health care. To date, at least nine states have passed legislation limiting insurers' ability to genetically test applicants for insurance coverage purposes. In Minnesota, two legislators introduced a bill known as the Genetic Discrimination Act to try to stop insurance companies from screening out people who have not even been diagnosed with a disease. A similar bill was passed in California. The two lawmakers in Minnesota argued that some people in the state were afraid to undergo tests that could reveal whether they carry the gene for a particular disorder because if the test is positive they may be unable to get health, disability, or life insurance. "If we don't pass this legislation now, it's very possible that we'll create a genetic underclass in this country for whom insurance is impossible," a legislator argued. But the insurance industry in the state fought the bill. A representative of the industry claimed, "This is anti-consumer. It is unfair to consumers to prohibit insurance companies from underwriting policies based on the best available information."[33] A 1993 American Council of Life Insurance study revealed the degree of mistrust among the public: 56 percent of those surveyed felt that insurance companies could not be trusted to keep the results of genetic tests confidential.[34] A national Harris poll conducted in 1995 found that 60 percent of those polled were "very concerned" that "organizations that want to know the state of your health—such as health and life insurance companies or employers—might require you to provide them with the [genetic] test results, so that they could decide whether to insure or hire you."

The use of genetic material as evidence in civil as well as criminal legal cases is expanding. For example, in 1996, two marines in Hawaii filed a lawsuit that could have a profound influence on the way our society handles genetic information. The marines refused to provide blood samples for the Defense Department's DNA data bank, a collection of DNA samples that are to be used to identify the remains of soldiers. The marines said they were concerned that genetic information about them would be used for other purposes. In California, a county judge decided to require a mentally retarded teenager to undergo genetic testing for evidence in a product liability lawsuit. The request came from a chemical supplier accused of causing the teenager's condition. DNA material has been used to circumvent a previous Supreme Court ruling that bars paternity actions against dead men. In what might be called "Who says dead men can't pay child support?" lawyers for plaintiffs argue that if the identity of an illegitimate child's father can be established, even in the absence of the father, motions against the property and the right to be supported can be claimed by the child. In 1994, a Connecticut judge ordered blood testing in a civil medical malpractice action against a psychiatrist accused of having sexual relations with a patient.

Given the powerful implications of genetic knowledge, some suggest that, within a few short years, most of us will have our DNA profile on record somewhere. A mid-1990s survey by the Northwest National Life Insurance Company found that 15 percent of employers planned to begin checking the genetic status of prospective employees by the year 2000. In a speech in 1998, proposing a genetic information privacy bill, Vice President Al Gore stated that "even hidden differences among people contain the potential for unleashing the impulse to compare and discriminate."[35] As the authors of the book *Dangerous Diagnostics* put it:

> The social meaning of this information in the 1990s must be reconsidered in the context of an increasing sense of crisis—over criminal violence, the cost of health care services, the quality of education and the general state of the economy . . . These economic and social imperatives are enhancing the social value of predictive testing and reinforcing the power of biological information well beyond the clinical context.[36]

AUTOMATED HISTORIES

This sci-fi world of DNA data banks will be built on the vast information network that is already in place. Most of us have little idea how much personal and medical knowledge about us is floating around in computerized databases. Corporate personnel files; hospital, mental health, and substance abuse agency records; and insurance company data banks join the demographic, financial, credit, and consumer-habits databases I covered in chapter 3. Much like the case of detailed employee review and evaluation files, this systematic monitoring and knowledge-gathering activity is being advanced by the use of relatively inexpensive computer technology. For example, take the software package called *Automated Social History*, marketed by Anderson Publishing Company. An advertisement card for the product shows a series of ten identical human heads, each turning from front view to portrait, and each drawn in a kind of fractal, geometric design that evokes a scientific gaze on the skull. The card states that the software provides an

> efficient and professional way to produce narrative social history reports . . . encompassing the most important areas of the subject's social and personal functioning. The program screens the subject for major forms of social, psychological, psycho-neurological, and medical illness.

> Completion of the ASH Plus questions generates five useful reports:
> Narrative Report. Used when a comprehensive social history is needed, this summary covers 13 areas of a person's life: religion, parents, family, education, marriage, personality traits, interests, sex, military, employment, crime history, alcohol/drug abuse, and medical history.
> Self-Reported Personality Traits Report. Provides an interpretation of the subject's self-description.
> Items Report. Produces a chart of the actual item responses to all questions administered.
> Risk Analysis Report. Produces a weighted risk analysis which can be used for any prediction scheme . . . This report can be extremely useful in probation/parole prediction. Can be utilized when determining the length of stay in residential substance abuse programs.
> Summary Report. A clinical summary weighing behaviors and attitudes that may contribute to the subject's current problems. This report infers a quick review and index of the current problems.

And, much like Bentham, who argued that the Panopticon could be adapted to fit a variety of institutional settings, this company sees wide-ranging uses for its product. "Who should use ASH Plus?" they ask, and then provide the answer: "Physicians, Psychologists, Social Workers, Hospitals, Mental Health Agencies, Substance Abuse Agencies, Probation and Parole Agencies, Correctional Institutions, Court Systems, and Security Departments."

With corporations "downsizing" in the context of a national health-care crisis, businesses are looking for places to cut costs while insurance companies are seeking as much information about prospective claimants as they can get. The result is new techniques and technologies designed to assess a person's physical, mental, and emotional health and to collect and store the information provided. For example, a growing number of Fortune 500 conglomerates are turning to so-called behavioral health-care companies to oversee the mental health care and alcohol and drug treatment programs of their employees. Marketers like these are selling a new system of measuring mental health-care treatments and their effects. Rather than relying solely on a mental health worker's experience or training to develop a treatment plan, new clients are asked to answer a battery of questions designed to assess their symptoms, state of well-being, and familial relations.

These data and the assessment of the therapist are entered into a computer software program that compares the symptoms of the new patient, say depression, with an extensive database of hundreds of similar cases. It also compares patients with a "standard of normal behavior" based on studies of healthy people. By having detailed data on other patients—how they were treated and what the results or "outcomes" were—a therapist can then follow a similar line of treatment with the new patient. A "case reviewer" at the company sends the therapist a simple chart that shows how the patient's symptoms compare with both the previously ill and the normal range of behavior. These charts may be shared with the patients "to compare the ups and downs of . . . symptoms with the standard of normalcy" so that they might understand the extent of their problem. After the therapist arrives at a course of treatment, similar charts are produced after every sixth session, based on new questionnaire data. Research in the field of "outcomes" in mental health care has been fostered by federally funded studies and by large insurance companies, hospitals, and health maintenance organizations that are "sifting through their own enormous files, analyzing the results of their treatment." A "pioneer" in the field, Dr. G. Richard Smith, a psychiatrist at the University of Arkansas, states that now "we are able to measure many more aspects of mental health care than anybody dreamed of five years ago."[37]

HOW ARE WE FEELING TODAY?

The area of medical records seems particularly vulnerable to privacy abuses, inaccurate data, and questionable insurance practices. Data "brokers" such as the Medical Information Bureau sell medical records to businesses and insurance companies so that they may determine whether a potential employee has a "preexisting condition" that warrants special consideration. Such information may be used to screen out potential "high-risk" employees and future expensive claims. As many as 35 percent of Fortune 500 companies check past medical records before they hire someone. According to one account, such files often contain not only information about previous medical treatments but also whether a person has sought psychiatric help, been treated for substance abuse, and even if he or she engages in "high-risk" leisure activities such as hang gliding. One person caught up in a nightmare of medical misinformation was Ben Walker, who dedicated thirty years of his life to the FBI. Fighting the occupational hazards of stress and depression, Walker began seeing a psychiatrist. "I was convinced that it should have remained confidential," says Walker. But when Walker's doctor was targeted in an unrelated investigation, state officials conducted a computerized search of pharmaceutical records and found allegations of prescription drug abuse. Although the allegations were false, the information was sent to the FBI and used to force Walker out. "I'm glad that I got help," says Walker. "But I don't think I should have paid the price." Most people do not realize that as part of the 1996 Medical Portability Act, the Department of Health and Human Services was to come up with a system that would assign each of us a unique medical identification number that would be linked to our complete medical history. Such a number could be used to pull records in an emergency, keep track of the spread of diseases, and the like. "But anyone with access to the number—from your dentist or your pharmaceuticals benefits manger—could know your genetic predisposition to Alzheimer's and the time you took emergency contraception."[38]

With increasing importance placed on medical data, even sharing details about your personal life on the job may come back to haunt you. While it is not likely that your coworker is a company spy, he or she may still be a source of information, particularly if the boss decides to challenge claims for medical or disability benefits. In one case in Oregon, a secretary who filed for compensation from repetitive-motion problems was surprised to find that, at a hearing, lawyers for the insurance company claimed her problem was caused by emotional stress and hormone fluctuations resulting from an abortion. "I had no idea that things you tell your friends in the office can be used against you," she said. But this "happens all the time," according to Pam Wear, a former director of a medical records trade association. "Sharing your personal lifestyle can be dangerous to your medical coverage." Pinkerton Security and Investigation Services and Wackenhut Corporation offer their clients—companies such as Northern Telecom, Merck, Boise Cascade, General Motors, and Allied Signal—toll-free phone lines, operated twenty-four hours a day, to encourage workers to "pass along accusations that their colleagues are using drugs, drinking, stealing, committing medical fraud or engaging in other illegal activity."[39]

Companies themselves are collecting vast amounts of detailed medical data on their employees. Each year American companies require employees to submit to millions of blood and urine tests, X rays, and other medical and laboratory procedures. Not only are files built during pre-employment physical and routine checkups, but some employers are using data collected in their "wellness centers" to confront employees' claims for benefits resulting from workplace injuries or stress. Workers often fail to realize that such medical records are not fully protected by doctor–patient confidentiality. For example, Adolph Coors Company in Golden, Colorado, operates a 23,000-square-foot wellness center devoted to keeping workers healthy with exercise programs, on-site medical personnel, and a counseling center. Coors estimates that by providing this "benefit" to employees the company saves $2 million a year by cutting sick leave and medical costs. But it also offers management a detailed source of medical information about its workers. Consider the example of longtime employee Richard Truman Fletcher. His case was described by *Wall Street Journal* reporter Ellen E. Schultz:

> The company knew he had the mumps at age eight, had lost his left eye in a fire-works accident at nine and had a vasectomy in 1962. It knew he smoked 30 cigarettes a day. It even had a note in its files saying he was embarrassed by smelly feet. One day in 1992, Mr. Fletcher died of a heart attack at the age of 54. His wife, Judy, filed for survivor's benefits . . . The widow thought she had a strong case. Her husband had died two weeks after being demoted from a desk job to manual labor . . . But Coors argued that Mr. Fletcher died from smoking—and all it had to do was flip open his extensive medical files to make its case. Coors had no need to hire a subpoena-wielding lawyer to go on a fishing expedition in hopes of finding a doctor to testify or a written record to bolster its position. It already knew that Mr. Fletcher had smoked a pack and a half a day since age 14—enough to persuade an administrative law judge to deny the widow's benefits.[40]

But the biggest saving, Schultz goes on to point out, comes from using the data to identify costly benefits that can be reduced, or to shift costs to employees. She cites, for example, the case of Hershey Foods Corporation, where workers now pay an extra $30 a month for health insurance if they have high blood pressure, $10 for high cholesterol, $10 if they don't exercise, $50 if they use tobacco, and $30 if they are overweight. Hershey caps the total of such extra charges at $840 a year per employee; the testing is mandatory. The data can therefore be used, according to one consultant, so that "management can now forecast where the ticking time bombs are in their employee population." Last year, a New York electronics firm began charging these so-called time-bomb workers higher premiums, instantly shifting $232,000 of health-care costs to employees. The 20 percent who refused to take the wellness test were charged the highest premium. "They were either smokers or had some condition they're trying to hide," said a company representative. "Now we need to evaluate the people with something to hide."[41]

BODY POLITIC(S)

While new and refined existing technologies and practices can be imposed on the body for purposes of surveillance and knowledge-gathering, they can also be used to ensure docility from the recalcitrant by taking control of the body. In other words, if the surveillance, evidence, or threat of knowledge is not enough to render people controlled, we can always convince, cajole, or force their bodies into submission with various "treatments" or physically repressive procedures and technologies. Increasingly, these measures appear in "medicalized" forms and are offered or forced on people in the name of care for them. This phenomenon was dramatically displayed in several cases in recent years related to birth control, welfare recipients, and drug users. In 1993 in Arizona, a so-called welfare mother had the contraceptive device, Norplant, surgically implanted in her arm under a court order to prevent her from having any more children. About that same time, another judge in Visalia, California, required a woman convicted of child abuse to use Norplant as a condition of her parole. These cases brought a call from conservative politicians and others that, as a matter of public policy, welfare eligibility should be linked directly to the use of Norplant.[42] In fact, twenty such measures were introduced in thirteen states during the early 1990s. None were ultimately passed, however. Of course, as I have pointed out earlier, the United States has for decades attempted to control the procreation of what were once quite openly called the "defective classes." What is so important now is that we need not go about rounding these people up in poorhouses and asylums, trying to watch and monitor their behavior as we did in the nineteenth and early twentieth centuries. The available technology has the potential to make the whole business quite simple and more politically viable, breaking down resistance and normalizing its implementation.

The latest iteration of technological eugenics is a program called CRACK, the acronym for Children Requiring a Caring Kommunity, a privately financed campaign. The organization puts up billboards in low-income neighborhoods claiming, "If you are addicted to drugs, get birth control—get $200 cash." The program attempts to entice drug-addicted women to get sterilized or get long-term birth control like Norplant or Depo-Privera in exchange for $200 in cash. The billboards have appeared in Florida, Minnesota, Pennsylvania, New Hampshire, and Michigan. The founder of the group says that getting private donations has not been a problem; she recently received $5,000 from Dr. Laura Schlessinger, the conservative radio talk show host. "It's simply a bribe for sterilization, and that's improper and it's wrong," said Steve Trombley, the president and chief executive officer of Planned Parenthood of Chicago. Some suggest that women may feel coerced into giving up their ability to have children, and not get any help to stop using drugs. "I don't care what they do as long as they get their tubes tied," said Frank Peard, a seventy-year-old retiree who helped arrange for CRACK billboards to be erected in Florida. "As far as I'm concerned they could buy a gun and shoot themselves with it." So much for a "Caring Kommunity." These tactics follow a movement by state governments to exert some form of social control on women whose behavior is seen as dangerous to unborn children. According to one account, "court cases in 21 states have sought to make it a crime for pregnant women to abuse alcohol or drugs . . . in 1997, the State Supreme Court ruled that a pregnant crack addict was guilty under the state's child-abuse laws. A similar case in Wisconsin is working its way through the appellate system. And three states, South Dakota, South Carolina and Wisconsin, passed fetal abuse laws last year, either mandating that substance-abusing pregnant women be forced into detoxification programs or subjecting them to jail time." [43]

Interestingly, while the government engages in determined efforts to stop the use of illegal "drugs," it sees fit to permit, even enforce by law, the use of legal "medication" regimes to control those bodies deemed out of control: "Just say no" becomes "Must say yes." The history of psychotropic "wonder drugs" is but one example. These anti-psychotic medications were used in the late 1950s and 1960s in state mental hospitals to control inmates' behavior and later helped to facilitate the emptying of those hospitals in that previously institutionalized individuals were released to lead "full and productive lives in the community." The medications were used extensively, despite the fact that they often produced debilitating physical side effects such as the "Thorazine shuffle" and Parkinson's disease. In the 1990s, the Supreme Court ruled that states have the legal right to compel prison inmates to submit to anti-psychotic drugs. In 1994, officials in New York state were considering a bill that would place those people being released from the state's mental hospitals—primarily the homeless and indigent— under court order to take anti-psychotic and neuroleptic medications.[44]

Like the anti-psychotic drugs, electroconvulsive therapy, or ECT, enjoyed a comeback of sorts in the 1980s; this psychiatric treatment creates epileptic-like seizures and convulsions as a result of an electric current being applied to the front or both sides of the brain. ECT began to be used systematically in the United States during the 1930s, and it was used extensively in state mental hospitals as a treatment for schizophrenia, despite the fact that doctors did not know why it seemed to relieve some of the symptoms. In the 1960s, however, ECT came under intense criticism as a cruel and controlling practice, and hospitals increasingly turned to the anti-psychotic drugs to treat patients. But ECT reemerged in the 1980s as an increasingly common treatment for depression, especially among the elderly.[45] How have anti-psychotic medications and ECT come back into favor?

In both cases, the contemporary versions of these techniques have emerged in seemingly more refined and palatable forms than their previous "modern" incarnations: a new generation of anti-psychotic drugs produces few of the crippling side effects that the former drugs did, and the ECT equipment and administering procedures are free of the horrifying images dramatized in films such as *One Flew Over the Cuckoo's Nest*. In fact, in the case of ECT—technically a "last-resort" treatment—private hospitals and clinics, otherwise known as "shock shops," dot the urban landscape. Both techniques, then, are being quietly normalized outside their association with the asylum, and they have become yet another disciplinary practice of everyday life. This point was well made in a *New York Times* article on the contemporary use of ECT that was entitled "With Reforms in Treatment, Shock Therapy Loses Shock." A practicing psychotherapist wrote to the newspaper a week later, stating, "Shock therapy (along with lobotomy, straight-jackets, shackles, and sterilization) is on the far right of the treatment spectrum. I believe it is symptomatic of a postmodern culture that there is a willingness on the part of some . . . to tolerate radical solutions to depression."

But that is precisely my argument; in such a postmodern culture, the procedure is no longer perceived as radical.[46]

Meanwhile, at the sound of the lunch bell at Nova Middle School in Davie, Florida, dozens of students form themselves into a line. But rather than scanning the lunch counter, these kids are waiting for their daily dose of Ritalin, a drug designed to control their distractible, hyperactive, or impulsive behavior. Most have been diagnosed with attention deficit disorder, or ADD. "Five years ago," a journalist reports, "10 students at Nova received the medication. Now the count is up to 40. No one knows how many more children start their day at home with a single dose, which peaks after about five hours."[47] Ritalin, despite the fact that it is a stimulant, supposedly works to help children focus on cognitive tasks, expanding their attention span. Dr. Daniel Safer, a mental health official in Baltimore County, Maryland, estimates that 3 to 4.2 percent of American youths—from ages five to eighteen—are being treated with the stimulant. (This does not include the ones who are taking it illegally. Ritalin has reportedly become popular in the illicit drug culture, as it can produce a burst of energy, even euphoria, which lasts several hours if snorted or ingested in relatively large quantities.) Dr. Safer claims that almost twice the estimated number of youths have ADD.

While some children (as well as some adults) may have benefited from the use of Ritalin, some experts contend that ADD is being vastly over-diagnosed and that Ritalin is over-prescribed. Thomas Armstrong, a psychologist who wrote *The Myth of the ADD*, states:

> My criticism is that this is a model coming from a medical disease-based perspective when we should be using a model that's much more health-based. I'm not against medication for some kids under certain circumstances or in a crisis situation or in a very severe case, but I feel we rush too quickly into medications for solutions . . . One reason for the popularity of ADD diagnosis is that it's kind of neutral. Nobody's to blame. It's not due to anything in the family, nothing to do with the classroom. Everybody is absolved of any responsibility, but the kid ends up with the label, which is a stigmatizing label . . . We have to be very suspicious of the fact that kids are being diagnosed using very subjective or very artificial and remote kinds of approaches.[48]

Dr. Eugenio Rothe, director of the child and adolescent psychiatry outpatient clinic at Jackson Memorial Hospital in Miami, says, "There's a danger of using [Ritalin] as a quick fix. Rather than sit down with a kid and find out what's bothering him, some may give a pill and that's it." He argues that some pediatricians may be writing prescriptions based primarily on parents' and teachers' complaints. "I'm sure there are kids medicated inappropriately for behavioral control and not true ADD," he says.[49]

In a very different mode of controlling behavior, defense contractors and research labs are turning their post-Cold War attention to the burgeoning high-tech security market in order to develop what are referred to as less-than-lethal weapons for police use. If successful, the police say, an arsenal of non-lethal weapons could save lives and spare them the cost of all those pesky excessive-force lawsuits. Los Angeles police and others have, in the past, deployed mace and pepper sprays and the infamous baton choke hold. But now, new devices are making headway. Various forms of stun guns are being deployed, including one prototype that shoots a stream of coffee-colored sticky goo that entangles an unruly arrestee. At Lawrence Livermore Labs in California, researchers are experimenting with high-intensity strobe lights that incapacitate people, low-frequency sounds that disorient and create nausea, and rapidly expanding foam that can fill a cell, for example, and block the sight and hearing of rioting prisoners. A similar device may be installed in the rear seat of police cars to subdue a violent passenger.

As states like California struggle to deal with exploding prison populations, officials are searching for ways to cut costs, such as reducing staff. For example, at the two-year-old Calipatria Facility just north of the Mexican border, authorities have installed an electrified fence that carries 4,000 volts and 650 milliamperes of power. About seventy milliamperes is enough to kill a human being. For anyone trying to escape, this amounts to an automatic death sentence. The warden of the facility states that unlike a guard, "The fence doesn't get distracted, it doesn't look away for a moment and it doesn't get tired." He has no problem using the fence, since the prison already has a lethal perimeter within which guards are instructed to shoot to kill an escapee. More than twenty additional California prisons are expected to get the fences in the next few years.[50]

Another device currently in use in about 150 locations in the country is an electronic stun belt that is strapped around a defendant's waist at trial or may be used on prisoners. The REACT belt, manufactured by Stun-tech, Inc., of Cleveland, is a four-inch-wide elastic band that is powered by a battery at the kidney and has a remote control. When activated, the device sends a shock of fifty thousand volts in eight-second bursts to a person's back muscles—enough to "make subjects scream and drop to the floor, writhing in pain." The company says that the feeling can be summed up in one word: devastation.[51] In the summer of 1998, Long Beach California Judge Joan Comparet-Cassini ordered her bailiff to activate one of the devices on forty-year-old Ronnie Hawkins when she became angry at his "constant talking." Mr. Hawkins, who was acting as his own attorney, was facing a twenty-five-year-to-life sentence for a third-strike petty theft charge. He was already chained and shackled and witnesses said he had made no aggressive moves toward anyone.[52] Amnesty International denounced the use of the device. Hawkins is filing a lawsuit.

Finally the ultimate devastation comes in the form of a death sentence. In the 1990s, state after state brought back executions as a supposed deterrent to criminal behavior (despite the fact that there is simply no evidence that capital punishment functions in this way). Yet it is clear that the revival of the death sentence is about public vengeance that, statistically, is more likely to be directed against African-Americans (and males) than against whites (and females) who commit the same crimes. While state-sponsored executions are obviously not a part of everyday life and have, fundamentally, little to do with my notion of meticulous rituals, there are certain similarities. Unlike the public display of brutality and reprisal that the scaffold provided, today's executions are sanitized, medical procedures that culminate in a bureaucratic death. In this way, they reflect—much like drug testing, the p-graph, Norplant, ECT, and the other techniques I have described—a surrender of the fundamental problem of social control to science and technology. A state execution, once medicalized, is no longer a horrible event; it becomes simply another pill swallowed, a test taken, or a medical procedure submitted to. Here is how one journalist described the execution of a man in Texas in 1994:

> Under brilliant florescent lights, Steven Ray Netherie, a 33-year-old Tennessean, convicted of killing a Dallas policeman, lies splayed on a gurney. The sight is stunning and confusing, not quite hospital, not quite death chamber. Gurney is a medical word for a cot or stretcher on wheels. But this is a stainless steel platform, bolted permanently to the floor. The medical illusion is further enhanced by the IV tubes running into each arm. One serves as a back up. But the nine thick leather restraints convey the reality. Netherie stares at the ceiling. He swallows, he wets his mouth. The warden calls for the last words. Netherie closes his eyes and recites a prayer in a halting drawl. Within seconds, the executioner, hidden behind a one-way mirror, starts to push eight syringes sequentially. In short order, they will induce unconsciousness, paralyze the diaphragm to stop breathing and cause cardiac arrest.

The chemicals in the IV are actually referred to as medicine by the prison director. After the inmate is killed and pronounced dead, a prison spokesman issues this statement in a dispassionate, almost mechanical voice:

> The execution of Steven Ray Netherie was carried out. He was taken from the holding cell at 12:06, strapped to a gurney at 12:07, was given an opportunity to make a last statement at 12:21, in which he said, "Well, I just wanted to ask people to pray for two families, my family and the family of Officer McCarthy. I appreciate their prayers. Lord Jesus, receive my spirit. Amen." The lethal chemicals were introduced at 12:22, completed at 12:24 and Steven Ray Netherie was pronounced dead at 12:30.

The bureaucratic administration of death is complete: file deleted.[53]

By medicalizing executions with lethal injection, Texas, like the twenty-four other states that have adopted the procedure, is attempting to humanize an inherently inhumane activity. "Lethal injection is usually brief, efficient and antiseptic," said the journalist who witnessed this killing. As a former attorney general for the state observed, "It's not a lot different from putting a dog to sleep." As Foucault once commented, a whole army of technicians joined the executioner: wardens, doctors, chaplains, and psychiatrists. He said that they reassure us that "the body and pain are not the ultimate object of punitive actions. Today a doctor must watch over those condemned to death, right up until the last moment—thus juxtaposing himself as the agent of welfare, the alligator of pain, and the official whose task it is to end life . . . take away life but prevent the patient from feeling it; deprive the prisoner of all rights but do not inflict pain; impose penalties free of all pain."[54] Criminologist James Marcourt states, "Electrocutions were violent. But electrocutions were less violent than public hanging. Now, we have lethal injection, which is obviously less violent than electrocution, so we're seeing this nice progression along a continuum of technology. Like I said, it's basically an anti-climatic event. It's much more palatable to the public."[55]

Indeed, Foucault suggests that punishments have become the most hidden part of the penal process. "As a result, justice no longer takes public responsibility for the violence that is bound up by its practice." And the chief of the Texas Prison System is quoted as saying, "We don't want to make a spectacle out of it, or give it the flavor of a circus or a carnival."[56] But apparently one TV talk-show host wanted to do just that; he is suing the state of California in an attempt to get an execution televised.

How do we experience a situation where our bodies are becoming central targets of knowledge and social control? It is said that the postmodern self personifies the multiple contradictions of the postmodern condition and may result in "intense emotional experiences shaped by anxiety, alienation, resentment, and detachment from others."[57] It seems to me that technologies or practices that permit our bodies to speak the truth, whether we want that voice to be heard or not, or alternatively, that control and restrict our bodies from being what they are, generate these very emotional states as they detach us from ourselves. Like the person whose capable mind is trapped in a degenerative frame, we are betrayed and abandoned by the physical expression of who we are. Hanson poetically describes this apparent double cross in the case of the lie detector:

> The two machines commune together as the polygraph reaches out to embrace the subject's body with bands, tubes, and clips. The body responds lover-like to the touch, whispering secrets to the polygraph in tiny squeezes, twinges, thrills, and nudges. Both the machines are treacherous. The body, seduced by the polygraph's embrace, thoughtlessly prattles the confidences it shares with the subject's mind. The polygraph, a false and uncaring confidant, publishes the secrets it has learned on a chart to read. The subject as mind, powerless to chaperone the affair, watches helplessly as the carnal entwine of the machines produces its undoing.[58]

What are our options to resist this courtship? One is, of course, to behave, to stay clean, to just say no. The other strategy is to try to trick our bodies into not giving us away—a process that is sure to reinforce the personal troubles of the postmodern self and, if successful, to send the technicians scurrying to perfect a more reliable instrument.

5

CU-See Me and the Internet

Ready or not, computers are coming to the people. That's good news, maybe better than psychedelics.

—Stewart Brand, *Rolling Stone*, 1972

Never lose your Web site contacts again! Sensor is a new software technology that allows you to identify your Web site visitors in "real time." Turn "quick" visitors into pure leads and increase your potential!

—Company press release, 1999

GET READY . . . VIRTURAL DORM IS COMING! LIVE—UNSCRIPTED, UNCENSORED. WEB-CAMS IN THE DORMS!

—Web advertisement, 2000

The history of the Internet—the so-called Information Superhighway—mimics the creation of the Interstate Highway System; both were late 1950s Cold War responses to the supposed post-Sputnik technological and nuclear threat of the former Soviet Union. Yet it was not until the late 1960s, with funding from the Pentagon's Advanced Research Projects Agency, that researchers managed to get several computers talking to each other. This nascent network expanded over the next few years, allowing Defense Department personnel and scientists at universities and research centers to communicate and exchange data.

What eventually became the Internet provides a basic communication service that conveys units of information in "packets" to and from computers attached to the network. The origins of the World Wide Web (Web)—the Internet's multimedia component combining text, sound, graphics, and video—came about in March 1989, when a British scientist working at a Swiss physics laboratory envisioned a system of networked "hypertext" documents. "Hypertext" is a form of non-sequential writing, where the text can branch in different directions allowing the reader to choose the path. A year later, the first piece of Web software was developed with the ability to view, edit, and send hypertext documents via the Internet. By the mid-1990s, researchers at the University of Illinois released a graphical Web "browser" called Mosaic, a version of which later evolved into the software Netscape Navigator.[1]

As we enter the new millennium, the number of Internet users worldwide will likely exceed 150 million; U.S. households are currently going online at a rate of 760 per hour. The number of Web pages "published" will soon top 300 million, with as many as 1.5 million pages posted every day. Estimates are that the number of commercial e-mail messages sent in the United States has exceeded more than 7.3 billion each day.[2] Results of a recent "Digital Citizen Survey" divided Americans into four categories depending upon their usage of the Internet, cell phones, laptops, beepers/pagers, and home computers. The survey found that 62 percent were "semi-connected"—that is, they exchange e-mail at least once a week, and use at least one of the other technologies regularly.[3] When I answered the survey questions for myself, I was chagrined to find out that I fell into the 2 percent considered "super connected." Having used Internet e-mail since the early 1980s, I have experienced that now common feeling of being "disconnected" when on vacation or away from the machines. These days, the culture seems saturated with talk of the Internet. Conversations are peppered with "I got that off the Web," "down load our application online," and so on. My plumber has a Web page. Every day I listen as my local National Public Radio station personnel stumble through their readings of awkward dot-domain names. There is little doubt that the Internet, for better or worse, ranks as one of the most important social, cultural, and economic developments of the late twentieth century. In this chapter, I examine several surveillance, social control, and privacy implications of Internet usage. Among these are the "dataveillance" capabilities of the network that facilitate the collection and exchange of information about individuals and monitor the activities of users on the network (at work, school, or home), as well as the extraordinary voyeuristic and exhibitionist activities emerging on the World Wide Web.

TECHNO-SPIRITUALITY

Like the video camera, the Internet is a quintessentially postmodern technology. It is at the center of our rapidly changing digitized communication and media storage and retrieval juggernaut. "Surfing" the Web is as hyperreal—fluid and anchorless—as it can be disorienting and disjointed (user: "What am I looking at now?" "Where did this come from?"). The Internet compresses time as well as social and geographical space, destroying the experience of distance and exacerbating "placelessness" (user: "So where am I now?" "How did I get here?"). With near instant access to a seemingly inexhaustible supply of information and images—on nearly every topic and from all over the planet—we are often left awestruck and overwhelmed, since little of it is organized or accessed in conventional ways (user: "Where did I start?" "Everything seems so jumbled"). Despite the presence of text, the dominant feature of the Web is, increasingly, its multimedia pastiche of images and sounds. The entire Internet is a virtual simulation, an "ecstasy of communication," where distinctions between "real" objects and their representations dissolve. It is a place where formerly unique objects, located in a particular space, lose their singularity, their "aura" as Walter Benjamin called it, as they become accessible to anyone from anywhere[4] (user: "I can see all the great works of art, right here on my computer screen!"). The Web does not simply present an image to its viewers, but rather it fundamentally alters the way people think about the world, determining what they see, and how they make sense out of it. And like television and other forms of mediated life before it, questions of authenticity and experience abound (user: "Have the images I am looking at been altered?" or "Is this 'real(ly)' the person she tells me she is in the chat room?").[5]

Kevin Kelly, one of the enthusiastic cheerleaders of the new "wired" culture, captures much of postmodern life on *and* off "the Net" when he claims that

> a person on the Internet . . . views the world decidedly decentralized, every far flung member a producer as well as a consumer, all parts of it equidistant from all others . . . and every participant responsible for manufacturing truth out of the noisy cacophony of ideas, opinions, and facts. There is no central meaning, no official canon, no manufactured consent . . . Instead every idea has a backer, and every backer has an idea, while contradiction, paradox, irony, and multifaceted truth rise up in a flood . . . People in a highly connected yet deeply fragmented society can no longer rely on a central canon for guidance. They are forced into a [post?] modern existential blackness of creating their own cultures, beliefs, markets, identities from a sticky mess of interdependent pieces. The industrial icon of a grand central or a hidden "I am" becomes hollow. Distributed, headless, emergent wholeness becomes the social ideal.[6]

According to promoters of Kelly's version of "techno-spiritualism," the Internet permits us to advance Marshall McLuhan's now classic idea of the "global village," offering us powerful new tools for fostering and sustaining social relations in new "cybernetic communities." Life on the Net, it is said, is a place, much like the rest of social life, where people can work, shop, fall in love, read the news, debate politics, and join in association with others who share common interests. On the Web, users can "pull" content from the medium, rather than

have it "pushed" at them as in existing media. This "pulling" supposedly empowers consumers since they have more choice to create their own reference
points through "book marking" and other personalizing features. And with no
central authority, clearinghouse, or censoring mechanism, the Net, many argue,
democratizes the technology of publication so that anyone can have a voice,
publish their own Web page, start a newsgroup, etc. And in this sense, the Web
has the potential to, as the saying goes, "subvert the dominant paradigm" by offering a place where alternative forms of social, cultural, and political expression
can flourish (assuming of course that those wishing to participate have the
knowledge and resources to do so). "States are powerless in the face of the new
technology." As one author characterizes the optimistic prophecy of the machines, "At a stroke, their regimes of censorship and surveillance are undermined—or at least by-passed as impotent."[7]

There *is* little doubt that the Internet is a truly amazing technology. I use the
Internet daily for library searches, easy and instant communication with colleagues around the world, ordering books, and consumer comparison shopping.
I used it extensively to do the research for this book. As a mechanism for effectively and efficiently distributing information, it is indeed quite remarkable. Yet,
like most utopian visions, myth and reality are often distant cousins. In fact, Internet "communities" look and function a lot more like the "gated communities"
I describe in chapter 3, where a few people who have control of the chat rooms,
bulletin boards, and other forums and can erase messages of those they disagree
with, or simply lock them out. Likewise, the promise of interactivity has never
materialized, leaving most Internet experiences about as interactive as channel
surfing the television. (It is little wonder that the first comprehensive study of
Internet usage found that the more hours people spend on the medium, the
more depressed, stressed, and lonely they feel.[8]) Increasingly it is difficult to pull
much of anything off the Web without being hit with a barrage of banners, flags,
junk e-mail, or other forms of pushing from advertisers and promoters. Political
debates and culture wars about pornography and sexual activity, hate speech,
and other issues such as viruses, spam and hackers have brought about calls for
regulatory legislation and censorship, euphemistically referred to as content fil-
tering. And finally, as I have argued about other new technologies, it seems there
is little public debate about the possible harmful social and cultural consequences that might come from a wholesale adoption of the wired life.

So, if the Web is quickly becoming "much like the rest of social life," we can
surely see where it is headed. Utopian visions aside, *cyber*space, the term
coined by dystopic science fiction writer William Gibson, is starting to look a
lot like the rest of our postmodern *social* space; both are deeply mired in con-
sumerism, surveillance, and voyeurism.[9] As I noted in previous chapters, postmodern surveillance practices tend to have four main characteristics: they are
technology-based, applied automatically and anonymously, and generate knowledge and evidence; they target the body as an object that can be watched and

assessed; they are local and dispersed, operating in everyday life; and they manage to bring wide-ranging populations, not just the official "deviant," under scrutiny. In what follows, I argue that the Internet is consistent with this descriptive type. It is indeed technologically driven and, as I will show, capable of collecting massive amounts of information (that can be used for a variety of purposes) "quietly" and anonymously. With its visual capabilities, the Internet can be used to watch, monitor, and display our bodies to millions of people, with or without the permission of the person being watched. And much like Michel Foucault characterized the capillary nature of disciplinary power, as a network, the Internet can extend out to the remotest corners of society, circulating throughout the social body. It is, for now at least, like Kevin Kelly says, "distributed" and "headless." It is not operated from the "top down," but functions "bi-directionally" (e.g., companies can monitor their employees' "Web surfing" behavior while "hackers" can use the Internet to corrupt the files of that same corporation. At the same time, others are making the details of their own lives available on the Web for others to see), appearing nearly everywhere, dispersed and fragmented. And, while not specifically designed as a surveillance tool, I will show how the Internet and its assorted components and practices are indeed being used for this purpose.

DATA MINING FOR E-GOLD

In the last few years, the Net, once a backwater network for a handful of academics, has been transformed into a commercial bonanza. Companies are scrambling to cash in on the network's promised capability to deliver goods and services to new and expanding markets. According to "e-commerce" experts, we have already entered the era of the "post-Web retailer," and the warning is that those businesses that do not stake their claim soon will lose out on the new gold rush. This new form of "dot-com capitalism" has produced some rather unorthodox economic formulas. For example, recently a Web site called Blue Mountain Arts.com, designed to let people send free animated greeting cards through e-mail, was bought by Excite@Home for $780 million. This staggering price was paid despite the fact that the family that owns the Web page has never made or even tried to make any money with it. What is so valuable about Blue Mountain that someone would pay nearly a billion dollars for it? Because of its original and free service, Blue Mountain attracted 9.2 million unique visitors in August of 1999, ranking them thirteenth overall of all Web sites around the world. During the 1999 holiday season, it expected more than fourteen million unique visitors per month. This kind of highly trafficked, "cyber billboard" is a "targeted" advertiser's dream, where potential customers are in a gift-giving mood and, based on the card that the customers select, the peddler has a good idea what the appropriate gift might be.

According to one marketing company, global spending for online advertising will reach $33 billion by 2004. Online retail sales "will continue to soar over the next five years" with the number of online shoppers in the U.S. topping fifty million households. Average online spending per household is expected to grow from $1,167 in 1999 to $3,738 in 2004 "as consumers shift from convenience and researched items to replenishment purchases like groceries."[10] Internet-related businesses generated more than $507 billion in revenues in 1999, surpassing for the first time traditional industries such as airlines, and contributing about 6 percent of the nation's gross domestic product.[11]

With this much at stake, the practitioners of e-commerce are willing to draw upon all the marketing schemes, "psychographics," and other "data mining" techniques I outlined in chapter 3, to identify, track, and collect data on potential customers while they attempt to shape and influence consumer behavior. For example, one marketing company, Forrester Research, Inc., sells information, what it appropriately calls "lenses," on different segments of consumers. In one "lens," the company surveyed more than 250,000 North American households to classify their levels of receptiveness to technology-based products and services. This segmentation "is designed to categorize consumers based on their attitudes, motivations, and abilities to use or acquire technology." In addition, more than 100,000 North American households completed their "Technographics Annual Benchmark Survey." It seems it is never too early to start tracking, and young people are a particularly hot target. "Technographics Young Consumers" is the result of a biannual survey of ten thousand young adults online, aged sixteen to twenty-two, about their online attitudes, behavior, and usage:

> This lens provides quantitative data and analysis about young consumers and the tremendous influence that the Internet has on their spending patterns. It helps companies understand both the immediate payoff of knowing young consumers' interest today as well as the potential long-term benefit for their corporate brands.[12]

The "tweens" age group, roughly eight to thirteen, are getting lots of attention these days. According to a recent Kaiser Family Foundation report of children in the media, this group consumes 6¾ hours of television, computer time, video games, movies, music, and print media per day. And consequently, the tweens will emerge as the driving force behind pop culture. *Spin* magazine declared recently that teenage girls now control the world's economy. By the year 2003, 56 percent of all children and 72 percent of teens will be online, and they will spend more than $1 billion there. Kathryn Montgomery, president, Center for Media Education, says, "I had a company executive tell me that parents should be happy about this 'cause their kids won't be spending all this time at the mall. But, in fact, they're bringing the mall to the kid." (And now "e-wallets" have arrived with names like DoughNET, RocketCash and iCanBuy that allow parents to put a specific sum of money into an account for their kids to spend online.)[13]

While the Internet presents some challenges to marketers, the "targetability" quotient of their campaigns can be enhanced if they collect more and more highly individualized consumer profiles based not just on our "psychographic" segments but on our actual online behavior. It just so happens that the best tool to collect that information is the very medium they are pushing their wares on: the Internet. "The World Wide Web is direct marketing on steroids," says Jason Catlett, president of *Junkbusters,* a Web site that helps people protect their privacy on line. "With the Web, the process of gathering information on consumers and messaging them with new offers is vastly accelerated in speed and reduced to a very low cost."[14] As one marketing company puts it:

> The key element to becoming a post-Web retailer will be a consolidated customer view to anticipate shoppers' needs. Merchants must *centralize the available information about shoppers—purchase history, direct mail responses, and Web store click-stream data—to identify their most profitable customer segments.* This information can be used to identify and adopt new product categories that will appeal to these customers. And by codifying merchandising rules, retailers can move beyond personalization into anticipatory selling. (Emphasis mine)[15]

"Web store click-stream data?" What the heck is that? Well, a click-stream is the electronic footprint that is created when someone goes about browsing on a Web site. From a marketing perspective, the click-stream contains sumptuous information about the pages and topics that people choose to read and even the time they spend lingering on them. "When you go to a Web site," says Eileen Gittins, CEO of a software company called *Personify,* "you leave a trail of bread crumbs that tells what you did . . . *Personify* tracks this and provides marketers [with a software interface] . . . to answer questions as fast as they can ask them." To analyze a customer's behavior on the site, *Personify* takes a select data set from a site's click-stream log file, from the registration database if there is one, and from the transaction database. In another version of Web snooping, Comet Systems, Inc., distributes free software that changes a Web browser's cursor into a cartoon character and other images. Yet, the estimated sixteen million people using the software are probably unaware that the program reports back, to the company's own computers, each customer's unique serial number each time they visit any of sixty thousand Web sites—including dozens aimed at children—that support its technology. Popular statistical analysis software maker SAS Institute now sells Web-reporting capabilities among its existing suite of data analysis tools. Under a program labeled *e-Intelligence,* SAS adds the capability, according to one press release, "of analyzing Web logs and click-streams to its entire line of data-warehousing and data-mining tools."

It seems that e-commerce companies are striving to achieve the merchandising nirvana of true "one-to-one marketing." The ideal is to create a "storefront" that is tailored to a particular individual. After gathering personal data—most of it supplied by the users themselves through online site registration requests—

and then tracking a shopper's movements within the site itself, the seller can then display products that fit the customer's profile. Getting customers to stay and shop is called "stickiness" in marketing parlance. One company, Andromedia, claims its *LikeMinds* software "improves site stickiness by personalizing each visitor interaction in real time. Levi Strauss used *LikeMinds* to increase repeat visit rate 225%, average time on the site 75% and average spend rate 33%." It goes on to claim that

> *LikeMinds Reporter* provides detailed reports on which *LikeMinds*-generated product recommendations customers are viewing, putting in their shopping carts, or buying. *LikeMinds Reporter* then calculates the conversion rates from products recommended by *LikeMinds* to products inserted into shopping carts or products purchased. Conversion rate reports help e-marketers gauge the effectiveness of product recommendations and determine which recommendations are best received by customers, enabling them to increase loyalty and drive revenue.[16]

Andromedia's *Smart eMarketing* solution combines sophisticated, real-time data monitoring, personalization, analysis and reporting, and the ability to integrate data captured online with traditional offline data resources. This helps companies identify and target the most qualified customers, understand their tastes and preferences, refine sales and marketing tactics, and predict likely cross-selling opportunities. *Smart eMarketing* drives higher response rates, improves retention, and builds loyalty, turning Web site browsers into buyers, and buyers into loyal customers.[17]

Even if the "just browsing" customer does not order any merchandise, the click-stream data can be quickly analyzed and the site reconfigured so that if the "window shopper" returns, a more refined and "personalized" sales pitch can be made or a follow up e-mail sent. One example: Onsale.com, an auction and retail site, tracks a visitor's travels from page to page and uses the information to send e-mail to customers who have registered with the site. "That's a very powerful thing," claims James McQuivey, with Forrester Research, an Internet research firm. "The trend toward capturing and using information is the future of on-line commerce."[18] The ultimate goal seems to be the creation of Web pages that immediately recognize an individual customer when he "enters the store" and then tailor the interface and offering to the customer's anticipated tastes.

Web firms defend their practices as not surveillance, but rather, the delivery of personalized service. As one marketing executive explains:

> In today's marketplace, we've lost the intimacy of that old neighborhood shopping district, and we've tried to replace that intimacy with knowledge to give us the same sense of unique service, unique value for the consumer, and information technology allows us to do that in ways that are revolutionizing the market.[19]

Yet Shari Steele from the privacy group Electronic Frontier Foundation asserts that any analogy to a well-meaning shopkeeper is off base:

It would be a shopkeeper who was watching you as you were browsing through their store. They're following you down the aisles, peering at everything you pick up and look at. It's also the shopkeeper who you've walked in and you've got stamped on your forehead all of the purchases that you've made at previous stores that you've gone.[20]

As McQuivey of Forrester Research points out, "In the old days, a customer's information stayed in the head of the local merchant. There was never a mechanism like the Internet to exploit it."[21] Indeed.

COOKIE MONSTERS AND FREE COMPUTERS

Few people fully comprehend the extent to which personal information and Web activity can be traced and collected. Each time you cruise to a Web page, the computer transmits packets of information that may reveal the last site visited, and other browsing and identity information. A new protocol (the language that permits computers to "talk" to each other) being developed by the Internet Engineering Task Force, Internet Protocol Version 6, may mean that every packet of information can be traced back to each user's unique network "fingerprints" address in it. This was never the case with the earlier versions. In addition, when visiting a site, computer files called "cookies" are often created and stored directly on a user's own computer (one can have the software issue a warning when this is happening but most people have no idea that this can be done). The data stored there may not only include your user name and password for the site and other personal preferences for that particular page, but also a tally of purchases made, interests and hobbies you entered while filling out product registration forms, and other tidbits of information. Douglas Rushkoff, author of *Playing the Future: What We Can Learn From Digital Kids*, says:

> If an ecommerce merchant puts a cookie on your hard drive, a little spy program, basically, that monitors your keystrokes, watches what you do, records all the transactions, it finds out, "Oh, you know, when we end prices in 88 cents, this person tends to buy more," or "When we use a red buy button instead of a blue one." And it's not that there's a human being looking and saying, "Oh, how did Johnny react?" It's a machine that's programmed to do nothing other than to extract more dollars from Johnny in less time.[22]

Some industry folks suggest that companies will soon devise a way to cross-reference cookie information with databases created when someone, for example, registers computer software, enters personal data on a health information page, or otherwise submits personal information. Detailed profiles of a person's buying habits, hobbies, and health concerns could emerge, allowing data miners to sell the information to the highest bidder. Beth Givens, director of the Privacy Rights Clearing House, suggests that this kind of monitoring is the digital equivalent of having an "invisible camera following you around through your whole life."[23]

Companies appear so keen on getting you online, shopping, and, of course, divulging personal information, that some are willing to give you a computer to do it. This past year an electronic commerce company, fronted as Free-PC.com, caused quite a stir when it announced it would be "giving away" ten thousand computers. The catch: recipients must be willing to let the company monitor the sites they visit and ads they check out, and users also must put up with advertisements that will appear onscreen whenever the computer is turned on. If the user doesn't log on to the Internet often enough, new ads will be automatically sent to the computer. "There's a cost barrier for people to buy a computer and to get Internet access, yet with the explosion of e-commerce, the Internet is the accepted medium to deliver advertising and content," said Don LaVigne, CEO of Free-PC.com. "We're simply getting the marketers and merchants to subsidize indirectly the access," says LaVigne. Company founder Bill Gross said that the company needs to collect personal information from its customers so that it can make enough money from advertising revenues to recoup the cost of the computers and earn a profit. Therefore the machines will not be handed out to just anybody, but rather to people who are the best match to what the advertisers want. Apparently, privacy issues were of little concern to the more than three hundred thousand people who swamped the company's Web site by mid-afternoon on the first day. With this kind of response, the company says it may give away as many as one million computers. If it works, others—such as America Online—are expected to follow with other "giveaway" schemes.[24]

In 1998, it was reported that some of the largest commercial sites on the Web had agreed to feed information about their customers' readings, shopping and entertainment habits to a Massachusetts company that was already tracking the "surfing" habits of more than thirty million Internet users.[25] This and other complaints about widespread privacy violations on the Internet prompted the Federal Trade Commission to investigate the issue. In the course of their research, the commission surveyed some fourteen hundred Web sites, and in its 1998 report, the authors stated that

> the vast majority of sites collect personal information from consumers—92% in the sample representing all U.S.-based commercial sites likely to be of interest to consumers. In addition, we found that a wide variety of detailed personal information is being collected online from and about children, often without actual notice to, or an opportunity for control by, parents. In our survey, 89% of the 212 children's sites surveyed collect personal information from children, but only 1% obtain parental permission prior to collecting such information. Here are a few examples of the kinds of information collection practices Commission staff discovered in the survey:

A medical clinic's on-line doctor-referral service invites consumers to submit their name, postal address, e-mail address, insurance company, any comments concerning their medical problems, and to indicate whether they wish to receive information on any of a number of topics, including urinary incontinence, hypertension, cholesterol, prostate cancer, and diabetes. The on-line application for the clinic's health education membership program asks consumers to submit their name, address, telephone number, date of birth, marital status, gender, insurance company, and the date and location of their last hospitalization.

An automobile dealership's Web site offers help to consumers in rebuilding their credit ratings. To take advantage of this offer, consumers are urged to provide their name, address, Social Security number, and telephone number through the Web site's on-line information form.

A mortgage company operates an on-line pre-qualification service for home loans. The on-line application form requires that each potential borrower provide his or her name, Social Security number, home and business telephone numbers, e-mail address, previous address, type of loan sought, current and former employer's name and address, length of employment, income, sources of funds to be applied toward closing, and approximate total in savings. The on-line form also requires the borrower to provide information about his or her credit history, including credit card, car loans, child support and other indebtedness, and to state whether he or she has ever filed for bankruptcy.

A child-directed site collects personal information, such as a child's full name, postal address, e-mail address, gender, and age. The Web site also asks a child extensive personal finance questions, such as whether a child has received gifts in the form of stocks, cash, savings bonds, mutual funds, or certificates of deposit; who has given a child these gifts; whether a child puts monetary gifts into mutual funds, stocks or bonds; and whether a child's parents own mutual funds. Elsewhere on the Web site, contest winners' full names, age, city, state, and zip code are posted.

Another child-directed site collects personal information to register for a chat room, including a child's full name, e-mail address, city, state, gender, age, and hobbies. The Web site has a lotto contest that asks for a child's full name and e-mail address. Lotto contest winners' full names are posted on the site. For children who wish to find an electronic pen pal, the site offers a bulletin board service that posts messages, including children's e-mail addresses. While the Web site says it asks children to post messages if they are looking for a pen pal, in fact anyone of any age can visit this bulletin board and contact a child directly.

The commission concluded that "unless industry can demonstrate that it has developed and implemented broad-based and effective self-regulatory programs by the end of this year, additional governmental authority in this area would be appropriate and necessary."[26]

PERFORMANCE MONITORING

The Web works its way into other areas of social life as well, delivering and circulating surveillance and accountability in the form of knowledge and information. These data can contribute to the maintenance of unbalanced and unequal
authority relationships and foster new forms of watching. For example, aug-
menting the surveillance practices already in place in schools across the country, some elementary and secondary schools are beginning to share student
records with parents via the Web. For about a year and a half the Uinta County
School District in Wyoming has offered parents access to everything from
grades to attendance records as part of a test of a product sold by PowerSchool
Technologies. The system is in place in more than ninety schools, mostly in
Utah. The company's home page boasts that the software has over thirty features including:

Attendance
PowerSchool has full period-by-period attendance capability.
User-defined attendance codes can be counted as absent, tardy/truant, or other.
Attendance totals are kept for each student in each class, and a variety of atten-
dance reports are available.

Parental access to student progress reports in real time over the Internet
PowerSchool has the built-in capability to allow parental access to student progress
data over the Internet. Parents can see current overall grades as well as student
progress reports that include assignment scores and teacher comments. Parents also
have access to both summary and detail attendance information. And data access is
real-time: If a teacher records scores for a test at 10 A.M., those scores are available
for parents and administrators to see at 10 A.M. The same goes for attendance: parents can log in at 10 minutes after the start of class and see if their student is in attendance. Of course, administrators have this same real-time data capability. Access
reports are available that show how many parents access the system, how long their
visits last, etc.

Transcripts, report cards, and cumulative data
PowerSchool maintains historical grade files which can be used to produce transcripts, report cards, graduation progress reports, class rankings, and other reports.

In this way, the technology—like the disciplinary power it facilitates—invests,
colonizes, and links together two institutions—family and school—that were
previously based on informal, personal arrangements. This linking creates a finer
mesh of social control, permitting administrators and parents to remotely and instantly monitor the whereabouts and performance of children and young adults.
In doing so, *all* these individuals are brought under greater scrutiny, not just the
recidivist "truants and troublemakers." This is all done under the guise of "improving" the educational environment. It does not take much imagination to see

the Web integrating and delivering images from the school's video camera system, ID bar-code scans, and instant drug testing results to a parent's desktop (see below). The fear and mistrust generated in a post-Columbine world are real, and these technological "solutions" present themselves as attractive options.

This kind of Web-facilitated "performance monitoring" can continue even after little Brandon or Brittany is off to college. Mom or Dad can still check up on their work, like Deborah A. Dixon whose son Eric attends Gettysburg College in Pennsylvania. "She can power up the computer at home or at work and visit the college's Web site. There, after punching in a user name and a private password, she can find information ranging from course descriptions and syllabi to her son's grades and his bill at the bookstore." The service is an addition to what the college has dubbed CNAV, a Web-based system developed by the school to give students easy access to their transcripts, bills, and other information. Through CNAV, students can also see a list of names and photographs of other students enrolled in the courses they are taking. Some kids may not be too anxious to share passwords with their folks. As one father put it during a parents' weekend demonstration, "I don't think my son will let me see his transcript. He likes to break that to me gently."[27]

The Web and "performance monitoring" come into play with a different twist in the workplace, revealing a certain paradox. On the one hand, we have hundreds of companies trying to get us online, visiting their Web pages, buying their products, reading their news, and trading their stocks. On the other hand, the very technology that permits us to do this is installed in our own workplaces, but managers of those businesses insist that computers must be reserved for appropriate productivity uses. The Web, then, is seen as both a source of and a threat to workplace productivity. According to the American Management Association's most recent survey in 1999, 45 percent of U.S. companies electronically monitor employees on the job, an increase from 35 percent in 1997. The increase is due mostly to concern over employee e-mail and non-work-related Web usage. This issue, as well as the cost of network resource consumption, and the threat of legal liability for the Internet content entering their network, have encouraged companies to look to "Internet access management systems" for help. These software systems, according to one vendor, Websense Enterprise, enable "corporations, schools and other organizations to monitor, report, and manage traffic traveling from their internal network to the Internet." Their systems include the following components:

Monitoring Module: Observes your network-to-Internet traffic and logs the information based on the parameters set in the Management Module. This log data includes network user information, type of sites visited, bandwidth consumed, and attempted violations of your Internet Access Policy.

Management Module: Allows you to set and enforce Internet access privileges for the users on your network. Settings may be configured by type of permitted sites, by user, by time of day or day of the week. This module also works in conjunction with the Monitoring Module to block access to undesirable sites and issue warnings of Internet Access Policy violations.

Reporting Module: Generates tabular and graphical reports on your network-to-Internet traffic. This module pulls the information from the logs created by the Monitoring Module and builds visual charts in a variety of formats for easy distribution among departmental managers, supervisors, and others in your organization. The Reporter can generate more than twenty different reports that provide information on observed traffic, type of sites visited (by user), network bandwidth consumed, etc. This module is also a "distributed module," meaning that departmental managers can use it from their desktop to create reports on their personnel and network consumption.

This vendor's "master database" includes the following categories that have been deemed "unacceptable, inappropriate, or undesirable" to access:[28]

Abortion Advocacy	Personals/Dating
Activist Groups	Politics [advocacy of any type]
Adult Entertainment	Racism/Hate
Alcohol/Tobacco	Religion
Alternative Journals	Sex
Cult/New Age	Shopping
Drugs	Sports
Entertainment	Tasteless
Gambling	Travel
Games	User Defined
Gay/Lesbian Lifestyles	Vehicles
Hacking	Violence
Illegal	Weapons
Job Search	Web Chat
Militancy	

This screening list of "unacceptable" behavior is an extraordinary example of the enforcement of "normalcy." "What are they going to do next? Track how many times I go to the bathroom?" grouses Howard Nordby, a twenty-six-year-old engineer at defense contractor Northrop Grumman Corporation. Last fall the young man was accused of being an "Internet abuser" after visiting sports Web sites on his lunch hour.[29] But just how many "Internet abusers" are there in any given workplace? These monitoring systems do not discriminate, but place everyone under suspicion and watch their activities whether or not they have any history of "abuse." Steve Sullivan, vice president of investment technology at T. Rowe Price in Baltimore, justifies the monitoring this way, "We want to make sure we're getting everything out of employees that we're supposed to be."[30] According to Stephen Dempsey, vice president of sales and marketing at Webster Network

Strategies in Naples, Florida, "We monitor every employee's Internet activity. We log every site they have visited and how long they have spent at each site. It's a hypertext log, so the network administrator can visit that site, too. It also logs sites that were denied."[31] Scott Paddock, manager of PC Brokers, a computer value-added reseller in Denver, had a different take on the trend. "I don't monitor Internet usage for two reasons. First, I trust my employees; that's why they work for me. If there were to be any problems with an employee, those problems would present themselves without the need for me to get involved in cloak-and-dagger shenanigans. And second, if I spent time monitoring their Web usage, I would be just as guilty of wasting time as my behavior implies they are," says Paddock.[32]

CU-SEE ME

In retrospect, the marriage of inexpensive video technology and the Internet was inevitable. The original, in a college computer lab in Cambridge, predates the Web itself. The "coffee camera" began with an experiment in networking in 1991, when researchers from several parts of the building put the technology they were developing to work to ensure that they knew when a fresh pot of coffee had been brewed. Output from a video camera pointed at the coffee machine was posted on their computers into still pictures, updated every second or two. Today, no one seems to know how many "webcams," as they are known, are out there, but Internet groupings or collections of hundreds of active, live, worldwide "feeds" include numbers in the thousands. Webcams, once again, reflect both our playful and serious fascination with the camera's gaze. What began as a novelty for some has been put to more "productive" use by others. For example, Webcams are being used for video conferencing, such as popular *CU-See Me* software, education and "distance learning," sales and marketing, and tele-medicine. As with other technologies I have discussed, these uses appear as significant innovations in human communication and practical solutions to social problems (e.g., delivering education or health care to people in remote areas). Yet, at the same time, the proliferation of Webcams "jacked" into the Net hints at the creation of a gigantic network of watchful eyes that offers unprecedented monitoring capabilities. "Insofar as it is a technology that people can own and direct themselves, it appears to be enabling and liberating; insofar as it is a technology that others can use to watch us, it is threatening," claims *Webcams In Society* magazine publisher Dr. Jim Cross of the University of Leeds. Cross says best estimates are that about 60 percent of all such cameras are trained on people or things inside homes.[33]

Security entrepreneur Damon Sleicher says Internet-capable cameras are "the hottest thing going." He cites, for example, how one major national retail chain has installed Webcams in its stores, enabling executives at remote headquarters to surveil business activities from their desktops.[34] Technologically speaking, it would seem a minor step to connect up all those store and workplace security camera systems throughout the country into the Internet. Construction workers at the WorldCom Corporation headquarters that was being built in Kansas City were monitored by a video camera mounted on poles overlooking the construction site. Here the project manager could "zoom in on any worker or any place. Every hour a picture is taken from the video and posted on the company internal Intranet allowing thousands of employees to check construction progress regularly."[35] William Johnson, founder of the Business Espionage Control and Countermeasures Association, envisions a day when industrial spies will be planting Webcams with wireless modems and then tracking executives' movements or securing details of manufacturing processes inside a seemingly well-guarded plant.

In yet another version of the nanny-watching obsession covered earlier, security consultant Sleicher also markets a service called *Kid-View*. For less than $300, he will temporarily install hidden cameras in your home and hook them to a modem that permits parents to watch the sitter from work any time of the day.[36] Extending this into day care centers, some centers have begun hooking parents up to similar systems permanently installed in the facility and charged as part of the monthly fees. This "virtual peek-a-boo" is characterized by one dealer of a system called *I See You* as "a succession of Kodak moments." His company, Simplex Knowledge, has teamed up with IBM to market the system nationwide.[37] At one center in White Plains, New York, there are cameras in six rooms and the playground; four more are on order. One parent's in-laws, who live a thousand miles away in Florida, can also check out their grandkid. "What we are selling is peace of mind for parents who feel guilty or are concerned about the quality of day care," claims Kathleen Vrona, who is selling another system dubbed *KidCam*. Indeed, parents are not only checking *in* on their kids but also checking *up* on day care workers. Claiming, on the one hand, that the cameras should help "improve the quality" of U.S. day care centers, Vrona asserts, on the other hand, that "we're not focusing on security—teachers slapping kids around or things like that—but that is certainly a benefit." Then what is the "improvement" the cameras are to magically create? One parent seems to reassure herself when she claims that the use of *KidCam* "shows that they have a lot of confidence in the people that work here if they're willing to have you log on and see what's going on." Yet clearly, if the day care operators and parents truly trusted the workers, they would not feel the need to keep such a close watch on them. In fact, they might start by paying the teachers more than grocery baggers at the local supermarket. As the director of one center put it, "It's a nice system but I'd rather give my teachers a raise."[38]

While the austere surveillance opportunities for Webcams seem endless, the vast majority of these cameras have been installed in private and public spaces for little more than the novelty that it can be done. Or, in other cases, they are in place for people to invite others to view them and/or their social space, sometimes for fun, and sometimes for profit. The diversity of Webcam gazes ranges from the most mundane public settings to the most intimate, private ones. Examples include:

- Buckman Elementary School, Room 100, Portland, Oregon
- Bus stop, Wilshire Boulevard, Beverly Hills, California
- Cambridge panorama, Cambridge, UK . . . you can zoom in on parts of the view or even call up Web servers in visible buildings. Courtesy of Olivetti Research Labs
- Car-Cam, view from a car which gets driven in Marin County, California
- East Carolina University, School of Education parking lot
- Kessell's Web Cam, shots of a car dealership in Cornwall, England
- Hauptbahnof train/bus terminal, Berlin, Germany
- KGW SkyCam Network, views from inside a Portland television station, and from around the area
- NASA Cams and Mission Displays from Kennedy Space Center
- Nerdman Show, a real-life version of The Truman Show
- NY-Taxi.com, take the ride of your life with cabbie, Clever Da Silva
- Random Camera points to a picture from a random camera
- SBT Accounting Systems, visitors' lobby, San Rafael, California
- Street corner (9th & Pearl), Boulder, Colorado

The list goes on and on.

As noted above, many of the sites are collected together on "Web rings" such as Eye On The World Spy-Cams.com, The Web Voyeur.com, Peeping Tom.com, and Big Brother on Demand.com to name a few. EarthCam.com claims to be

your complete guide to live Internet cameras and Webcam events from around the world. There are an ever-increasing number of live video cameras supplying diverse and exotic images on the World Wide Web. EarthCam is the first searchable directory that specifically locates live images from thousands of indoor and outdoor Internet cameras. EarthCam's extensive database allows users to search by keyword or simply browse through our categories and subcategories. You can also search via 16 local U.S. cities guides or world map. Camera sites are categorized under thirteen general subjects: Event Cams, Arts & Entertainment, Business, Computers, Education, News, People & Society, Scenic, Space & Science, Sports & Recreation, Traffic, Weather, and Weird & Bizarre. *Users can see what is happening around the world right now—24 hours a day, 7 days a week.*

A search of home pages devoted to "voyeurism" revealed dozens involved in the distribution, exchange, and sale of erotic pictures and video taken of people without their knowledge. One site called The Peep Hole.com includes "hidden" camera footage from restrooms, hotels, clothing-store dressing rooms, tanning booths, and high school locker rooms as well as clips from "up skirts" (where cameras are positioned in such a way to look up women's clothing in public places), "eye in the sky" security cameras of gambling casinos, department stores, elevators, and other public places. In one case in California, a man spent sixteen hours at Disneyland angling a concealed video camera under the skirts of women waiting in lines. Security guards finally noticed the man and police took the camera, but authorities found no law with which to prosecute him. "With video, there's not a whole lot of restrictions," says one fellow who sells miniature video cameras. "You can do it anywhere except where someone can reasonably expect privacy." Wiretapping and eavesdropping laws are much more restrictive, he says. "But I can basically follow you around all day, as long as I don't follow you into your home or a public restroom or something."[39]

But this kind of invasion into "private" space is happening as well. For example, unauthorized videotapes of hundreds of naked male athletes in the locker rooms of more than fifty universities are being produced, sold and distributed on sexually oriented sites on the Web. Without their knowledge, the athletes were videotaped by employees or students working for video companies, posing as athletic trainers and carrying hidden cameras in gym bags. The videos of the students, including their faces, are now marketed through Web sites under such titles as Voyeur Time.com, After the Game.com, Wrestle Time.com and Shower Time.com. "I know that we have at least 1,000 kids on eight tapes," says Louis S. Goldstein of Chicago, who filed a lawsuit in Illinois state court. One former varsity athlete learned from a roommate that he had been taped a few years ago in a locker room at his school. "I pulled up the home page and I am looking at myself naked on the Internet," said the former athlete, who spoke on the condition that neither his name nor his sport be identified. "And everyone in the world has access to it. My parents have seen it now, and they are very upset. It is terrible because I have no control over it." This young man said locker rooms are not the same to him anymore. "You know, you see a gym bag and you don't think twice about it," he said. "But now I do." Still, lawyers are not exactly sure what criminal laws were violated in the case. There is no federal eavesdropping law regarding hidden video cameras, so prosecutors have turned to the interstate distribution of pornography or indecent material and racketeering statutes. At present, there are no laws governing control over images and words on the Internet.[40]

One utterly fascinating phenomenon has been the proliferation of Web pages set up by people who install cameras in their own homes and charge others a fee to watch them go about their daily lives. Catching the most notoriety and media attention was JenniCam.org. Two years ago college junior Jennifer Ringley of Washington, D.C., thought it would be fun to hook up a digital camera to her computer and let it post a photo to the Web every two minutes. Her life has been broadcast to the world ever since. Now a home-based Web page designer, Ms. Ringley claims she gets five hundred thousand visits a day to her server (at $15.00 per month membership). The cameras in her apartment, one in the bedroom and one in the living room, are on twenty-four hours a day, seven days a week. How does this young woman feel about her public performance?

Why are you giving up your privacy like this?
Because I don't feel I'm giving up my privacy. Just because people can see me doesn't mean it affects me—I'm still alone in my room, no matter what. And as long as what goes on inside my head is still private, I have all the space I need. On the other hand, if someone invented a TelepathyCam where you could hear everything I was thinking, I must admit I'd be a bit more squeamish. *wink*

You're naked sometimes, is this pornography?
Pornography is in the eye of the beholder. Myself, I do not think this constitutes pornography. Most often, pornography is defined as something explicit which is made with the clear intention of arousing the viewer. Yes, my site contains nudity from time to time. Real life contains nudity. Yes, it contains sexual material from time to time. Real life contains sexual material. However, this is not a site about nudity and sexual material. It is a site about real life.[41]

Hollywood picked up on the theme of entertainment voyeurism with the film, *The Truman Show*. The movie's central character, Truman Burbank, has his entire life, from birth on, broadcast live to the world "without commercial break and without interruption." Five thousand cameras record Truman's life, yet in this case, he does not have a clue that wife, boss, friends, and strangers are all actors. Speaking of the film, yet possibly indicative of the postmodern JenniCam phenomena, film critic Janet Maslin defines "Trumania" as an "obsessive national interest in the surreal ordinariness of Truman Burbank" that is manifested "by a willingness to find the most nondescript of Truman's experiences more poignant and meaningful than one's own."[42]

Ever since Jenni became an "eWebrity," hundreds of personal erotic camera sites have appeared touting "true" and "real" amateur exhibitionists (as opposed to professionals from the adult entertainment industry) such as Alanna's Bedroom Spy.com, AZBoy WebCam.com, BadGirlCam.com, Isabella@Home.com, and Mistress Rene's Web Cam.com. This virtual sexcape appears to follow the postmodern adage: "The illusion has become real and the more real it becomes, the more desperately they want it."[43] Enterprising "ePornographers" have tried to convert the "bored housewife" and other adolescent male fantasies into eCash by setting up "real life" voyeuristic scenarios. For example, one Kansas City man offered local college women free room and board to live in a house with Webcams in every room. He's charging forty-nine dollars a month for unlimited access to his Bikini Dorm.com where he claims, "It's about as spontaneous as it can be." Like other kinds of Internet activities that transcend traditional boundaries, these kinds of virtual peepshows present a problem to local authorities concerning zoning infractions. The Tampa City Council ruled that the owner of a similar house had to obtain an adult-use variance to continue operating.

Other simulated voyeuristic examples include sites such as ONTAP.com's Virtual Dorm where

students around the world live together online. Just like your own dorm (but without the smell), these roommates represent different lifestyles, majors, and backgrounds. They are wired together, 24 hours a day, seven days a week, using high-tech streaming video and audio, desktop computers and a connection to the Internet.

At Virtual Dorm, you can open a window on life at other colleges. . . . You can even chat with the Dormers in the OnTap chat rooms or read about their lives in their online V-dorm journals.

There's no editing in Virtual Dorm—what you see is all real, all the time. The Dormers keep their cameras on 24-7—go see if you can catch them between classes, or lure them away from their studying.[44]

In a recent crafty publicity antic, Hollywood movie promoters tantalized fans and potential viewers with a bit of voyeurism of their own:

Welcome to the secret Webcams set up by *Three to Tango* director Damon Santostefano . . . Damon has been assembling this candid footage for the past few months, placing hidden Webcams in trailers, offices, gyms, and other secret locations in an attempt to bring you candid footage of Matthew Perry, Neve Campbell, Dylan McDermott, and Oliver Platt . . . as you've never seen them before.

One video clip had a home movie feel that was shot from under a table and exposed just the legs of several female fans of actor Dylan McDermott supposedly waiting in his trailer on the set of the movie and making plans to greet him in their underwear.[45]

In what was billed as the world's first live birth on the Internet, forty-year-old Elizabeth Oliver delivered a baby in front of two cameras, a cameraman, a producer, a narrator and an audience of hundreds of thousands. America's Health Network, a cable TV network with 7.2 million subscribers, broadcast the delivery of Elizabeth's baby boy on its Web site. The Orlando-based company said it wanted to show the birth for people curious about how babies are born and to calm the nerves of expectant mothers. "It's such a miraculous and wonderful event," said Dr. Walter Larimore, the show's host. "If there's a problem, we'll show a problem. It's live. Nothing has been rehearsed," said Liz Poole, the producer who was in the delivery room. "We're being very flexible, following Mother Nature. This is a real family and real people." Ms. Oliver said, "It's neat that anybody can watch." Yet her notoriety and visibility on the Internet turned out to be not so "neat" for Ms. Oliver after all. Shortly after giving birth, Ms. Oliver disappeared after authorities claimed that she was wanted for writing bad checks. She later walked into the police station, was arrested, and freed on bond after a brief stay in jail.[46]

The birthing stunt was followed up by a live broadcast of gastric bypass surgery performed on Carnie Wilson, the daughter of Beach Boy founder, Brian Wilson. "Carnie has fought a weight problem her whole life," claims a promotional blurb, "Now, in collaboration with A Doctor In Your House.com, celeb-featured health and wellness service . . . Weighing the Alternatives with Carnie Wilson."

It takes a courageous person to open her heart and let us in on the pain and suffering endured by an obese person in this weight-obsessed culture. Yet Carnie Wilson, singer with the successful musical group Wilson Phillips, host of her own daytime TV talk show, and daughter of legendary Beach Boy Brian Wilson, does. She takes us on a journey through her thoughts and feelings as she meets with several specialists, including endocrinologists, surgeons, psychologists, physiciatrists [*sic*] and nutritionists on her way to her difficult decision to undergo gastric bypass surgery on August 10, 1999, cybercast, live, on this site, watch the archive here![47]

Other "celebs" lending their names to the cause of health and wellness on A Doctor In Your House.com include the Roger Moore Skin Cancer Support Group, the Calvin Hill Sports Medicine & Injury Support Group, the Jill Eikenberry Breast Cancer Support Group, and the Pat Boone Prostate Cancer Support Group.

Finally, On January 1, 2000, a twenty-six-year-old former computer systems manager, Mitch Maddox, who legally changed his name to DotComGuy, sequestered himself away in an empty Dallas house, planning to live exclusively online—including ordering food, furniture and clothes—for one year, without leaving the house. "Our vision is that new online shoppers will go to our site to learn how to utilize ecommerce," said DotComGuy. Moreover, part of the escapade involves twenty-four-hour streaming video from dozens of digital cameras set up throughout the house. "We certainly don't recommend that people lock themselves away from the world, but we will prove that it can be done,'" said Len Critcher, a friend of Maddox's and president of DotComGuy, Inc. Sponsors of the gimmick include Gateway computers, which donated a laptop, and Peapod.com, which agreed to keep the house stocked with groceries. The sponsors are listed on the project's Web site, www.DotComGuy.com. Previous versions of "living online" promotion included TV show "Good Morning America" housing two New Yorkers in an "e-cave" for a week with a refrigerator, a $500 daily stipend, a computer and Internet access, but Mr. Maddox claims he will break the record living off e-commerce longer than anyone else. On New Year's Day, the Web site video showed a somewhat pathetic looking DotComGuy, sitting alone on the floor of an empty room "chatting" online.[48]

RESTLESS VOYEURS

While the Panopticon exemplified modern social control within the confines of the disciplinary institution, one could argue that the Internet is, in part, prototypical of *post*modern social control that circulates throughout society. "[T]he massive, compact disciplines are broken down," as Foucault reminds us, "into flexible methods of control, which may be transferred and adapted."[49] Power, in this case, is exercised in a multi-directional, capillary network. It appears nearly everywhere, dispersed and fragmented. At the same time, it links individuals and organizations in a complex web of social relations. The Net, then, for all its hyperbolic promise of liberation and freedom, must also be understood as a *potential* tool for fostering and maintaining unbalanced and unequal authority relationships.

As I have shown above, the Internet facilitates meticulous rituals of power across our continuum of social control. On the "soft side," it helps companies ritualize knowledge-gathering activities that build case files out of the smallest, mundane details of our lives, often without us even knowing about them. By increasing the amount of information they have about us, and by decreasing the amount of control we have over that information, private companies shift the balance of power in their favor. We are thus vulnerable to being "targeted" for marketing campaigns that bring all the "intelligence" gathered about us together with the power of the human sciences in an attempt to shape and influence our choices, behaviors, and social and cultural activities. But the Internet enables more direct surveillance and monitoring practices as well. The act of linking people together within a network enhances hierarchical observation and fosters normalizing judgments. For example, the behavior of a preschool staff can be monitored by a parent sitting at work while, at the same time, their employer can be keeping track of their Web usage and judging its "acceptability." Similarly, a parent can log on and check their teenager's school attendance for the day ("truant/tardy/present") while school administrators see how many times that parent has accessed the system and how long his or her visits last, thus giving them a measure of just how involved the parent is in the child's life.

But more, Webcams "jacked in" to the Net contribute to the "ecstasy of communication": the deluge of images—voyeuristic gazes and exhibitionist delights—cascading into our computers from anywhere at anytime. "The postmodern person is a restless voyeur," asserts Denzin, "a person who sits and gazes (often mesmerized and bored) at the [computer] movie or TV screen. This is a looking culture, organized in terms of a variety of gazes."[50] The Internet promotes these gazes, gazes that not only unveil the private and make it public, but that obliterate the very distinction between the two. Much like typical security cameras, Webcams, once installed in "public" spaces, do not distinguish between those who *choose* to be on camera and those who do not. Anyone walking by one is vulnerable to its lens and to having their image or activities captured and circulated to millions across the Internet. Likewise, others can be preyed upon by video voyeurs who position their cameras in "private" locker rooms and the like and sell their tapes to e-pornographers. At the same time, Web exhibitionists can display their bodies—for fun or profit—to anyone willing to watch them eat breakfast, change their clothes, or have major surgery. This is a media where anyone can be an "eWebrity"—a bored college student, a pregnant woman, or a "one hit wonder" rock star. "Obscenity begins when there is no more spectacle," Baudrillard reminds us, "no more illusions, when everything becomes immediately transparent, visible, exposed in the raw and inexorable light of information and communication."[51] This may be the true "pornography" of JenniCam.org: that the invisible has become visible and that nothing is secret or sacred any longer.

6

The Revolution Will
Not Be Televised

It had to be like a faceless gaze that transformed the whole social body into a field of perception: Thousands of eyes posited everywhere, mobile attentions ever at the alert, a long hierarchized network.

—Michel Foucault[1]

What I apprehend immediately when I hear the branches cracking behind me is not that there is someone there; it is that I am vulnerable; that I have a body which can be hurt; that I occupy a place and I cannot in any case escape from this space in which I am without defense—in short, I am seen.

—Jean-Paul Sartre[2]

In the future, everyone will be famous for fifteen minutes.

—Andy Warhol

The purpose of this book has been to examine some of the surveillance techniques that have become part of contemporary life. Following the work of Michel Foucault, I have centered my observations on the practices at the intersection of power, knowledge, and the body. Most generally, I have included microtechniques of discipline—often enhanced by the use of new information and visual, communication, and medical technologies—that target and treat the body as an object to be watched, assessed, and manipulated. These local, meticulous rituals of power are the knowledge-gathering activities that involve surveillance, information, and evidence collection and analysis that increasingly compose our daily lives as workers, consumers, and community members. I have argued that these new disciplinary techniques must be understood as a product both of important, long-term processes set in motion with the onset of modernity, and of the emerging cultural context of postmodernity.

I have drawn my examples from and moved back and forth between the official justice system and everyday life. Much like the reformers of nineteenth century, contemporary advocates of "community-based" punishment and social control seek to make justice more effective and more efficient. Yet, as I have shown, as they have gone about decentralizing the justice system, we have seen how some the discourses, techniques, and procedures used in the justice system have been adapted for use in schools, workplaces, and other community institutions. One of my goals has been to show how we appear to be building a community *of* corrections, a tendency to normalize and accept the presence of formal social control in our daily lives. "But perhaps the most important effect of the carceral system and its extension well beyond legal imprisonment is," according to Foucault, "that it succeeds in making the power to punish natural and legitimate, in lowering at least the threshold of tolerance to penalty."[3]

But how did all this happen? "There was no revolution," one journalist declares, "no totalitarian takeover, no war bringing the collapse of world-wide democracy. But by an invention here and a new computer application there, American culture is nearing the point forwarded by those who feared technology could breed a new kind of oppression." Yet, while many of us are subjected to this new despotism, few, it would seem, see or appreciate the implications of this "quiet" revolution. We seem to exhibit what Marshall McLuhan called "narcissus narcosis," a syndrome in which people appear oblivious to how new technologies are invading and changing every aspect of their daily lives.[4] One reason, as I have tried to show, is that these surveillance and disciplinary practices often work in the background; we may not even know they exist, and even if we do, they rarely, in and of themselves, give cause for serious concern. Take, for example, the "tagging" of merchandise in stores to prevent shoplifting. If we were confronted as we left a business and were "patted down" physically, people would be outraged. Yet, since the technology permits us to be "electronically" frisked, we generally consent to this surveillance ceremony. But at the same time, the ritualistic removing of the tags at the checkout line and the presence of the barrier-like scanners at the doors remind us that we are in fact being watched. How many of us still cringe when we exit, knowing that we have done nothing wrong, but still slightly afraid of the alarms, fearful that an absentminded clerk might have forgotten to remove a tag? Even the more confrontive disciplinary rituals such as random drug screens are quickly routinized into common, everyday practices that soon lose their sense of transgression. "Who cares if someone tapes my conversation at the local donut shop?" someone will declare; "What difference does it make if some big company knows all about me?" another asks. "People should be tested for drugs," most seem to say; "They can test me, I have nothing to hide." Fragmented and piecemeal, quiet and habitual—and often convincingly productive—meticulous rituals elicit only minor resistance.

Yet these new habits, no matter how small or seemingly trivial, have their own significance, for they define a certain mode of political investment in the body. That is, meticulous rituals of power are the concrete ways in which our bodily lives are shaped, manipulated, and controlled by public and private organizations and by the people who have authority over us. These are the politics of social control in the workplace, the school, the home, and the community. They are also the politics of our "virtual" database(d) identities and who controls them.[5] But since these kinds of practices often appear as a "nudge" here and a "twist" there, few of us experience them as anything like "oppression." Yet, taken together, these "small acts of cunning" constitute the building blocks of what I would argue is a rapidly emerging disciplinary society; a society increasingly lacking in personal privacy, individual trust, or viable public life that supports and maintains democratic values and practices.

I do not claim that the surveillance techniques I have identified are put in place with impunity, that they are universally accepted, or even that they work in accordance with their proponents' claims. Development is uneven; some resistance is always present. People do fake drug tests, employers make exceptions, and probation officers work with violators trying to avoid revocations. There is competition among providers of new technology, some of it designed to thwart the efforts of others. While the phone companies sell us *CallerID* and *CallTrace,* for example, they also market *CallBlocker* to prevent these other functions. Like the invention of the penitentiary itself, the new techniques are said to embody all the ideal virtues of justice—preventing crime or deviance, protecting property, or insulating us from harm—while being more effective, less expensive, and more "civilized" than what came before. The prison, for example, was more "humane" than the scaffold; now that the reality of the penitentiary can no longer be concealed (or its cost tolerated), the electronic anklet bracelet is "kinder and gentler" and more practical than the institution. Or take drug testing. Urine analysis is relatively cumbersome and invasive; people resent it. Testing hair follicles is not only more effective, it is less intrusive. Each failure, it seems, only serves to justify and bring about a new generation of disciplinary devices.

FORGET BIG BROTHER

When I speak about "everyday surveillance," someone invariably asks, "Who is doing all this? Who's behind it? Who is 'Big Brother'?" "There is no 'Big Brother,'" I tell them; "we are him." Rather than appear simply "from the top down" or originate from a small group of identifiable individuals or even a particular organization, the new surveillance and social control practices, I argue, are advanced, directly or indirectly, by all of us. They are not orchestrated by only a few or as part of some master plan that is simply imposed on us; rather, disciplinary power expands "bi-directionally," flowing from top to bottom and vice versa. So while

President Ronald Reagan can issue an executive order that demands that all federal workers be tested for drugs, an ex-auto mechanic can start marketing and selling video cameras to school districts for their buses. While the FBI can help push a wiretap bill through Congress, an employer in your hometown may initiate "integrity" testing of all job applicants. A government agency or giant corporation may set out to create a new surveillance gadget, but it seems just as likely that a university professor will develop one—or, importantly, the basis for a potential one—for no other reason than "curiosity," or to get a promotion. A young computer software designer may develop a new program because its capabilities are "cool," rather than seeing it as an employee-monitoring tool. A grade school teacher may get a grant to adopt bar-code scanning in the classroom simply because the technology is there and because to use it "sounds like a good idea."

This is not to suggest that everyday surveillance emerges "by accident." Some people have a vested interest in creating and selling new surveillance technologies, while others may be in a position to exercise this kind of control and benefit from it. Yet even they are, ultimately, not exempt from the gaze of that "long hierarchized network" Foucault refers to. We are all involved and enmeshed within a grid of power relations that are highly intentional and purposeful, arrangements that can be more or less hierarchical and unequal but are never simply one-directional. So while a police officer can surveil suspects with a new high-tech scanner, the department can "keep an eye" on that very officer by installing a videocam in the patrol car. Similarly, a teacher can make "normalizing judgments" about students using a computer program, only to find that school administrators can use the same program to assess the teacher's "performance" in the classroom.

Everyday surveillance, I would argue, is being built on a foundation of seduction, desire, fear, and salvation. We all advance disciplinary power when we go about naively—and with blind faith and sometimes arrogance—trying to "make things better" and always assuming that, in fact, we can. This applies to anyone, across the political spectrum. "The road to hell," the saying goes, "is paved with good intentions." While some of the effects I have described in this book may be the "unintended consequences" of such good intentions, they are consequences nonetheless, and, it seems, they are rarely considered in public debate or discourse. We extend the bounds of everyday surveillance when we turn our backs on the important relationship between knowledge and power, when we take science—physical, medical, and social—at its word or assume that all technological change is always "for the better." There are often seemingly very compelling reasons why decisions are made to test people for drugs, to fingerprint welfare recipients, or to put surveillance cameras on school buses. After all, we need to "deal with the problem" (even if we have little idea of just what the problem actually is) or, better yet, because "something might happen." Why not take steps to prevent it? We are easily seduced by the image of a protected, peaceful order. We are a people who like things to "work," to be efficient, to be predictable, to "make sense." We are easily persuaded and charmed by politicians promising social stability, school administrators ensuring well-behaved children, and developers offering us the "serene fortress" of the gated community. We desire to eliminate risk, but at what price? Listen to those who become crusaders after a tragedy strikes their lives: the phenomenon (whatever it is—drug addiction, drunk driving, child abduction—it doesn't matter) will be stopped "at all cost," "to prevent this tragedy from happening to someone else"; "if one life can be saved, it will be worth it." Will it? Obviously, we want to stop the needless loss of life and injury, but on what basis and with what values do we evaluate the choice between reducing life's risks and tragedies by some unknown amount versus limiting our constitutional rights and personal freedoms? Put another way, is it worth surviving the risks of life only to end up "living" in a surveillance society?

We support, actively or passively, the creation of disciplinary practices, irrationally believing that they will be deployed exclusively "on those other folks," only to find that we have become the next targets. We facilitate everyday surveillance as well when we consume products that either make us the potential targets of surveillance or, alternatively, give us the tools to watch others. Here, the daily act of consumption—so central to the organization of late capitalism—becomes directly tied to the distribution and spread of disciplinary technology. If the company hasn't already done so, we are quite willing to "wire" ourselves in with "cell" phones, pagers, and e-mail, and we rush to buy the latest products that offer us access to the "Net" and the "Web" (the irony of this new terminology should not be ignored). We post pictures of our families and ourselves on the Web so anyone can see us. We also bring home the machines to monitor our kids' phone calls, to keep an eye on their driving, or even to test them for drugs. We buy the videocams and use them to document our own movements, or we turn them on our friends, neighbors, or strangers. *America's Funniest Home Videos* receives more than two thousand clips a day. According to the host, "everybody gets their Andy Warhol fifteen minutes. It's like driving by and looking into people's windows."[6] News networks will pay handsomely for amateur tapes of "important" events that they can then broadcast over and over again. In a culture of voyeurs, there is always plenty of footage. Interestingly, as the case of the Rodney King beating illustrates, we can even use these devices to "turn the tables" on those who abuse their position. Some have argued that this signals the democratization of surveillance, offering ordinary citizens the power to challenge authorities.[7] Yet, this strikes me as a contradiction in terms. A democratic society ensures and protects everyone's personal privacy, elites and commoners alike; it does not facilitate universal visibility.[8]

The imperative of more and more social control is also a function of fear. Steven Nock claims that increased formal surveillance results from our need to establish "reputations" and trust because, in a society of strangers, "How can we trust the people we see but do not know; those who live near us, who work near us, who must sometimes be counted on to help us?"[9] Yet, I would argue that, in our contemporary culture, it would seem that the "stranger" is more than someone without a reputation; what we really fear is the stranger assumed to exist within us all. In our sometimes hysterical culture, everyone is a potential suspect; otherwise, why would people who have established, "good" reputations still be subjected to surveillance ceremonies? Nock cites the example of the "highly respected civic leader" who is trusted. "His word is believed; his promise accepted."[10] Yet, at the height of the war on drugs, a proposal was made in my hometown that five city commissioners present themselves for drug screening in order to make a public statement that the town was "drug-free." The commissioners voted against the proposal, three to two, and the editor of the local newspaper proceeded to question the motives of those who had voted against it. The message is clear: If you refuse to consent to disciplinary rituals, you must have something to hide.

It seems that we indeed trust no one. As I have argued, our primary sources of cultural knowledge, the popular media and cinema, have turned everyday life into a theatrical drama where the most compelling stories are those that recount lives filled with uncertainty, unpredictability, and tragedy. "Watch out! You could be next!" the media scream out. We therefore become convinced that our only recourse against the apparent tide of problems we face is to "keep an eye on" everyone. We are therefore seduced into believing that even our own subjection is an unfortunate but necessary condition. Is fear an irrational response then? No. Not only are the media accounts powerfully convincing, but also our fears are grounded in a certain reality. The United States is a relatively dangerous place; I am not suggesting that crime, youth violence, drugs, and other social ills are not "real." What I am saying is that we need to be aware of the role played by the media in shaping the process of how we come to "know" and believe we understand the nature of those problems.

This cultural hysteria—generated by docudramas, prime-time sensational journalism, and made-for-TV movies "based on the true story"—creates a fertile market for those selling "science" and the technological "fixes" they claim will bring knowledge and certainty to ease our fears. Political problems become technical ones when we are gripped by fear and we long for the salvation of easy "solutions." But what have we bargained for when we surrender the fundamental problem of social control to science and technology? Ironically, while the videocam is used to "create" this hysteria through television and the cinema, it is offered as our salvation as well. "Just put up a camera," they say, and the problems will go away. In the case of the school bus, for example, once the camera is in place, no one has to bother teaching children *why* they should behave, it's enough just to get them to do it. This begs the question, how will they act when they are not under the gaze of the camera? Of course, the logical outcome of this "solution" is to make sure that they are always under its watchful eye.

How do we maintain anything deserving to be called a democratic society in the face of all this? I am not referring simply to the act of voting (although that is at issue also) as much as I am to the notion of democracy as an ongoing, daily accomplishment that is practiced and maintained both in human relationships and by mediating institutions. Democracy in this sense means not only ensuring our constitutionally given rights but also fostering what we might call the characteristics of a "good society"; a society where citizens are able to maintain a degree of trust in the individuals and organizations that they encounter; a society that is "civil" in every sense of the word; a society that ensures human rights and respects individual privacy and dignity, while at the same time balancing a concern for the "common good."[11] For years, social and political scholars have asserted that a fundamental characteristic of such a society is a viable public life— one that includes both public space (e.g., streets, parks, community markets, meeting places, schools, and the like) and a civic discourse (i.e., something such as "public opinion"). If Enlightenment reason and democratic ideals offer us any hope, it is in the notion that people can come together and rationally decide what is in their best interest and for the common good.

But in today's culture, how is this possible? As more and more of this "public" space is brought under the gaze of surveillance, and as meticulous rituals permeate our daily lives, "there is nowhere to hide," as Gary Marx puts it. "A citizen's ability to evade this surveillance is diminishing. To venture into a shopping mall, bank, subway, sometimes even a bathroom is to perform before an unknown audience."[12] Even if this kind of surveillance is relatively "seamless," as I have argued, it may function to undermine our willingness to participate in civic life and "to speak our minds as clearly, openly, and imaginatively as we can."[13] Like those subjected to the gaze of the Panopticon, we are increasingly "awed to silence," systematically manipulated and progressively unable to question private authority, challenge public officials, or engage in political dissent. We become, in essence, a "docile" citizenry, "disciplinary" subjects rather than democratic ones.

Driven out of the public sphere, we retreat to the "private life" of home only to find that, increasingly, it is not private at all. Here, public opinion has been replaced by the mass-mediated "storytelling" of high-profile media stars who "inform" us about how to vote and what is and what is not a "social problem." Our homes will be increasingly "hardwired" with new telecommunication links that offer corporations unprecedented access to our habits, buying preferences, and financial status. Meanwhile, some of the same technologies can be used to convert some people's homes into "virtual" prisons as they are remotely monitored under the watchful eye of authorities or, in other instances, similar devices enable suspicious parents to listen in on their teenagers' phone calls, to videotape the baby-sitter, or to rifle through each other's e-mail. With the contemporary blurring of boundaries between notions of "public" and "private," between "real"

freedom and its simulation, it is easy to see how "democracy" could become little more than a media illusion on the postmodern landscape.

BACK FROM THE ABYSS

All this sounds pretty bleak, doesn't it? Now that we have arrived at the crumbling edge of the cliff, it's time to turn to me and say, "OK, now what? You
brought us here; what do we do about it?" This is the point in which many cultural critics end their book by offering some vague and hopeful agenda for the
future, evoking some ideal society that will somehow mysteriously spring forth
from the rubble. Well, I have no such agenda to offer. To do so would contradict
much of what I have written here. Some readers may respond to this by saying,
"See, it's easy to be critical and much harder to come up with solutions." But I
don't agree; both criticism and solutions are extremely difficult. The first step, I
would argue, is understanding; to learn that there is, indeed, a crumbling ledge
out there to be cautious of; to see it through the haze of confusion, accepted wis-
dom, and just plain foolishness.

Since advocating leaping into the abyss would effectively end our discussion
here, let's assume we choose to confront the surveillance society. Let's further
assume that, while possible, a radically different culture is not likely to emerge
anytime soon. After all, as I have tried to show, much of what we live with today
is grounded in a legacy of Western thought and practice dating back several centuries. It is also firmly lodged in the basic day-to-day functioning of the society.
Given these assumptions, what can we do, as individuals, to counter disciplinary
practices? One strategy is to simply drop out of the culture entirely. This is the
tactic of many that have retreated to remote areas as part of the so-called radical survivalist movement. Interestingly, these predominately right-wing "coun-
terculture" groups characterize themselves as living "off the grid" of credit cards,
television, public utilities, and the consumer society. While these folks appear to
be alert to some of the issues I have raised, their often racist attitudes and ram-
pantly conspiratorial Big Brother paranoia about the government miss the mark
completely, and this makes them quite an unattractive lot to sign on with.

An alternative position, however, is one of active resistance. If we accept the
premise that much of the exercise of this kind of power takes place in the form
of "local" micropractices that are present in our everyday lives, then the sites of
opposition are right before us. They are in our own homes, workplaces, schools,
and communities. We don't need, necessarily, to form a counterinsurgency
movement to storm Washington, D.C. Rather, when some school board members in your community assert that student athletes should be tested for drugs,
demand that they demonstrate that drug abuse is indeed a problem. Next time
you telephone a business and a recording tells you that your call is being monitored "for your protection," ask to speak to a supervisor, and tell that person that

you disapprove of the practice. When your state legislature debates the merits of fingerprinting driver's license applicants, call your representative's office and ask her or him to vote against it. The next time someone carries on about the wonders of the latest digital gadget, acknowledge its potential benefits but remind the speaker that there may be privacy or surveillance implications to the product's use. Talk with your kids, openly and honestly, about both the allure and the dangers of drug use. In fact, turn off the television, log off the computer, unclip the beeper, and take your kid for a walk around the block. Wave to your neighbors. Well, you get the point.

Endnotes

CHAPTER 1

1. The term *social control* has a long history in the sociology. See Jack Gibbs, *Norms, Deviance, and Social Control: Conceptual Matters* (New York: Elsevier, 1981); Stanley Cohen and Andrew Scull, *Social Control and the State* (New York: St. Martin's Press, 1983); and Donald Black, *The Social Structure of Right and Wrong* (New York: Academic Press, 1999).

2. These ideas were pursued in some of my earlier work. See William G. Staples, "Small Acts of Cunning: Disciplinary Practices in Contemporary Life," *Sociological Quarterly* 35, no. 3 (Summer 1994): 645–64; and Dan Krier and William G. Staples, "Seen but Unseen: Part-time Faculty and Institutional Surveillance and Control," *American Sociologist* 24, nos. 3–4 (Fall/Winter 1993): 119–34.

3. Our "hyperreal" personas stored in the databases may be "better" representations of our "real" selves. Can you remember all the videos you rented last year? I would bet that your local video store's computer system could recall them.

4. Mark Poster, "Databases as Discourse; or, Electronic Interpellations," in *Computers, Surveillance, and Privacy*, ed. David Lyon and Elia Zureik (Minneapolis: University of Minnesota Press, 1996), 175–92.

5. Donald Lowe, *The Body in Late Capitalism USA* (Durham: Duke University Press, 1995).

6. This perspective is rooted in recent "neo-liberal" models of managing the "risk society" where, as Ericson puts it, "deviance gives way to risk as the concept for the understanding of how dangers are both identified and responded to technologically. The concern is less with the labeling of deviants as outsiders, and more on developing a knowledge of everyone to ascertain and manage their place in society." This perspective strikes me as positively frightening. See Richard V. Ericson's review of an earlier edition

of this book in *Social Forces* 76, no. 3 (1998): 1154, as well as his, *Policing the Risk Society* (Toronto: Toronto University Press, 1997).

7. Some contend that in no other area of the law is the Fourth Amendment being eroded as it is in the case of "sobriety checkpoints." In Kansas City, police stopped nearly 10,000 cars at checkpoints in 1998 and arrested 449 persons for driving under the influence of alcohol, a 4.5 percent rate. This seems to be typical nationally. "Sobriety checkpoints: Police stops may deter drunken driving. Some consider them illegal," *Kansas City Star*, 31 August 1997, 1(A).

8. The U.S. Supreme Court has upheld the constitutionality of sobriety checkpoints but established specific guidelines for their use. Police are required to give notification of a checkpoint, and they cannot detain motorists for an unreasonable amount of time. The court has also indicated that an arrest rate of less than 5 percent would raise questions of whether there is a legitimate government interest in the procedure (see note 5 above). "Excerpts from Supreme Court Decision." *New York Times*, 15 June 1990, 11(A).

9. This country is awash in so many guns that they have been declared a public health hazard. In 1997, more than 35,000 Americans died by gunfire. (By comparison, handguns were used to murder 2 people in New Zealand, 15 in Japan, 30 in Great Britain, and 106 in Canada.) Guns kept in the home for self-protection are forty-three times more likely to kill someone in the home than to kill in self-defense. More than twice as many women are shot and killed by their husbands or lovers than by strangers. And for every "justifiable homicide" where a citizen used a gun in defense, 131 lives were ended in firearm murders, suicides, and unintentional shootings. See <http://www.handguncontrol.org> [accessed 6 June 2000].

10. Michel Foucault, *Discipline and Punish: The Birth of the Prison*, trans. A. M. Sheridan (New York: Pantheon, 1977).

11. Diana Crane, *The Sociology of Culture* (Cambridge: Blackwell, 1994), 15. See also Clifford Geertz, *The Interpretations of Cultures* (New York: Basic, 1973).

12. Some recent books include Philip Agre and Marc Rotenberg, eds., *Technology and Privacy: The New Landscape* (Boston: MIT Press, 1997); Fred H. Cate, *Privacy in the Information Age* (Washington, D.C.: Brookings Institute, 1997); Ann Cavoukian and Don Tapscott, *Who Knows: Safeguarding Your Privacy in a Networked World* (New York: McGraw-Hill, 1996); Judith Wagner Decew, *In Pursuit of Privacy: Law, Ethics and the Rise of Technology* (Ithaca: Cornell University Press, 1997); Whitfield Diffie and Susan Landeau, *Privacy on the Line: The Politics of Wiretapping and Encryption* (Boston: MIT Press, 1998); Brian Kahin and Charles Nesson, eds., *Borders in Cyberspace: Information Policy and the Global Information Infrastructure* (Boston: MIT Press, 1997); David Lyon, *The Electronic Eye: The Rise of Surveillance Society* (Minneapolis: University of Minnesota Press, 1996); David Lyon and Elia Zureik, eds., *Computers, Surveillance, and Privacy* (Minneapolis: University of Minnesota Press, 1996); Bruce Schneier and David Banisar, eds., *The Electronic Privacy Papers: Documents on the Battle for Privacy in the Age of Surveillance* (New York: Wiley & Sons, 1997); and Reginald Whitaker, *The End of Privacy: How Total Surveillance Is Becoming a Reality* (New York: New Press, 1999).

13. Of course, historians and other analysts of culture have been using newspapers as legitimate sources for years. See Vernon Dibble, "Four Types of Inference from Documents to Events," *History and Theory* 3, no. 2 (1963): 203–221; Hyman Mariampolski and Dana Hughes, "The Use of Personal Documents in Historical Sociology," *The Amer-*

ican Sociologist 13, no. 2 (May 1978): 104–113; and John Milligan, "The Treatment of an Historical Source," *History and Theory* 18, no. 2 (May 1979): 177–196.

CHAPTER 2

1. Alice Morse Earle, *Curious Punishments of Bygone Days* (Rutland, Vt.: Charles E. Tenant, 1972), 144–45.

2. W. David Lewis, *From Newgate to Dannemora* (Ithaca: Cornell University Press, 1975), 117–20.

3. It should also be pointed out that the "birth of the prison" did not end physical punishment. Inmates at penitentiaries, mental asylums, and poorhouses as well as children in houses of refuge and reformatories were subjected to systematic corporal punishment and physical and mental abuse, to say nothing of various "treatments." See David J. Rothman, *The Discovery of the Asylum: Social Order and Disorder in the New Republic* (Boston: Little, Brown, 1971) and his *Conscience and Convenience: The Asylum and Its Alternatives in Progressive America* (Boston: Little, Brown, 1980).

4. "Applying the Death Penalty," *New York Times*, Letters to the Editor, Ernest van Den Haag, 18 November 1994, 34(A). See, for example, "Six Lashes in Singapore," *Newsweek*, 14 March 1994, 29.

5. Steven Best, "Foucault, Postmodernism, and Social Theory," in *Postmodernism and Social Inquiry*, ed. David R. Dickens and Andrea Fontana (New York: Guilford, 1994), 28.

6. Foucault, *Discipline and Punish: The Birth of the Prison*, trans. A. M. Sheridan (New York: Pantheon, 1977).

7. Michel Foucault, "Afterword: The Subject of Power," in *Michel Foucault: Beyond Structuralism and Hermeneutics*, ed. Hubert L. Dreyfus and Paul Rabinow (Berkeley: University of California Press, 1983), 209.

8. For a summary of the U.S. experience with institutional social control during the pre- and postcolonial periods, see Rothman, *The Discovery of the Asylum,* and his *Conscience and Convenience.*

9. Lawrence Friedman, *A History of American Law* (New York: Simon and Schuster, 1973), 250.

10. I wrote about these developments in a previous book entitled, *Castles of Our Conscience: Social Control and the American State, 1800–1985* (New Brunswick: Rutgers University Press, 1991), 19–25. I reproduce some of this history here, since I think it crucial to our understanding of our present-day situation.

11. Orlando Lewis, *The Development of American Prisons and Prison Customs, 1776–1845* (1922; reprint, Albany: Prison Association of New York, 1967) 18; Staples, *Castles of Our Conscience,* 19–25.

12. See Staples, *Castles of Our Conscience,* 19–25.

13. Staples, *Castles of Our Conscience,* 19–25.

14. Staples, *Castles of Our Conscience,* 19–25.

15. Thomas Dumm, *Democracy and Punishment: Disciplinary Origins of the United States* (Madison: University of Wisconsin Press, 1987), 120.

16. "At Work, a Different Test for Drugs," *New York Times*, 21 January 1996, 11(F).

17. Robert M. Emerson and Sheldon M. Messinger, "The Micro-Politics of Trouble," *Social Problems* 25, no. 2 (1977): 121-34.

18. Jeremy Bentham, "Preface," in *The Panopticon Writings*, ed. Miran Bozovic (London: Verso, 1995), 32; Foucault, *Discipline and Punish*, 195.

19. Foucault, *Discipline and Punish*, 211.

20. Foucault, *Discipline and Punish*, 297.

21. Dreyfus and Rabinow, *Michel Foucault*, xxvi.

22. Foucault, *Discipline and Punish*, 209.

23. See Fredric Jameson, *Postmodernism, or, The Cultural Logic of Late Capitalism*. (London: Verso, 1992), and Ernest Mandel, *Late Capitalism* (London: Verso, 1978).

24. Donald Lowe, *The Body in Late Capitalism USA* (Durham: Duke University Press, 1995), 20.

25. Vaclav Havel, "The New Measure of Man," *New York Times*, 8 July 1994, 29(D).

26. In the world of art, architecture, and the cinema, "postmodern" generally refers to the mixing, blending, and bending of traditional styles and media(s), the creation of pastiche, "re-mixing" older songs in music, and the like.

27. Jean Baudrillard, *The Ecstasy of Communication* (New York: Semiotext(e), 1988).

28. Sherry Turkle, *Life on the Screen: Identity in The Age of the Internet* (New York: Simon & Schuster, 1995), 235.

29. Meyerowitz, cited in Lili Berko, "Surveying the Surveilled: Video, Space, and Subjectivity," *Quarterly Review of Film and Video* 14, no. 1–2 (1992): 61–91.

30. Norman K. Denzin, *Images of Postmodern Society: Social Theory and Contemporary Cinema* (Newbury Park, Calif.: Sage, 1991), 9.

31. Actual text from local TV news, Channel 9, Kansas City, 10 P.M., 10 June 1997.

32. See Gavin de Becker, quoted in *USA Weekend*, 22–24 August 1997, 8. See also Gavin de Becker, *The Gift of Fear* (New York: Little, Brown, 1997).

33. For recent work on fear in the culture, see Barry Glassner, *Culture of Fear: Why Americans Are Afraid of the Wrong Things* (New York: Basic Books, 1999); and Jeff Ferrell and Neil Websdale, *Making Trouble: Cultural Constructions of Crime, Deviance, and Control* (Hawthorne, N.Y.: Aldine De Gruyter, 1999).

34. See the General Social Survey, a personal interview survey of U.S. households conducted by the National Opinion Research Center: <http://www.icpsr.umich.edu/GSS99/home.htm> [accessed 12 November 1999].

35. "Heroin Ads Are Needle-Sharp," *Lawrence Journal-World*, 18 June 1996, 4(A).

36. Keith Humphreys and Julian Rappaport, "From the Community Mental Health Movement to the War on Drugs: A Study in the Definitions of Social Problems," *American Psychologist* 48, no. 8 (1993): 892–901.

37. According to Humphreys and Rappaport (1993: 895) budget authority for federal spending on interdiction, law enforcement, treatment, and prevention of drug abuse rose 679 percent during the decade 1981–91. In 1988 the majority of people arrested in America's twenty-two largest cities were classified as "cocaine users."

38. "Get tough" suddenly meant "Go broke!" according to Ronald Corbett and Gary T. Marx, "Critique: No Soul in the New Machine: Technofallacies in the Electronic Monitoring Movement," *Justice Quarterly* 8, no. 3 (September 1991): 399–414. By 1987 thirty-seven states were under court-ordered mandate to end prison overcrowding, claims Joan Petersilia in *Expanding Options for Criminal Sentencing* (Santa Monica: RAND, 1987).

39. David Altheide, "Gonzo Justice," *Symbolic Interaction* 15, no. 1 (1993): 69–86. See also his "Electronic Media and State Control: The Case of Azscam," *Sociological Quarterly* 34, no. 1 (1993): 53–69; and *Media Power* (Newbury Park, Calif.: Sage, 1985).

40. Stanley Cohen anticipated some of these developments in his important works *Visions of Social Control: Crime, Punishment and Classification* (Cambridge: Polity Press, 1985) and "The Punitive City: Notes on the Dispersal of Social Control," *Contemporary Crisis* 3, no. 4 (1979): 339–63.

41. "Idle Hands within the Devil's Own Playground," *New York Times*, 16 July 1995, 3(E).

42. Mike Davis, *City of Quartz* (London: Verso, 1990), 257.

CHAPTER 3

1. Jean Baudrillard, *Simulations* (New York: Semiotext(e), 1983), 25.

2. "For Some Convicts, Wires Replace Bars," *New York Times*, 22 February 1990, 1(A).

3. On "hyperreality" see Baudrillard, *Simulations*, 11; John Holman and James Quinn, "Dysphoria and Electronically Monitored Home Confinement," *Deviant Behavior* 13, no. 1 (Jan–Mar 1992): 21–32. Using a "psychometric instrument," Holman and Quinn assessed the extent of "dysphoria" (or "a generalized feeling of anxiety, restlessness, and depression") among seventy-seven clients in EMHC programs in two states. They report no significant difference between this and a comparison group of forty-nine offenders under "traditional forms of community supervision." Both groups post-tested at the "high end of the normal range" (1992: 29). A student of mine told me that even being around someone under house arrest was nerve-racking. Describing a roommate he said, "They're always jumpy. The phone rings, and they run."

4. "New Growth in a Captive Market," *New York Times*, 31 December 1989, 12(E); and *Arizona Republic*, 13 May 1992, 5(B).

5. Bureau of Justice Statistics Bulletin, *Prisons and Jail Inmates at Mid-Year 1998*, (Washington, D.C.: Department of Justice, March 1999).

6. "New Growth in a Captive Market."

7. "New Growth in a Captive Market," 12(E).

8. "Jail Has Alternatives," *University Daily Kansan*, University of Kansas, Lawrence, 18 September 1990, 1.

9. "For Some Convicts, Wires Replace Bars," 1(A).

10. Ronald Corbett and Gary T. Marx, "Critique: No Soul in the New Machine: Technofallacies in the Electronic Monitoring Movement," *Justice Quarterly* 8, no. 3 (September 1991): 399–414.

11. Michel Foucault, *Discipline and Punish: The Birth of the Prison,* tr. A. M. Sheridan (New York: Pantheon, 1977), 200.

12. Foucault, *Discipline and Punish*, 206.

13. A former student, who is an ISO officer, supplied this information. I must ensure confidentiality of this individual and of the agency.

14. See note 13.

15. V. G. Hodges and B. Blythe, "Improving Service Delivery to High-Risk Families: Home-Based Practice," *Families in Society: The Journal of Contemporary Human Services* 73, no. 5 (May 1992): 259–65.

16. L. J. Woods, "Home-Based Family Therapy," *Social Work* 33, no. 3 (May/June 1988): 211–14.

17. Foucault, *Discipline and Punish*, 211.

18. Shaun Assael, "Robocourt," *Wired*, March 1994, 106.

19. Assael, "Robocourt," 106.

20. Corbett and Marx, 400.

21. "Sheriff's Video Patrol Auditioning Begins," *Lawrence Journal-World*, 6 March 1994, 3(B).

22. "Sheriff's Video Patrol Auditioning Begins," 1(B); Foucault, *Discipline and Punish*, 177.

23. "Using Cable TV to Get Child Support," *New York Times*, 14 November 1993, 12.

24. " '*Life on the Beat*' Bolsters Police Image," *Lawrence Journal-World*, 29 May 1998, 6(D).

25. "New Police Policy Puts a Precinct on Cable TV," *New York Times*, 17 July 1994, 13.

26. "New Scanners May Redefine 'Strip Search,' " *New York Times*, 5 May 1995, 7(A).

27. "High-Tech Crime Fighting Making Way to Kansas," *Lawrence Journal-World*, 20 October 1993, 12.

28. "Driver's License Photos Would Be Open to Police," *Lawrence Journal-World*, 16 February 1995, 4(B).

29. "Colorado to Halt Sale of Driver's License Photos," *Reuters News Service*, 3 February 1998.

30. "Ion-Scanner," *Motor Week*, Public Broadcasting System, 5 May 1995.

31. "High-Tech Police Car Battles Bad Drivers," *Lawrence Journal-World*, 23 November 1997, 10(A).

32. Michael Fumento, "Road Rage vs Reality," *The Atlantic Monthly* 282, no. 2 (August 1998):12–17.

33. "Pot Farmer Says Agents Intruded," *Lawrence Journal-World*, 22 June 1995, 8(A).

34. "In Sarajevo, Victims of a 'Postmodern' War," *New York Times*, 21 May 1995, 1.

35. "High-Tech Devices Utilized by U.S. Military in Bosnia," National Public Radio, *All Things Considered*, 15 March 1996.

36. "Bayonets Given to Police Force," *Lawrence Journal-World*, 2 November 1997, 9(A).

37. "If You're Heading to California, Better Be Careful What You Say on the Phone." <http://www.abcnews.com.> [accessed 11 November 1999].

38. "Clinton Gets a Wiretap Bill Covering New Technologies," *New York Times*, 9 October 1994, 15.

39. "Privacy Issues Collide with Law Enforcement," *New York Times*, 15 October 1995, 14.

40. "New Turnpike System Lets Drivers Glide Past Lines at Toll Booth," *Lawrence Journal-World*, 7 October 1995, 10(B).

41. "The Road Watches You," *New York Times*, 13 May 1995, 15(A).

42. "A New Way to Sniff Out Automobiles That Pollute," *New York Times*, 22 October 1995, 33(A).

43. "No Place to Hide," *Forbes*, 22 September 1997, 226.

44. "KHP Goes High-Tech to Monitor Troopers," *Lawrence Journal-World*, 28 August 1998, 8(B). Of course, the "low-tech" version of this brings the public in as watchers. "1-800 How's my driving?" stickers have been around for about ten years.

45. "Consumer Privacy and Smart Cards—A Challenge and an Opportunity." <http://www.The Smart Card Forum.org> [accessed 15 May 1997].

46. David Lyon, "The New Surveillance: Electronic Technologies and the Maximum Security Society," *Crime, Law and Social Change* 18, no. 1–2 (September 1992): 159–175.

47. Lili Berko, "Surveying the Surveilled: Video, Space, and Subjectivity," *Quarterly Review of Film and Video* 14, no. 1–2 (1992): 61–91.

48. "A High-Tech Dragnet," *Time*, 1 November 1993, 43.

49. "Thousands of Eyes for State Police," *New York Times*, 19 May 1994, 8(A).

50. NYCLU Surveillance Camera Project Report, New York, 1998 <http://www.nyclu.org> [accessed 2 October 1999].

51. "Baltimore Plans to Install 200 Cameras in Downtown," *Kansas City Star*, 20 January 1996, 20(A).

52. "Baltimore Installs Cameras for Public Area Surveillance," *Lawrence Journal-World*, 20 January 1996, 5(A).

53. "Big Brother Enters Debate about Traffic Cameras," *Lawrence Journal-World*, 13 February 1996, 6(A).

54. "The Electric Arm of the Law," *New Scientist*, 8 May 1993, 19–20.

55. "Britain's Raciest Surveillance Videos Stir Outrage," *Lawrence Journal-World*, 18 March 1996, 8(D).

56. "Are You Being Watched?" <http://www.abcnews.com> [accessed 11 November 1999].

57. "Violence at High School Video Taped," *Lawrence Journal-World*, 7 June 1996, 6(A).

58. "Videotape of Rape Leads to Charges, Expulsions," *Lawrence Journal-World*, 16 November 1999, 8(A).

59. "Doctors Fear Suits via Video of Births," *Lawrence Journal-World*, 19 June 1998, 1.

60. "Camera Keeps Eye on Treasurer's Office," *Lawrence Journal-World*, 17 December 1997, 5(B).

61. "Stores' Growing Use of Audio Surveillance Raises Concerns," *Kansas City Star*, 3 May 1994, 21(D).

62. In a "turn the tables" on privacy move, gadfly journalist and documentary filmmaker Michael Moore later set up a "Webcam" (see chapter 5) aimed at the windows of Ms. Goldberg's New York apartment asserting that she "does not respect the privacy rights of others. She believes in keeping an eye on persons who are a threat to the country. So do we. From now on, twenty-four hours a day, seven days a week, you can come to this web site to see what Lucy is up to. Log on anytime and keep an eye on her activities. Hopefully, if we spot anything fishy, we can stop her before she strikes again." <http://www.iseelucy.com> [accessed 3 October 1999].

63. "Entrapment and Manipulation . . . How Monica Was Betrayed," *The Times* (London) 27 October 1998.

64. "At the Bar: Secret Tape-Recording," *New York Times*, 16 September 1994, 14(D).

65. FAQ, <http://listen.to/eargram> [accessed 10 October 1999].

66. "Many Seek Security in Private Communities," *New York Times*, 3 September 1995, 1(A).

67. Yet one visitor comments: "Before I came here my sister told me it creeped her out, it was too perfect. It is kinda Stepford Wife-like." "At Celebration, Reasons to Celebrate," *New York Times*, 7 March 1999, 42.

68. "Secretly Taping Nannies Becomes Big Business," *Lawrence Journal-World*, 19 November 1997, 3(A).

69. "Cloak and Dagger from the Home and Hearth," *New York Times*, 30 July 1995, 8(F).

70. "Children Under Surveillance: When Parents' Trust Wears Out, Some Resort to Spying on Their Teens, " *Washington Post*, 28 February 1999, 1(A).

71. "Children Under Surveillance."

72. "Teen-Agers in Washington Face New Curfew," *New York Times*, 7 July 1995, 9(A); "Use of Curfews Growing against Youth at Night," *New York Times*, 8 November 1993, 13(A); and "Philadelphia Adopts Tough New Truant Policy, with Handcuffs, Too," *New York Times*, 9 February 1994, 12(A).

73. Peter Conrad and Joseph Schneider, *Deviance and Medicalization: From Badness to Sickness* (St. Louis: Mosby, 1980), and Malcolm Spector, "Beyond Crime: Seven Methods to Control Troublesome Rascals," in *Law and Deviance*, ed. H. L. Ross (Beverly Hills: Sage, 1981), 127–58.

74. William G. Staples, *Castles of Our Conscience: Social Control and the American State, 1800–1985* (New Brunswick: Rutgers University Press, 1991), 138–145; William G. Staples and Carol A.B. Warren, "Mental Health and Adolescent Social Control," in *Research in Law, Deviance and Social Control: A Research Annual*, eds. Steven Spitzer and Andrew Scull (Greenwich, Conn.: JAI Press, 1988), 113–126; William G. Staples and Carol A.B. Warren, "Fieldwork in Forbidden Terrain: The State, Privatization and Human Subjects Regulations," *The American Sociologist* 20, no. 3 (Fall 1989), 263–267.

75. "Even Small Schools Adding Security," *Lawrence Journal-World*, 25 January 1994, 8(B).

76. "For Many Students, a High School's New Security Rules Have the Opposite Effect," *New York Times*, 9 May 1999, 27(Y).

77. "Schools Requiring ID Code to Pick Up Children," *Lawrence Journal-World*, 30 October 1995, 8(A).

78. "Buses Host 'Candid Camera,'" *Lawrence Journal-World*, 14 June 1994, 2(B); Jeremy Bentham, "Preface," in *The Panopticon Writings*, ed. Miran Bozovic (London: Verso, 1995), 32.

79. "Videocams on School Buses Becoming More Widespread," *Lawrence Journal-World*, 11 September 1993, 11(A). I read a while back that in St. Louis, school authorities took another tack: They put video monitors on the buses, rather than cameras, and played tapes that kept the children's attention. The accompanying photo showed a row of docile students staring blankly at the screens.

80. "Drug/Weapon Finder Is a Fraud, FBI Says," *Kansas City Star*, 19 January 1996, 1(A).

81. "Computer Project Seeks to Avert Youth Violence: Columbine Spurs Pilot Program at Schools," *New York Times*, 24 October 1999, 16(Y).

82. "Schools Are Relatively Safe, U.S. Study Says," *New York Times*, 19 November 1995, 20(A).

83. See Carl Milofsky, *Testers and Testing: The Sociology of School Psychology* (New Brunswick: Rutgers University Press, 1989), and F. Allan Hanson, *Testing Testing: Social Consequences of the Examined Life* (Berkeley: University of California Press, 1993).

84. "Grades Go High-Tech in Cordley Class," *Lawrence Journal-World*, 23 October 1994, 1(B).

85. Of course, there never seems to be any question about such software being "progress." The headline reads, "KU-Developed Software Beneficial to Schools: Computer Helps in Classroom," *Lawrence Journal-World*, 26 November 1995, 8(B).

86. "Mr. Edens Profits from Watching His Workers' Every Move," *Wall Street Journal*, 1 December 1994, 9(A).

87. *AMA Survey on Workplace Monitoring and Surveillance*, (New York: American Management Association, 1999). The greater share of this oversight is focused on selected job categories and is most often performed as spot checks rather than ongoing surveillance, the survey found, and an average 84 percent of companies with such practices inform their employees of their policies. The financial services sector, including the banking, brokerage, insurance, and real estate industries, lead in electronic monitoring (68%), followed by business and professional service providers (51%) and wholesalers and retailers (47%). As defined by the AMA, electronic monitoring includes storage and review of e-mail (27%, up from 15% in 1997); recording and review of telephone conversations (11%, vs. 10% in 1997); storage and review of voice mail messages (6%, vs. 5%); storage and review of computer files (21%, vs. 14%); and video recording of employee job performance (16%, as in 1997). Additional surveillance practices include tracking telephone numbers called and time spent on calls (39%, vs. 34% in 1997); computer time and keystrokes entered (15%, vs. 16%); and video surveillance to counter theft, violence, or sabotage (33%, vs. 34% in 1997). The annual survey included 1,054 AMA-member organizations, and was conducted in January–March 1999. The survey's margin of error is ±3.5%.

88. "Privacy Clashes with Employer Need to Monitor E-Mail," *Dallas Morning News*, 22 July 1998.

89. " 'Virtual Affair' Leads to Divorce," *Lawrence Journal-World*, 2 February 1996, 3(A).

90. "What's on Your Hard Drive?" *New York Times*, 8 October 1998, 1(G). The article also points out that "examples abound of sensitive information going out the door when government agencies, pharmacies, doctors' offices and other businesses donate or sell used computers without erasing the computers' memories. For example, a woman in Nevada bought a used computer from an Internet auction company and was surprised to find that it contained names, addresses, Social Security numbers and prescription information for 2,000 people, including people being treated for AIDS, alcoholism and mental illnesses. A pharmacy had failed to erase the information when it sold the computer."

91. Michel Foucault, *Power/Knowledge: Selected Interviews and Other Writings, 1972–1977*, ed. Colin Gordon (New York: Pantheon, 1980), 156.

92. "Corporate Delete Keys Busy As E-Mail Turns Up in Court," *New York Times*, 11 November 1998, 1(A).

93. "High-Tech Spy Equipment in the Workplace," National Public Radio, *All Things Considered*, 1 April 1996.

94. "Labor Pains," Kansas City, *Pitch Weekly*, 7 October 1999, 12.

95. "Modern Business Technology Becoming Electronic Leash," *Lawrence Journal-World*, 5 November 1995, 6(E).

96. "You're Not Paranoid: They Really Are Watching You: Surveillance in the Workplace Is Getting Digitized—and Getting Worse," *Wired*, March 1995, 85.

97. "How Deep Should Employers Dig?" *Grand Forks Herald*, 11 February 1995, 7(D).

98. *AMA Survey on Job Skill Testing and Psychological Measurement* (New York: American Management Association, 1998), 3.

99. "Employee Beware: The Boss May Be Listening," *Wall Street Journal*, 29 July 1994, 1(C).

100. "Firms Walk Tightrope on Privacy Issues," *Los Angeles Times*, 20 December 1987, 1(P).

101. The extent that marketers rely on the social sciences was demonstrated recently when sixty psychologists and psychiatrists sent a letter to the American Psychological Association objecting to colleagues who lend their expertise, not to mitigate the causes of human suffering but to "promote and assist the commercial exploitation and manipulation of children." See "Study by the Kaiser Family Foundation," *National Public Radio*, 17 November 1999.

102. Oscar Gandy, Jr., *The Panoptic Sort: A Political Economy of Personal Information* (Boulder: Westview, 1993), 2.

103. Zygmunt Bauman, *Intimations of Postmodernity* (London: Routledge, 1992), 49; David Lyon, *Postmodernity* (Minneapolis: Minnesota University Press, 1994), 66. See also Pierre Bourdieu, *Distinction: A Social Critique of the Judgement of Taste* (London: Routledge, 1984).

104. "Spy Commerce: The Surveillance Society: Part Three," *Village Voice*, 9–15 December 1998.

105. "Consumers Wake up to Privacy Intrusions," *St. Petersburg Times*, 7 February 1999, 1(H).

106. "Missouri Officials Put Bell Plan—Selling Data—on Hold," *Lawrence Journal-World*, 6 October 1995, 5(D).

107. H. Jeff Smith, *Managing Privacy: Information, Technology, and Corporate America* (Chapel Hill: University of North Carolina Press, 1994), 2.

108. Smith, *Managing Privacy*, 3.

109. "Spy Commerce," 9–15 December 1998.

110. "Jordan: Use Computers to Track Immigrants," *Lawrence Journal-World*, 4 August 1994, 12.

CHAPTER 4

1. *AMA Survey on Workplace Drug Testing and Drug Abuse Policies* (New York: American Management Association, 1994).

2. "At Work, a Different Test for Drugs," *New York Times*, 21 January 1996, 11(F).

3. *Abuscreen Ontrack* by Roche Diagnostic Systems, 1989.

4. Steven L. Nock, *The Costs of Privacy: Surveillance and Reputation in America* (New York: De Gruyter, 1989).

5. Nock, *The Costs of Privacy*, 102.

6. F. Allan Hanson, *Testing Testing: Social Consequences of the Examined Life* (Berkeley: University of California Press, 1993), 128.

7. Hanson, *Testing Testing*, 128.

8. "At Work, a Different Test for Drugs."

9. "Drug-Test the Chess Club?," *USA Weekend*, 20–22 November 1998.

10. Mark E. Brossman, "Workers Gain Privacy Rights by Legislation, Judicial Action," *National Law Journal*, 9 April 1990, 28.

11. "Justices to Take Up Case of Schools Drug Testing," *New York Times*, 29 March 1995, 12(A).

12. David T. Lykken, *A Tremor in the Blood: Uses and Abuses of the Lie Detector* (New York: Plenum, 1998), xxi.

13. Hanson, *Testing Testing*, 68.

14. Lykken, *A Tremor in the Blood*, xvi; U.S. Congress, Office of Technology Assessment, 1983, in Nock, *The Costs of Privacy*, 89–90.

15. Nock, *The Costs of Privacy*, 90–91.

16. "Debatable Device: Privacy, Technology Collide in a Dispute over Intimate Test," *Wall Street Journal*, 3 February 1993, 1.

17. "Debatable Device"; Michel Foucault, *Discipline and Punish: The Birth of the Prison*, tr. A. M. Sheridan (New York: Pantheon, 1977), 193.

18. "Debatable Device."

19. "The Indelicate Art of Telling Adults How to Have Sex," *New York Times*, 16 May 1993, 18(E).

20. "The Indelicate Art."

21. Dorothy Nelkin and Laurence Tancredi, *Dangerous Diagnostics: The Social Power of Biological Information* (1989; reprint, Chicago: University of Chicago Press, 1994), 160–61.

22. "Faster, More Accurate Fingerprint Matching," *New York Times*, 11 October 1992, 9(F).

23. "Fingerprint System Extends Arm of the Law," *New York Times*, 12 November 1993, 11(B).

24. "UNISYS Bioware: The Heart Accurate Identification," <http://www.unisys.com> [accessed 22 February 1999].

25. "Fingerprinting Targets Welfare Fraud," *Lawrence Journal-World*, 23 January 1994, 9(A).

26. "Bank Cards Facing Uncertain Future," *Lawrence Journal-World*, 8 June 1993, 1.

27. <http://www.sensar.com> [accessed 23 September 1999].

28. "The Hand's Shape: Unique and Useful for Identity Check," *New York Times*, 21 October 1992, 5(C).

29. NYCLU Surveillance Camera Project Report, New York, 1998, <http://www.nyclu.org> [accessed 2 October 1999].

30. "Wanted for Rape: John Doe, Known Only by DNA," *The Plain Dealer*, 7 October 1999, 1(A).

31. Press release, Myriad Genetics, Inc. <http://www.myriad.com> [accessed 18 February 1999].

32. <http://www.aclu.org> [accessed 12 December 1999].

33. "Minn. Debates Bill to Prohibit Genetic Testing," *National Underwriter* (Property & Casualty/Risk & Benefits Management Edition, March 20, 1995), 24.

34. "Rebuilding Confidence in Confidentiality," *National Underwriter* (Life & Health/Financial Services Edition, 23 October 1995), 35.

35. "Genetic Information Privacy Bill Proposed," *Lawrence Journal-World*, 21 January 1998, 7(A).

36. Nelkin and Tancredi, *Dangerous Diagnostics*, ix–x.

37. "Business Using Therapy Data to Lower Costs," *New York Times*, 12 April 1994, 1(A).

38. "Privacy a Healthy Prescription," *Lawrence Journal-World*, 14 August 1998, 8(B).

39. "Employee Beware: The Boss May Be Listening," *Wall Street Journal*, 29 July 1994, 1(C).

40. "Medical Data Gathered by Firms Can Prove Less Than Confidential," *Wall Street Journal*, 19 May 1994, 1(A).

41. "Medical Data Gathered."

42. It would seem that, according to the conservative right, some segments of the population should be stopped, by force if necessary, from having what these moral entrepreneurs consider to be "illegitimate" families. As Nancy Fraser predicted several years ago, the "coming welfare wars will be wars largely about, even against women . . . [who are] claiming benefits not as individuals but as members of failed families, these recipients are effectively denied the trappings of social citizenship." Nancy Fraser, *Unruly Practices: Power, Discourse, and Gender in Contemporary Social Theory* (Minneapolis: University of Minnesota Press, 1989), 144, 152–53; "Where the Norplant Debate Hits Home," *New York Times,* 7 March 1993, 17.

43. "Cash-for-Sterilization Plan Draws Addicts and Critics," *New York Times,* 24 July 1999, 8(A).

44. Peter Breggin, "Let's Not 'Treat' the Problem of Homelessness with Drugs," Letters to the Editor, *New York Times,* 26 June 1994, 6(E).

45. Carol A. B. Warren and Kathleen A. K. Levy, "Electroconvulsive Therapy and the Elderly," *Journal of Aging Studies* 5, no. 3 (1991), 309–27; and Timothy Kneeland and Carol A. B. Warren, *Push-Button Psychiatry: A History of Electroconvulsive Therapy* (Westport, Conn.: Greenwood Press, 2000).

46. "With Reforms in Treatment, Shock Therapy Loses Shock," *New York Times,* 19 July 1993, 1(A); and Hugh L. Polk, M.D., "Shock Therapy Still Causes Brain Damage," Letters to the Editor, *New York Times,* 1 August 1993, 14(E).

47. "As More Children Use Ritalin, Debate over Drug Grows," *Dallas Morning News,* 29 December 1995, 15(C).

48. "School Watch; Psychologist: ADD is Abused Diagnosis," *Atlanta Journal and Constitution,* 16 January 1996, 3(B).

49. "Ritalin: What Parents Need to Know," *The Miami Herald,* 8 December 1995, 4. "A Wonder Drug's Worst Side Effect; Kids Turning to Easy-to-Get Ritalin for a Quick and Sometimes Deadly High," *Washington Post,* 5 February 1996, 1(A). See also "Reading, Writing and Ritalin," *New York Times,* 21 October 1995, 21(A).

50. "New Fence Could Kill Escapees," *Kansas City Star,* 20 November 1993, 9(A).

51. "Order in the Court with Shocking Restraint," *Lawrence Journal-World,* 9 April 1994, 10(D).

52. "Stun Belt Use Stuns Courtroom," *Lawrence Journal-World,* 11 July 1998, 10(A).

53. "Capital Punishment: Part Two," National Public Radio, *All Things Considered,* 27 September 1994.

54. Foucault, *Discipline and Punish,* 9.

55. Foucault, *Discipline and Punish,* 9.

56. Foucault, *Discipline and Punish,* 9.

57. Norman K. Denzin, *Images of Postmodern Society: Social Theory and Contemporary Cinema* (Newbury Park, Calif.: Sage, 1991), vii.

58. Hanson, *Testing Testing,* 93.

CHAPTER 5

1. See David J. Eck, *The Most Complex Machine: A Survey of Computers and Computing* (New York: A. K. Peters, Ltd., 1995); Katie Hafner and Matthew Lyon, *Where Wiz-*

ards Stay Up Late: The Origins of the Internet (New York: Simon & Schuster, 1996). Gregory R. Gromov, "The Roads and Crossroads of Internet's History," <http://www.internetvalley.com> [accessed 12 November 1999].

2. *The Internet Index*, Number 24, 31 May 1999, <http://new-website.open-market.com/intindex/index.cfm> [accessed 3 October 1999]. Like many resources in our society, access to and use of the Internet reveals a persistent inequality. One government report suggests that a "digital divide" exists between the "information rich" (Whites, Asians/Pacific Islanders, those with higher incomes, those more educated, and dual-parent households) and the "information poor" (such as those who are younger, those with lower incomes and education levels, certain minorities, and those in rural areas or central cities). See "Falling Through the Net: Defining the Digital Divide," National Telecommunications and Information Administration, U.S. Department of Commerce, 1999, <http://www.ntia.doc.gov/ntiahome/fttn99/> [accessed 11 October 1999].

3. See "The Wired/Merrill Lynch Forum Digital Citizen Survey," <http://hotwired.lycos.com/special/citizen/> [accessed 3 November 1999]. The Digital Citizen Survey was fielded by the Luntz Research Companies during the second and third week of September, 1997. Luntz conducted telephone interviews with one thousand randomly selected U.S. adults eighteen or older, along with an additional 444 interviews with likely technology users. The margin of error for the entire survey was plus or minus 2.6 percent.

4. See Walter Benjamin's "The Work of Art in the Age of Mechanical Reproduction," in Walter Benjamin and Hannah Arendt, eds., *Illuminations: Essays and Reflections* (New York: Harcourt, 1968), 219–253. In the end, Benjamin asserts that the loss of authenticity may be advantageous because it democratizes and politicizes art. His Frankfurt School colleagues, however, were convinced that the capitalist culture industry would commodify and standardize art to its and society's detriment.

5. A *New Yorker* magazine cartoon illustrates this problem. Speaking of his cyber-friend, a dog seated at a computer says to another dog, "On the Internet, she doesn't know I'm a dog." Further, some assert, as this transcript for National Public Radio suggests, that "Pitchmeisters masquerading as teenagers frequently slip into chat," say Esther Drill, Heather McDonald and Rebecca Odes of gURL.com. Unidentified Girl #4: "A lot of, you know, record labels now, the sort of underground type of marketing that they're trying to do . . . where they're coming and posting on our community . . . to be, like, 'I love Britney Spears.' " Unidentified Girl #5: "Right. We have an area on our site where you can send us e-mail about who you'd like to see featured, and we think probably 75 percent of it comes from record label people." See "Marketers Devise Ingenious Ways to Reach Kids on the Web," *All Things Considered*, National Public Radio, 18 November 1999.

6. Kevin Kelly, "The Electronic Hive: Embrace It," in *Computerization and Controversy: Value Conflicts and Social Choice* (2nd ed.), ed. Rob Kling (San Diego: Academic Press, 1996), 76–77.

7. Krishan Kumar, *From Post-Industrial to Post-Modern Society* (Oxford: Blackwell, 1995), 160.

8. "Hours Spent on Internet Add to Depression, Stress," *Associated Press Wire Service*, 31, August 1998, reporting on a study from Carnegie Mellon University.

9. As the Web becomes "much like the rest of social life" it mimics what Kuntsler calls the "Sameness of the Suburban Landscape" where "we drive up and down the gruesome, tragic suburban boulevards of commerce, and we're overwhelmed at the fantastic,

awesome, stupefying ugliness of absolutely everything in sight." In this case, we "surf" up and down a mediascape that looks increasingly like those suburban thoroughfares, plastered with the familiarity of franchised advertisements, company logos, and virtual "box stores" ready to sell or, popularly, auction, any conceivable commodity. And we see Disney and other media conglomerates teaming up with the likes of powerhouse Microsoft to saturate the Web with their cultural products, making it look like the all-too-familiar mainstream of Hollywood, cable and tabloid television, HBO, MTV, and the rest. See James Howard Kuntsler, *Home from Nowhere: Remaking Our Everyday World for the Twenty-first Century* (New York: Simon & Schuster, 1996).

10. Forrester Research, Inc. <http://www.forrester.com> [accessed 2 December 1999].

11. "Study—Internet Revenues to Top $507 Billion," *Associated Press Wire Service*, 28 October 1999.

12. Forrester Research, Inc. <http://www.forrester.com> [accessed 2 December 1999].

13. "Kids & Media @ The New Millennium," Kaiser Family Foundation, 1999, <http://www.kff.org/content/1999/1535/> 10 December 1999; "Marketers Devise Ingenious Ways to Reach Kids on the Web," *National Public Radio*, 18 November 1999.

14. "Do You Know Who's Watching You? Do You Care?" *New York Times*, 11 November 1999, 1(G).

15. Forrester Research, Inc. <http://www.forrester.com> [accessed 2 December 1999].

16. Andromedia, Inc. <http://www.andromedia.com> [accessed 4 December 1999].

17. Andromedia, Inc. <http://www.andromedia.com> [accessed 4 December 1999].

18. "Targeted Marketing Confronts Privacy Concerns," *New York Times*, 10 May 1999, <http://www.nytimes.com/library/tech/99/05/cyber/commerce/10commerce.html> [accessed 10 November 1999].

19. "Courts and Lawmakers Struggle to Provide Protections for Privacy as Technology Makes Personal Information More and More Accessible," *All Things Considered*, National Public Radio, 27 December 1999.

20. "Courts and Lawmakers Struggle."

21. "Targeted Marketing Confronts Privacy Concerns," *New York Times*, 10 May 1999, <http://www.nytimes.com/library/tech/99/05/cyber/commerce/10commerce.html> [accessed 10 November 1999].

22. "Marketers Devise Ingenious Ways to Reach Kids on the Web," *All Things Considered*, National Public Radio, 18 November 1999.

23. "Confronting the Cookie Monster; The Issue of Privacy Confounds Business and the Consumer," *San Diego Union-Tribune*, 22 August 1999, 9(I).

24. "No Holding Back as Public Opts for PCs Over Privacy Internet," *Los Angeles Times*, 9 February, 1(C); "Free Computers, for the Price of Personal Disclosure," *AP News Wire Service*, 9 February 1999.

25. "Big Web Sites to Track Steps of Their Users," *New York Times*, 16 August 1998, 1.

26. "Consumer Privacy on the World Wide Web." Federal Trade Commission, Washington, D.C., July 21, 1998, <http://www.ftc.gov/privacy/index.html> [accessed 12 November 1999].

27. "College Opens Student Records to Mom and Dad," *New York Times*, 11 November 1998, 26.

28. "Internet Access Management Solutions," WebSENSE Enterprise, Inc. <http://www.netpartners.com> [accessed 23 November 1999].

29. "Boss May Lurk as You Surf the Web," *Los Angeles Times*, 9 August 1999, 3(E).

30. "Boss May Lurk."

31. "Big Brother, Web Style," *PC Week*, 9 April 1996, 24.

32. "You Are Being Watched," *PC World*, November 1997, <http://www.pcworld.com/workstyles/online/articles/nov97/1511p245.html> [accessed 12 November 1999].

33. "Someone to Watch Over You: Webcams Are Cropping Up Everywhere," *San Diego Union-Tribune*, 24 August 1999, 6.

34. "Clandestine Cams," <http://www.discovery.com> [accessed 4 December 1999].

35. "Sprint Is Building Huge HQ in Kansas," *New York Times*, 12 July 1998, 30.

36. "Clandestine Cams," <http://www.discovery.com> [accessed 4 December 1999].

37. "Internet Lets Parents See Their Children at Day Care," *Lawrence Journal-World*, 8 July 1997, 4(A).

38. Ibid., 3(A).

39. "Someone to Watch Over You: Webcams Are Cropping up Everywhere," *San Diego Union-Tribune*, 24 August 1999, 6.

40. "Secret Videotapes Unnerve Athletes," *New York Times*, 9 August 1999, 4(D).

41. <http://www.jennicam.org> [accessed 10 October 1999].

42. Janet Maslin, "So, What's Wrong With This Picture?" *New York Times*, 5 June 1998, 1(E). Maslin goes on to say, "What if our taste for trivia and voyeurism led to the purgatory of a whole life lived as show-biz illusion? What if that life became not only the ultimate paranoid fantasy but also achieved pulse-quickening heights of narcissism?"

43. From the film *Wall Street*, quoted in Norman K. Denzin, *Images of Postmodern Society*, (Newbury Park, Calif.: Sage, 1991), 82.

44. <http://www.ontap.com> [accessed 4 December 1999].

45. <http://www.warnerbros.com/webcams/> [accessed 2 December 1999].

46. "Woman Will Give Birth on Internet," *Associated Press Wire Service*, 12 June 1998; "Internet Mom Turns Herself in to Police," *Associated Press Wire Service*, 1 July 1998.

47. <http://www.adoctorinyourhouse.com> [accessed 9 December 1999].

48. "Man Plans to Live Year Online," *Associated Press Wire Service*, 1 January 2000.

49. Michel Foucault, *Discipline and Punish: The Birth of the Prison*, tr. A. M. Sheridan (New York: Pantheon, 1977), 211.

50. Denzin, *Images of Postmodern Society*, 9.

51. See Jean Baudrillard, *The Ecstasy of Communication*, (New York: Semiotext(e), 1988).

CHAPTER 6

1. Michel Foucault, *Discipline and Punish: The Birth of the Prison*, tr. A. M. Sheridan (New York: Pantheon, 1977), 214.

2. Jean-Paul Sartre, "The Other and His Look," in Justin Treller, ed., *To Freedom Condemned* (New York: Philosophical Library, 1960), 37.

3. Michel Foucault, *Discipline and Punish: The Birth of the Prison*, tr. A. M. Sheridan (New York: Pantheon, 1977), 301.

4. "Surveillance Extends Everywhere," *Lincoln Star*, 19 May 1994, 7; Marshall McLuhan, *Understanding Media: The Extensions of Man* (New York: McGraw-Hill, 1964).

5. Our "hyperreal" personas stored in the databases may be "better" representations of our "real" selves. Can you remember all the videos you rented last year? I would bet that your local video store's computer system could recall them.

6. Quoted in Lili Berko, "Surveying the Surveilled: Video, Space, and Subjectivity," *Quarterly Review of Film and Video* 14, no. 1–2 (1992): 61–91.

7. See David Brin, *The Transparent Society* (Reading, Mass.: Addison-Wesley, 1998).

8. Of course, we must also ask the more fundamental and political questions raised by organizers of a conference of privacy: "Should privacy be valued as an essential condition of individual dignity, the integrity of personality, intimacy, trust, autonomy, creativity, and social diversity? Or does it serve primarily to protect hypocrisy, sexual immorality, political subversion, class and gender privilege, exploitation, domestic violence, and/or sexual harassment?" *The Question of Privacy*, Dartmouth College, 1999.

9. Steven L. Nock, *The Costs of Privacy: Surveillance and Reputation in America* (New York: De Gruyter, 1989), 3.

10. Nock, *The Costs of Privacy*, 2.

11. See Robert N. Bellah, Richard Madsen, William M. Sullivan, Ann Swindler, and Steven M. Tipton, *The Good Society* (New York: Knopf, 1991). The communitarian sociologist Amitai Etzioni argues that excessive protection of individual privacy, in certain situations, may threaten the common good. See Amitai Etzioni, *The Limits of Privacy* (New York: Basic Books, 1999). Deciding what is best for the "common good," however, is a political process.

12. Gary T. Marx, quoted in Berko, 86.

13. Jeffrey C. Goldfarb, *The Cynical Society* (Chicago: University of Chicago Press, 1991), 182.

Selected References

Agre, Philip, and Marc Rotenberg, eds. *Technology and Privacy: The New Landscape*. Boston: MIT Press, 1997.

Altheide, David. "Gonzo Justice." *Symbolic Interaction* 15, no. 1 (1993): 69–86.

———. "Electronic Media and State Control: The Case of Azscam." *Sociological Quarterly* 34, no. 1 (1993): 53–69.

———. *Media Power*. Newbury Park, Calif.: Sage, 1985.

American Management Association. *AMA Survey on Job Skill Testing and Psychological Measurement*. New York: American Management Association, 1998.

———. *AMA Survey on Workplace Drug Testing and Drug Abuse Policies*. New York: American Management Association, 1994.

———. *AMA Survey on Workplace Monitoring and Surveillance*. New York: American Management Association, 1999.

Baudrillard, Jean. *The Ecstasy of Communication*. New York: Semiotext(e), 1988.

———. *Simulations*. New York: Semiotext(e), 1983.

Bauman, Zygmunt. *Intimations of Postmodernity*. London: Routledge, 1992.

Bellah, Robert N., Richard Madsen, William M. Sullivan, Ann Swindler, and Steven M. Tipton. *The Good Society*. New York: Knopf, 1991.

Benjamin, Walter. "The Work of Art in the Age of Mechanical Reproduction." In *Illuminations: Essays and Reflections*, edited by Walter Benjamin and Hannah Arendt, 219–253. New York: Harcourt, 1968.

Bentham, Jeremy. *The Panopticon Writings*. Edited by Miran Bozovic. London: Verso, 1995.

Berko, Lili. "Surveying the Surveilled: Video, Space, and Subjectivity." *Quarterly Review of Film and Video* 14, no. 1–2 (1992): 61–91.

Best, Steven. "Foucault, Postmodernism, and Social Theory." In *Postmodernism and Social Inquiry*, edited by David R. Dickens and Andrea Fontana, 25–52. New York: Guilford, 1994.

Black, Donald. *The Social Structure of Right and Wrong*. New York: Academic Press, 1999.

Bourdieu, Pierre. *Distinction: A Social Critique of the Judgement of Taste*. London: Routledge, 1984.

Brin, David. *The Transparent Society*. Reading, Mass.: Addison-Wesley, 1998.

Cate, Fred H. *Privacy in the Information Age*. Washington, D.C.: Brookings Institute, 1997.

Cavoukian, Ann, and Don Tapscott. *Who Knows: Safeguarding Your Privacy in a Networked World*. New York: McGraw-Hill, 1996.

Cohen, Stanley. *Visions of Social Control: Crime, Punishment, and Classification*. Cambridge: Polity Press, 1985.

———. "The Punitive City: Notes on the Dispersal of Social Control." *Contemporary Crisis* 3, no. 4 (1979): 339–363.

Cohen, Stanley, and Andrew Scull. *Social Control and the State*. New York: St. Martin's Press, 1983.

Conrad, Peter, and Joseph Schneider. *Deviance and Medicalization: From Badness to Sickness*. St. Louis: Mosby, 1980.

Corbett, Ronald, and Gary T. Marx. "Critique: No Soul in the New Machine: Technofallacies in the Electronic Monitoring Movement." *Justice Quarterly* 8, no. 3 (September 1991): 399–414.

Crane, Diana. *The Sociology of Culture*. Cambridge: Blackwell, 1994.

Davis, Mike. *City of Quartz: Excavating the Future in Los Angeles*. London: Verso, 1990.

de Becker, Gavin. *The Gift of Fear*. Boston: Little, Brown, 1997.

Decew, Judith Wagner. *In Pursuit of Privacy: Law, Ethics and the Rise of Technology*. Ithaca: Cornell University Press, 1997.

Denzin, Norman K. *Images of Postmodern Society: Social Theory and Contemporary Cinema*. Newbury Park, Calif.: Sage, 1991.

Dibble, Vernon. "Four Types of Inference from Documents to Events." *History and Theory* 3, no. 2 (1963): 203–221.

Diffie, Whitfield, and Susan Landeau. *Privacy on the Line: The Politics of Wiretapping and Encryption*. Boston: MIT Press, 1998.

Dumm, Thomas. *Democracy and Punishment: Disciplinary Origins of the United States*. Madison: University of Wisconsin Press, 1987.

Earle, Alice Morse. *Curious Punishments of Bygone Days*. Rutland, Vt.: Charles E. Tenant, 1972.

Eck, David J. *The Most Complex Machine: A Survey of Computers and Computing*. New York: A. K. Peters, Ltd., 1995.

Emerson, Robert M., and Sheldon M. Messinger. "The Micro-Politics of Trouble." *Social Problems* 25, no. 2 (1977): 121–134.

Ericson, Richard V. "Review: *The Culture of Surveillance*." *Social Forces* 76, no. 3 (1998): 1154–1156.

———. *Policing the Risk Society*. Toronto: Toronto University Press, 1997.

Etzioni, Amitai. *The Limits of Privacy*. New York: Basic Books, 1999.

Ferrell, Jeff, and Neil Websdale. *Making Trouble: Cultural Constructions of Crime, Deviance, and Control*. Hawthorne, N.Y.: Aldine De Gruyter, 1999.

Foucault, Michel. "Afterword: The Subject of Power." In *Michel Foucault: Beyond Structuralism and Hermeneutics*, edited by Hubert L. Dreyfus and Paul Rabinow, 208–226. Berkeley: University of California Press, 1983.

——. *Power/Knowledge: Selected Interviews and Other Writings, 1972–1977.* Edited by Colin Gordon. New York: Pantheon, 1980.

——. *Discipline and Punish: The Birth of the Prison.* Translated by A. M. Sheridan. New York: Pantheon, 1977.

Fraser, Nancy. *Unruly Practices: Power, Discourse, and Gender in Contemporary Social Theory.* Minneapolis: University of Minnesota Press, 1989.

Friedman, Lawrence. *A History of American Law.* New York: Simon & Schuster, 1973.

Gandy, Oscar, Jr. *The Panoptic Sort: A Political Economy of Personal Information.* Boulder, Colo.: Westview, 1993.

Geertz, Clifford. *The Interpretations of Cultures.* New York: Basic, 1973.

Gibbs, Jack. *Norms, Deviance, and Social Control: Conceptual Matters.* New York: Elsevier, 1981.

Glassner, Barry. *Culture of Fear: Why Americans Are Afraid of the Wrong Things.* New York: Basic Books, 1999.

Goldfarb, Jeffrey C. *The Cynical Society.* Chicago: University of Chicago Press, 1991.

Gromov, Gregory R. "The Roads and Crossroads of Internet's History." <http://www.internetvalley.com/intval.html> [accessed 4 December 1999].

Hafner, Katie, and Matthew Lyon. *Where Wizards Stay Up Late: The Origins of the Internet.* New York: Simon & Schuster, 1996.

Hanson, F. Allan. *Testing Testing: Social Consequences of the Examined Life.* Berkeley: University of California Press, 1993.

Harris, Lewis, and Associates. *Work Place Health and Privacy Issues: A Survey of Private Sector Employees and Leaders.* New York: L. H. & Associates, 1994.

Hodges, V. G., and B. Blythe. "Improving Service Delivery to High-Risk Families: Home-Based Practice." *Families in Society: The Journal of Contemporary Human Services* 73, no. 5 (May 1992): 259–65.

Holman, John E., and James F. Quinn. "Dysphoria and Electronically Monitored Home Confinement." *Deviant Behavior* 13, no. 1 (January–March 1992): 21–32.

Humphreys, Keith, and Julian Rappaport. "From the Community Mental Health Movement to the War on Drugs: A Study in the Definitions of Social Problems." *American Psychologist* 48, no. 8 (1993): 892–901.

Jameson, Fredric. *Postmodernism, or, The Cultural Logic of Late Capitalism.* London: Verso, 1992.

Kahin, Brian, and Charles Nesson, eds. *Borders in Cyberspace: Information Policy and the Global Information Infrastructure.* Boston: MIT Press, 1997.

Kelly, Kevin. "The Electronic Hive: Embrace It." In *Computerization and Controversy: Value Conflicts and Social Choice,* 2d ed., edited by Rob Kling, 76–77. San Diego: Academic Press, 1996.

Kneeland, Timothy, and Carol A. B. Warren. *Push-Button Psychiatry: A History of Electroconvulsive Therapy.* Westport, Conn.: Greenwood Press, 2000.

Krier, Dan, and Willliam G. Staples. "Seen but Unseen: Part-time Faculty and Institutional Surveillance and Control." *American Sociologist* 24, no. 3–4 (Fall/Winter 1993): 119–34.

Krishan, Kumar. *From Post-Industrial to Post-Modern Society.* Oxford: Blackwell, 1995.

Kuntsler, James Howard. *Home from Nowhere: Remaking Our Everyday World for the Twenty-first Century.* New York: Simon & Schuster, 1996.

Lewis, Orlando. *The Development of American Prisons and Prison Customs, 1776–1845.* 1922. Reprint, Albany: Prison Association of New York, 1967.

Lewis, W. David. *From Newgate to Dannemora*. Ithaca: Cornell University Press, 1975.

Lowe, Donald. *The Body in Late Capitalism USA*. Durham: Duke University Press, 1995.

Lykken, David T. *A Tremor in the Blood: Uses and Abuses of the Lie Detector*. New York: Plenum, 1998.

Lyon, David. *The Electronic Eye: The Rise of Surveillance Society*. Minneapolis: University of Minnesota Press, 1996.

——. *Postmodernity*. Minneapolis: Minnesota University Press, 1994.

——. "The New Surveillance: Electronic Technologies and the Maximum Security Society." *Crime, Law, and Social Change* 18, no. 1–2 (September 1992): 159–175.

Lyon, David, and Elia Zureik, eds. *Computers, Surveillance, and Privacy*. Minneapolis: University of Minnesota Press, 1996.

Mandel, Ernest. *Late Capitalism*. London: Verso, 1978.

Mariampolski, Hyman, and Dana Hughes. "The Use of Personal Documents in Historical Sociology." *The American Sociologist* 13, no. 2 (May 1978): 104–113.

Milligan, John. "The Treatment of an Historical Source." *History and Theory* 18, no. 2 (May 1979): 177–196.

Milofsky, Carl. *Testers and Testing: The Sociology of School Psychology*. New Brunswick: Rutgers University Press, 1989.

National Telecommunications and Information Administration. "Falling Through the Net: Defining the Digital Divide." Washington, D.C.: U.S. Department of Commerce <http://www.ntia.doc.gov/ntiahome/fttn99/>, 1999 [accessed 23 November 1999].

Nelkin, Dorothy, and Laurence Tancredi. *Dangerous Diagnostics: The Social Power of Biological Information*. 1989. Reprint, Chicago: University of Chicago Press, 1994.

Nock, Steven L. *The Costs of Privacy: Surveillance and Reputation in America*. New York: De Gruyter, 1989.

Petersilia, Joan. *Expanding Options for Criminal Sentencing*. Santa Monica, Calif.: RAND, 1987.

Rothman, David J. *Conscience and Convenience: The Asylum and Its Alternatives in Progressive America*. Boston: Little, Brown, 1980.

——. *The Discovery of the Asylum: Social Order and Disorder in the New Republic*. Boston: Little, Brown, 1971.

Schneier, Bruce, and David Banisar, eds. *The Electronic Privacy Papers: Documents on the Battle for Privacy in the Age of Surveillance*. New York: Wiley & Sons, 1997.

Smith, H. Jeff. *Managing Privacy: Information, Technology, and Corporate America*. Chapel Hill: University of North Carolina Press, 1994.

Spector, Malcom. "Beyond Crime: Seven Methods to Control Troublesome Rascals." In *Law and Deviance*, edited by H. L. Ross, 127–157. Beverly Hills: Sage, 1981.

Staples, William G. "Small Acts of Cunning: Disciplinary Practices in Contemporary Life." *Sociological Quarterly* 35, no. 3 (Summer 1994): 645–64.

——. *Castles of Our Conscience: Social Control and the American State, 1800–1985*. New Brunswick: Rutgers University Press, 1991.

Staples, William G., and Carol A. B. Warren. "Mental Health and Adolescent Social Control." In *Research in Law, Deviance and Social Control: A Research Annual*, edited by Steven Spitzer and Andrew Scull, 113-126. Greenwich, Conn.: JAI Press, 1988.

——. "Fieldwork in Forbidden Terrain: The State, Privatization and Human Subjects Regulations." *The American Sociologist* 20, no. 3 (Fall 1989): 263–267.

Turkle, Sherry. *Life on the Screen: Identity in the Age of the Internet.* New York: Simon & Schuster, 1995.

Warren, Carol A. B., and Kathleen A. K. Levy. "Electroconvulsive Therapy and the Elderly." *Journal of Aging Studies* 5, no. 3 (1991): 309–327.

Whitaker, Reginald. *The End of Privacy: How Total Surveillance Is Becoming a Reality.* New York: New Press, 1999.

Woods, L. J. "Home-Based Family Therapy." *Social Work* 33, no. 3 (May/June 1988): 211–14.

Index

About the Author

William G. Staples grew up on the south shore of Long Island, New York. He has been a commercial fisherman, taxicab driver, plumber's apprentice, and pizza chef. He studied sociology at the University of Oregon, went on to receive his Ph.D. from the University of Southern California, and spent two years as postdoctoral fellow at the University of California, Los Angeles. He is currently professor of sociology at the University of Kansas and is the author of *Castles of Our Conscience: Social Control and the American State, 1800–1985* (1991), and, with Clifford L. Staples, *Power, Profits, and Patriarchy: The Social Organization of Work at a British Metal Trades Firm, 1791–1922* (forthcoming). He lives in Lawrence, Kansas.